Neston
1840–1940

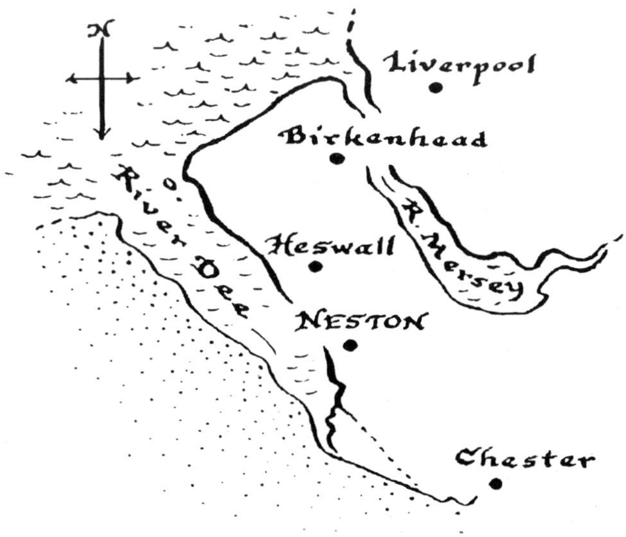

The Town Hall, High Street, Neston, *c.*1920.

Neston
1840–1940

edited by
Geoffrey W. Place Geoffrey Place

cover painted by
David Scott

The Burton and South Wirral
Local History Society
1996

Published by
The Burton and South Wirral Local History Society

ISBN 0 9509145 1 7

Designed, copy-edited and set in TrueType Book Antiqua
by David Morris

Printed in Great Britain by
Bemrose Shafron Ltd, Chester

Table of Contents

Illustrations

page

Acknowledgements

Grateful thanks are due to all those people or institutions who provided either information or material for illustrations, without which this book would be a slimmer volume, or gave assistance in other ways.

As regards illustrations, Michael Barton's drawings were used for Figs 54 and 70; 68 came from a drawing by Bernadette Bowes; the paintings for the cover and Fig. 112, and the other drawings, were executed by David Scott.

Photographs, postcards and other documents belonged to R. E. Benbow (40, 115), Birkenhead Central Library (25), George Bridson (110), Cheshire County Record Office (69), Ellesmere Port and Neston Borough Council (76, 79), Mrs Mary Francis (62), Mrs Kathleen Gray (49), Miss Molly Gray (102), Mrs Gill Jackson (8), the late Mrs Helen Mealor (20), the Midland Bank, Neston (frontispiece), Mrs Margaret Pritchett (13, 74), Ralph Robinson (119), Mrs Stuffin (43), Charles Swanborough (107), Major R. N. Topham (64), the Williamson Art Gallery and Museum (33), Mrs Doris Wilson (16), and the late Mr Woodward (50). The remaining illustrations were provided by members of the research group.

The names of all the local people who freely contributed with advice, anecdotes, etc. are included among the sources at the end of each chapter.

Finally, we express our gratitude to the Parkgate Society for its generous and timely loan, which by assisting us with the immediate financial demands of publication has allowed us to dispense with the added burden of arranging fund-raising activities.

HOW THIS BOOK CAME TO BE WRITTEN

When Paul Booth first came to Burton in Wirral in 1971 as a lecturer from Liverpool University, he started a research group which has so far published two books, formed a local history society and produced some fifteen annual bulletins. We are proud that the Burton and South Wirral Local History Society has always been actively engaged in research, and we firmly intend that our commitment to research shall continue.

Our first book — *Burton in Wirral, a History*, edited by P. H. W. Booth — had seventeen authors. When the strain of the publication process and the delight at seeing our labours in print had faded a little, we determined to turn our attention to Neston. Twenty-two people attended our first meeting, and ten stalwarts were still there at the finish. They were Susan Chambers, Clive Edwards, Edward Hilditch, Clare Johnson, Kate Kelly, David and Hilary Morris, Geoffrey and Valerie Place, and David Scott.

Bryan Heatley, Lyn Miles and Norman Cullen also stayed with the group for several years, and many other people, whose names will be found in the notes on sources at the end of each chapter, gave their help.

The authorship of the book eventually devolved almost wholly on three people. These were Susan Chambers, Edward Hilditch and Geoffrey Place. The sources for each chapter indicate which author was responsible.

Neston is a very different place from its near neighbour, Burton, and has a very different history, which has been divided into distinct segments by its changing fortunes. The reasons for taking the hundred years from 1840 to 1940, rather than starting with Neston's Saxon origins and working our way forwards, are given in the first chapter. And we were also anxious to tap the memories of our older neighbours before it was too late.

The research group has already earmarked its next project, and we hope that that too will turn into a book.

Most of those who have researched this book were not born in Neston, and they are conscious that the true flavour of a place can be conveyed best by a native. David Scott was indeed born here: his poetic description of Neston in the 1930s ends the book, and here is his introduction to it:

> **The purpose of this book is to survey a span of a hundred years. Very few now living in Neston were born in the days of Queen Victoria, whose reign covered sixty years of our period. Surely it is a good thing that this brief history has been undertaken before any further loss of memories. We have already missed many gems of local knowledge, and we hope that this book will act as a stimulus to keep alive those hundreds of facts, anecdotes and snippets of information which remain treasured only in folklore.**

CHAPTER ONE

THE NESTONIANS

In 1840, Neston's days of prosperity were, for the time being, over. Its status as the only town in Wirral had been emphatically crushed by the rise of Birkenhead. The shipping and the Customs men were only a memory, and Parkgate's fame as a seaside resort was being eclipsed by the creation of New Brighton. The town of Neston reverted to being a village and became an inward-looking backwater. From this sleepy state it was gradually rescued by the railway and by the energy of some of its citizens, but Neston remained somewhat isolated, at least in temperament, until the Second World War. That is why this span of a hundred years, from 1840 to 1940, has been chosen to tell our story.

This introductory chapter sets Neston in its historical context; discusses its population, its character, and the influence of wealthy families on the locality; and finally relates one lady's memory of the impression made on her by the Neston of a hundred years ago. Then, in subsequent chapters you will read about the way in which Nestonians earned their living; the development of the schools and the churches; the growth of local government and the provision of health and welfare; how Nestonians spent their free time; Neston's communications with the outside world by road, rail and telephone; and how the unique flavour of Neston was modified by the modern world.

The ancient parish of Neston was made up of the eight townships of Great Neston, Little Neston, Ness, Ledsham, Willaston, Thornton Hough, Raby and Leighton. These parts still made up the parish of Neston in 1840, but later the outer parts were hived off, leaving Great Neston, Little Neston and Leighton together. Parkgate, being a more recent settlement, straddled the boundary of Great Neston and Leighton. Most of this book concentrates on the town of Neston, but illustrations are drawn from the other areas too, as, for example, when agricultural life in Raby, Willaston, Little Neston and Ledsham is described.

In medieval times, the eight parts of the parish were just villages or hamlets, like many other villages in Wirral. Nearby Burton was much more important in the fourteenth century, when it had a weekly market

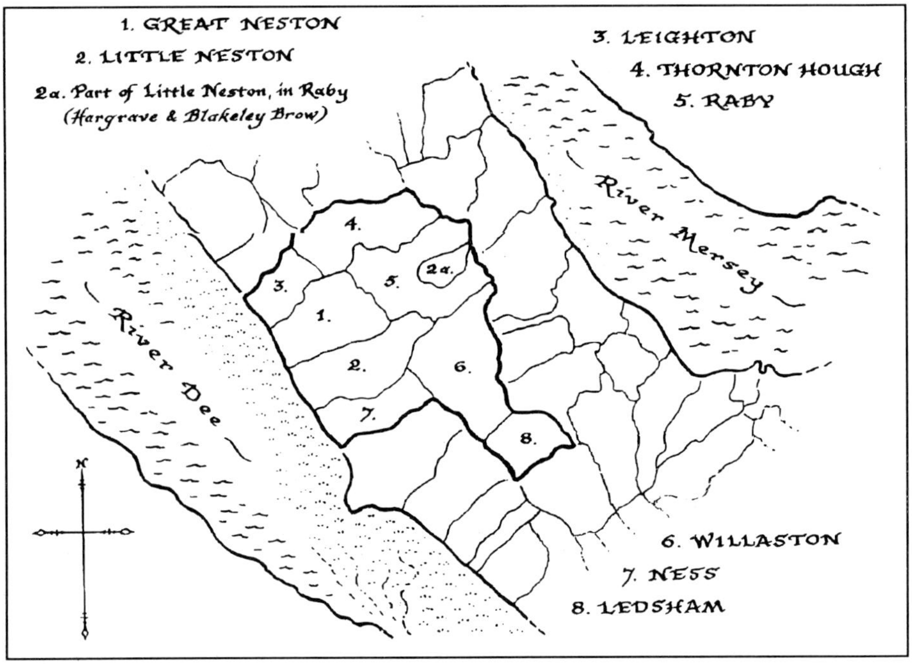

Fig. 1 The eight townships of the ancient parish of Neston. These administrative districts were in use from Saxon times until the advent of the Local Board of Health for Neston in 1867.

and an annual fair. Neston's status rose in the mid-sixteenth century, when the City of Chester began to build Neston Quay, originally known as the New Haven or New Quay, as the principal anchorage in the Dee estuary. The resulting trade, the travellers and the growth of supporting services, such as craftsmen to repair the ships, and Customs officers, raised Neston from a village to a town. Eventually Neston was able to put the seal on its importance by being granted a royal warrant to hold a weekly market and annual fair in 1728. By that time the shipping had moved to Parkgate, which was soon specializing in the passenger traffic to Dublin. After about 1760 Parkgate was also flourishing as a seabathing resort. In these years Neston was a busy town.

The decline came quickly. Owing to the loss of water in the Parkgate channel, the shipping ceased to come by 1815, and the last Customs officer finally departed in 1828. In 1830 James Atherton bought 170 acres of sandhills opposite Liverpool and created the new resort of New Brighton, which had taken away most of Parkgate's summer visitors by 1840.

Meanwhile Birkenhead was growing rapidly. In 1821 its population was only 200, while Neston and Parkgate had six times as many people. Then the introduction of steam ferries across the Mersey led to rapid development at Birkenhead, which by 1841 had 8,000 inhabitants.

At that time, most of Neston and all of Parkgate was owned by the Mostyn family of North Wales. It was in the 1840s that they sniffed the winds of change, sold all their Cheshire lands and developed Llandudno as a new resort. This is how it happened.

When Sir Thomas Mostyn died unmarried in 1831 he was the last male member of the family that had owned the Neston estate since 1672. His five sisters went to the High Court of Chancery to claim £10,000 each under their father's will. The eldest daughter had no children, and her husband administered the estate until his death in 1839. The second daughter had married Sir Edward Lloyd, who had been created the first Baron Mostyn. Their son Edward adopted the surname Mostyn when he took control of the estate in 1839. Not only did he have to pay his aunts, but the estate had been heavily mortgaged for decades, and was in debt for £100,000. It was therefore decided to sell the Cheshire estate. Meanwhile, Edward Lloyd Mostyn had received a recommendation that the empty beach at Llandudno would make a fine watering-place. In 1843 an Enclosure Act had apportioned most of the Llandudno common land to the nearby Gloddaeth estate which belonged to the Mostyns. The award was finalized in 1848, and the need to finance the new development was pressing. And so, over six days in June 1849, the Mostyn estate of 1,500 acres in *"Great Neston, Parkgate, Leighton, Thornton Hough and Hinderton"* was auctioned in 284 lots, at the Mostyn Arms Hotel in Parkgate.

As the *Liverpool Albion* asked:

> *Who'll buy a town? A pretty town indeed – the town of Parkgate, which above all other towns has the singular privilege of being sold by auction. Many a town has been battered to pieces, but Parkgate has only to be brought to the hammer.*

Such a large amount of property could not be sold in one go, and two further auctions were needed in the next few years. The effect on the neighbourhood can be imagined, as new owners moved in and former tenants struggled to find the money to buy their own property. For example, Esther Briscoe set out to buy the hotel she had run for nearly forty years, and which she had transformed from the George Inn to the Mostyn Arms Hotel in 1818. She took out a mortgage with Thomas Brassey, the railways contractor, and when Mrs Briscoe died in 1854 Brassey's agent had to buy the hotel to save the investment. There were too few customers to keep a hotel going now that New Brighton was flourishing, so the building was leased as a school. Mostyn House School was eventually able to buy its freehold when Brassey died, after he had used the building as collateral to build the Danish State Railway.

THE situation of PARKGATE, and the adjoining Lands can scarcely be equalled in the kingdom; the air is most salubrious and healthy; and it is one of the principal Summer Resorts in this part of England. A Railway is now in course of formation to unite the whole of these Estates with Liverpool, Chester, Manchester, &c., by joining the Chester and Birkenhead Railway at Spital Station. The Estates are intersected with several Turnpike Roads, to which most of the Lots have considerable Frontage; amongst them may be named the Neston and Woodside,—Chester and Hinderton,—Chester and Gayton,—Parkgate,—Thornton Hough,—*via* Clatterbridge to the Rock Ferry, &c. &c.

Most of the ERECTIONS are of a substantial character, and amongst the FARM BUILDINGS will be found many extremely well arranged and commodious, The Lots have been so divided as to offer to even the smallest Capitalist an opportunity of investment; while to those of more extended means.

THE THORNTON HOUGH ESTATE,

In a perfectly Ring Fence, surrounded by Roads,

THE LEIGHTON HALL,

HINDERTON and other FARMS, are well worthy of their most particular attention.

THE MOSTYN ARMS HOTEL is deserving of marked observation, being replete with every accommodation and convenience; besides this, (to Brewers especially) the SHIP INN, and the PENGWERN ARMS FERRY HOUSE, in Parkgate, the LION INN, Neston, and other small Inns are each so well established as to be a source of great profit.

A piece of LAND has been allotted in the centre of Parkgate by the Honourable Mr. Mostyn, as a Site for the erection of a Church.

A FLOATING FERRY, upon a new principal, is also likely soon to be placed upon the Dee, to convey Passengers at any state of the Tide to join the Holyhead Railway at Bagillt.

COAL is to be had in this locality at a very low rate. BRICK CLAY, excellent building STONE and SAND are to be found on the property thus rendering these Estates most desirable to the Speculator, the Inhabitants of large towns in the neighbourhood, or the retired Tradesman.

Fig. 2 Extract from the sale catalogue of the Mostyn estate, 1849.

During the hundred years of this book's survey, the population of Birkenhead soared from 8,000 to 140,000, a multiplying factor of 17.5. In the same period, the population of Neston increased by 2.25 times, from 2,513 to 5,676. The population of England and Wales rose from 16 million to 40 million, a factor of 2.5. In national terms, therefore, Neston grew only a little slower than the national average, but in terms of its neighbourhood, especially Liverpool and Birkenhead, it increased relatively modestly.

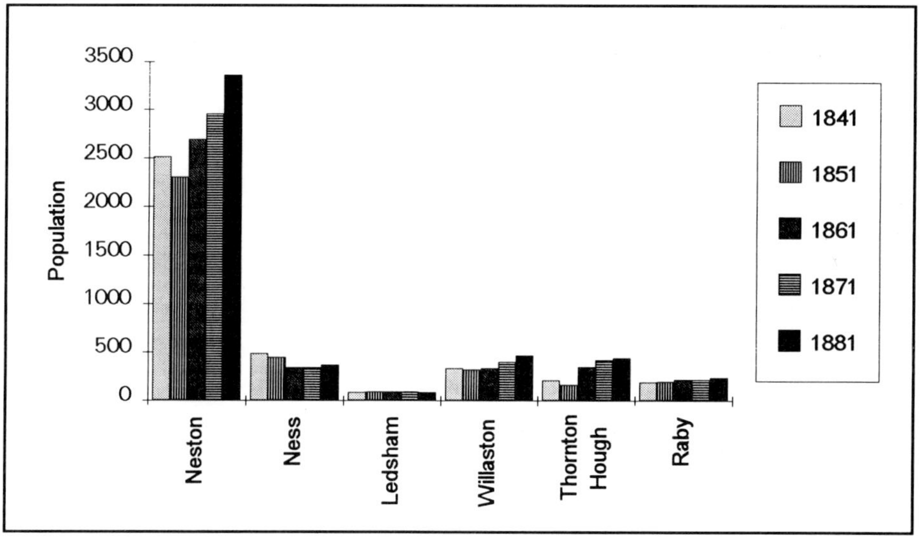

Fig. 3 Comparative population growth in the ancient parish of Neston, based on census returns from 1841 to 1881. (Direct comparisons of population figures are not always reliable because the boundaries may alter. Until 1881 the numbers from the ten-yearly censuses are usually given by township, whereas from 1891 they are the electoral wards of Neston Council. Hence the population figures quoted on this page for "Neston" are for Great Neston, Little Neston and Leighton with Parkgate.)

The troubled times in the 1840s caused the population to go down a little, from 2,513 in 1841 to 2,304 in 1851. There was a steady recovery in the next twenty years (2,692 in 1861, 2,954 in 1871), followed by a larger jump to 3,359 in 1881, owing mainly to the opening of the colliery in Little Neston, where the population rose by 55%.

By 1901 the population was 4,154, as the growth of housing encouraged by the railway began to take effect.

A more detailed grouping of population numbers for the two census years 1851 and 1881 reveals how differently individual townships developed.

Township	1851				1881				Increase/ Decrease		
	A		B		C		D		E	F	G
	No.	%	No.	%	No.	%	No.	%	%	%	%
Great Neston	845	69	385	31	1,082	66	551	34	28	43	33
Leighton	315	55	254	45	371	53	334	47	18	31	24
Little Neston	406	80	99	20	591	58	430	42	46	334	102
Ness	373	83	76	17	282	76	87	24	-24	14	-18
Ledsham	71	76	22	24	63	78	18	22	-11	-18	-13
Willaston	253	81	59	19	318	69	142	31	26	141	47
Thornton Hough	92	57	70	43	230	52	211	48	150	201	172
Raby	135	70	58	30	130	56	103	44	-4	78	21
Total parish	2,490	71	1,023	29	3,067	62	1,876	38	23	83	41

Cols A and C are persons born in Wirral; Cols B and D are persons born elsewhere; Cols E and F show the percentage change between A and C, and B and D, respectively; Col. G shows the percentage change for each whole township and the parish.

Fig. 4 Comparison of township populations, between 1851 and 1881, by numbers and percentages.

In the town of Neston itself, the growth of population between 1851 and 1881 was mainly by natural increase, but in two townships the increase was caused by incomers.

In Little Neston and its surroundings, the reopened colliery had attracted over a hundred new faces — some sixty from Wales and thirty from Lancashire — so that the population doubled. In Thornton Hough, where two-thirds of the heads of households were immigrants, the population had swollen from 162 to 441. The run-down Thornton estate had been revitalized by its landowner, Joseph Hirst.

Neston had a reputation for rowdiness in the nineteenth century, and to a lesser extent as late as the Second World War. Early photographs of Neston Cross usually show a group of idlers sitting round the Bushell fountain, and it seems that sometimes youths who loitered there and at street corners would intimidate passers-by with offensive remarks. The vicar, R. W. Gleadowe, called on the magistrates to do something about this nuisance in 1878, and indeed the magistrates' court at that period was constantly busy with cases concerning drunkenness, fighting and tramps. A man summoned for assault in that same year explained to the Bench that it was a common custom in Neston to pick a quarrel with a stranger, like himself, and get up fights. He had therefore taken care to get his own blow in first! The same attitude was echoed nearly sixty years later, in 1934, when a man was fined after knocking down someone in Brook Street and then offering to fight anybody in the crowd, some sixty strong, which had eagerly gathered to watch. The newspaper account spoke of *"Neston's pugnacious reputation"*.

Another example of local rowdiness was the customary New Year jollifications. It was reported in 1884:

> *Never was this night* [New Year's Eve] *known to be so quiet. The usual gangs of roughs who commonly, at an untimely hour, alarm quiet folks by boisterously hammering at doors or excruciating ringing at bells, were singularly absent.*

We hear about the rowdy goings-on at Neston Races, the drunken aftermath of the annual hiring fair, and the fears aroused by dancing on the Green behind the Golden Lion on the evening of Ladies' Day. There was also a serious riot in 1880, on the occasion of the parliamentary election for the West Cheshire constituency. The day started innocently enough, with Liberal supporters parading with loaves stuck on the ends of yellow-ribboned staffs. For the Conservatives, a makeshift band was pulled round the streets in a cart, *"each player playing his own tune"*. But fighting soon broke out, and the police sent to Birkenhead for reinforcements. The crowd, many of them drunk, grew to a thousand, and faced thirty policemen who patrolled the streets four deep. Stones were thrown, and the police charged the crowd and sent for a magistrate, Uvedale Corbett of Ashfield Hall. He spoke to the crowd and threatened to read the Riot Act, which would have enabled him to call on the military for help. Fortunately the crowd had had enough sport and quietly dispersed.

A part of Neston's rowdiness was related to its plentiful supply of pubs; but another part related to the colliery at Little Neston. It was a tough area, and the miners, many of whom after 1874 were not originally from Neston, were suspicious of strangers. Gangs of youths calling themselves the colliery bulldogs would wait for strangers coming down Colliery Lane, or "Lousy Hill" (now Marshlands Road). The look-outs would give warning that visitors were approaching, so that their companions lower down the road could attack and rough them up. Once a lady wearing a wide hat walked down the road, and as she passed under the railway bridge, a boy sitting on the parapet did something unprintable on her hat. This tale was related for years with much relish.

A far more serious confrontation took place in 1879 between a group of miners and two local policemen. Sergeant Hugh O'Donnell and PC John Dillon found themselves surrounded by a threatening crowd, who appeared to be looking about for stones to attack them. The ground was so hard with frost that the stones could not be lifted, but both policemen drew revolvers and fired over the heads of the crowd. For this improper use of firearms, O'Donnell and Dillon were reprimanded and stripped of their merit badges.

There were a few occasions when Neston's propensity for violence took an uglier turn. Just before Christmas in 1903, two young men were drinking at the bar in the Liberal Club, which is now the Civic Hall. They argued, and when they left the club the argument turned into a fight. Ernest Grundy gave Harry Pritchard a black eye, but the injury turned out to be a fractured skull. Both young men took to their beds, Grundy with nervous depression. Harry Pritchard soon died, and when he heard the news Ernest Grundy cut his own throat.

A suspicion of strangers was not, of course, unique to Neston, but it was a noteworthy feature of Neston life before 1940. Mrs Kate Ryder spent every August at Parkgate throughout the 1920s, and she has described the insularity caused by lack of transport except by train. The relative isolation of villages in those days accentuated the differences in modes of speech. She used to follow the local children, but

> *their way of talking disturbed me. I couldn't understand it and despised it. I knew it was ugly and wrong. Of course I did not realize that my Shropshire accent may have had a similar effect on them.*
>
> *There were so many nephews and nieces from Shropshire that we formed a gang. There was a big family called Mealor, and the only reason for causing trouble between us was our accents. They teased us for being Welsh, which we weren't, but to oblige we gabbled nonsense loudly and they thought we were speaking Welsh. Only once was there violence. One of them threw a dead plaice at the group, and a dead plaice's fin can cause a sharp cut!*

Neston had a distinctive accent and vocabulary of its own. "Yowlers" were Heswall folk, for example, and Neston folk were "Yousers", derived from the greeting *"How do youse?"* (or, according to legend, from *"You, sir!"*). George became Judder and Joseph became Jotter. Many of the working population had nicknames which became distinguishing features between families for more than one generation, even to this day. Many a Jones acquired a prefix, like Plodger, Musty, Kydo (the shepherd with Jim Kemp for years), Monk, Slow, and Muddy, whose job was to pile waste slag at Neston colliery at the turn of the century (hence Muddy's Tip). Joe Mirac was Miraculous Jones to whom nothing was impossible. Other surnames gathered titles like Pan-fry, Pop-the-letterbox, Moco, Jimmy Knowledge-box. Women attracted names like Nanny Dent, Mrs Whisky, and Mrs Parcel-delivery, who ran a delivery service for a small fee to Tozer the pawnbroker for those ashamed to be seen by their neighbours on such an errand themselves.

When Mrs Saladine recorded her memories, she explained the inward-looking feel of Neston:

> *They intermarried too much in Neston. You couldn't talk to anybody, they were either first or second cousins. You were afraid to say anything, you see.*

This problem was not eased until the great influx of new residents after the Second World War, but even in 1960 Mr Cross, the watch repairer, complained that if you offended one person in Neston, you offended them all. Inbreeding was held to be responsible for an element of dullness among some of the local population, which inspired Mrs Barrett to found a Home for Feeble-minded Girls. More will be learned of this home later, in the description of the laundry.

But Mrs Saladine went on to say *"They were very nice. I liked Neston"*. This is a prevailing theme of memories before 1914, both in Neston and Parkgate. Everybody knew everybody else and looked after each other. There was often cause for help, because there was a good deal of poverty in nineteenth-century Neston. Fishing in particular was a seasonal trade; fishing families would have money until November, but might run out by Christmas. There was a charity – Monk's Charity – administered by the vicar, which could provide coal and vouchers for food. One Parkgate shopkeeper used to cook dishes and pass them over the fence for the children of the fishing family that lived next door, and people used to go to the kitchen window of Mostyn House School to see if there were any leftovers after the evening meal. It was quite common to see people with bare feet in summer. The children of Benjamin Higgins, fisherman, never went hungry, but they would take off their shoes as soon as they returned from school. The schools would not admit children without footwear, so shoes had to be kept for school. One Neston resident remembered:

> *My mother's people were fishing people and when the weather was bad they could not go out in the boats. They were very hard times. They would have no money to buy food. My gran would take my grandad's suit to be pawned; there used to be an old pawnshop nearby run by Tommy Tozer, but gran always managed to get the suit out by Sunday for grandad to go to church, for it was the only suit he had.*
>
> *My gran used to go cockling early frosty mornings with pony and cart to earn money for food. My grandad had chest trouble and so was always sick. The gentry were very good to them. Mother used to tell me they would give them*

> *nice clothes and food and hair ribbons for the girls which were popular in those days. Otherwise they would have starved. No hand-outs then – people were very poor.*

But she also said *"They were happy days!"*

Many such memories recall the important part played in the life of Neston by the "gentry", and the sharp divisions between classes that existed in the nineteenth century. Let us now see who these gentlefolk were.

Fig. 5 Ashfield Hall was probably built in 1818 by Joseph Hayes Lyon. It was largely demolished after the Second World War, although parts were converted to farm buildings. Several people of local importance lived here at different times, including Robert Macfie, Uvedale Corbett and Sir John Harmood Banner, MP.

It has already been stated that a large part of Neston and the whole of Parkgate was owned by the Mostyn family of North Wales until they sold it in 1849. As an absentee landlord during the 1840s, Edward Lloyd Mostyn may be presumed to have taken out a great deal more economic value than he put in, although he did attempt to develop Parkgate by completing the Parade and providing a landing-stage for the ferry to Bagillt. The Mostyn estate was divided for sale into lots which were designed to encourage house building *"to suit large and small capitalists"*. At the time it was expected that a railway would soon be built, but the link to

Hooton was not opened until 1866, and "capitalists" were slow to settle in the district. Those who did, particularly Liverpool businessmen, brought considerable economic benefit by spending money earned outside the Neston area. And because they had money, and in many cases a sense of their obligation to the community — not *noblesse oblige*, but *richesse oblige* — their wealth resulted in considerable social benefit as well.

One of the first such newcomers was Robert Macfie, a Scot and keen Presbyterian, who owned a sugar-refining business in Liverpool. He bought Ashfield Hall in 1857, and used his wealth to insert Presbyterianism into the religious life of Neston. When he retired to Scotland, the financial loss was keenly felt by the congregations he had supported.

A similar effect was caused by Captain Henry Ward, of the St George Steamship Company, Liverpool, who lived at Woodpark. He built a chapel at the top of the High Street, and when he died in 1890 his congregation tried but failed to buy the building.

The most influential of the Liverpool businessmen to buy land at Neston was Christopher Bushell, a wine merchant. In 1856 he employed the young architect Alfred Waterhouse to design Hinderton Hall, a sandstone mansion in the High Victorian Gothic style. As well as the employment Bushell created at his house and estate, he gave liberally in both Liverpool

Fig. 6 Hinderton Hall was designed for Christopher Bushell by Alfred Waterhouse. Building started in 1856.

and Neston. In 1874 he founded the Liverpool Council of Education, over which he presided until he died in 1887. He gave generously to the elementary schools established in Neston, Parkgate and Little Neston, to the church in Willaston, and to the rebuilding of Neston church. He gave £400 for the building of Bushell Road, completed in 1885 to link Neston station with Hinderton Road.

In Liverpool, Bushell was honoured by a marble statue, now in the Victoria Building of Liverpool University. His memorial in Neston is the Bushell Fountain at the Cross, erected in 1882 on the site of a public well sunk at his expense in 1865. The memorial fountain, designed by the Local Board's surveyor, John Morris, was made by Shearer, Field & Company at the Dalbeattie Granite Works near Dumfries. The fountain was not connected to Bushell's well, but to the mains water supply which he, as chairman of the Neston Local Board in its early days, had done much to promote.

Christopher Bushell was generous with his time as well as his money. When he died, aged 76, he was chairman of fifteen committees and boards.

Fig. 7 The Manor House, Moorside Lane, was probably built, or rebuilt, in the first two decades of the nineteenth century, and demolished *c*.1969. It is thought to have been on the site of Neston Lodge, the Earl of Derby's hunting lodge for Neston Park until 1600. John Churton, the moving spirit behind the erection of Neston's town hall, lived here.

Neston parish church contains memorials to three generations of the Bushell family: a window to Christopher Bushell; a pair of gates to the tower commemorating his son Reginald, who died in 1904; and a marble tablet to Reginald's son Christopher, who was killed in 1918 and was awarded the Victoria Cross.

Other local residents of substance used to make their money work for the community. Reginald Haigh of Leighton Banastre, a cotton broker who came to Parkgate about 1880, helped to found Neston Cricket Club and threw open his own grounds for the recreation of the navvies building the railway. He also regularly arranged concerts for the local fishermen. John Churton of the Manor House in Moorside Lane, another wine merchant, arranged Christmas meals for the elderly, stated in 1892 to be an annual affair. It was Churton who proposed that a town hall should be built to celebrate Queen Victoria's Golden Jubilee in 1887, and his wife laid the foundation stone.

Fig. 8 The Lydiate, Duncan Graham's residence, built on the site of an older farmhouse, and now owned by the Home Farm Trust.

The wives of the gentry were often ready to play their part in the community. It will be seen, for example, that the Ladies' Club (the Neston Female Friendly Society) depended on the financial support of its "honorary members", who subscribed but did not expect to draw benefits.

During severe winters, the ladies of Neston would help to organize soup kitchens; in January 1887 Mrs Churton supervised the cooking of 150 quarts of soup, sold at one penny a quart. The previous year, Mrs Bushell of Hinderton Hall had organized the distribution of soup, bread and coal.

"In those days," said one Parkgate resident, referring to the years before the First World War, *"everybody knew everybody else, and they helped each other."* Although there was plenty of charity and social support among Nestonians (for example, Mr and Mrs Wolton Gray, timber merchants, were proverbial for their kindness to those in need), it was inevitable that the wealthy households, whose income usually came from outside Neston, took the lead. A good example was Duncan Graham of the Lydiate, Willaston, a Liverpool merchant who dealt in South American trade and insurance, and who died in 1901. He was the first chairman of Cheshire County Council, formed in 1889, and had been a magistrate since 1861. He paid for Willaston's vicarage and the Village Institute, gave assistance to the provision of a church and school, and paid for a water supply to be piped from the water tower at Hinderton to Willaston.

Fig. 9 The village of Thornton Hough was very decrepit until it was rebuilt, first by Joseph Hirst, and then by William Lever. These old thatched cottages, photographed *c.*1870, stood on the north side of the village. They were all replaced in the rebuilding, from the present smithy to the Congregational chapel.

Another village of the old Neston parish was to be totally transformed by two wealthy landowners. In 1847 William Mortimer described Thornton Hough, with its single street cut through the solid sandstone, as

> *presenting a very unpleasant appearance, and though it possesses a few tolerably good houses, the greater portion are of a very inferior description.*

In the 1860s a Yorkshire textile manufacturer named Joseph Hirst came to live in Thornton Hough. He built All Saints church in 1867, and then had a fifth clock face added to its tower because he could not see the lower face from his house. He also built the vicarage, a school, and a row of cottages and shops called Wilshaw Terrace.

Hirst died in 1874, and the estate was bought in 1891 by William Hesketh Lever, who became Lord Leverhulme in 1917. He rebuilt almost the whole of the village, apart from Hirst's buildings, using some of the architects whom he was employing at the same time on his model village at Port Sunlight. He pulled down the existing Thornton Manor, and built, indeed continually rebuilt, a new house there. He built Hesketh Grange for his father, and his brother, J. D. Lever, bought Hirst's house, Thornton House, and rebuilt that. William Lever also provided a Congregational chapel and another school.

In Neston itself he paid for the building of the Liberal Club that became Neston Institute, and supported various local nonconformist and other enterprises, and his son gave Stanney Fields to Neston as a public park.

Apart from Lord Leverhulme, who died in 1925, the most notable wealthy patron between the wars was Arthur Bulley of Mickwell Brow, Ness, a cotton merchant, and the founder of Ness Gardens and of Bees Seeds. As he remarked to Dr Yeoman, *"I have made more money than the heart of man can desire and I want to do something with it."* Examples of his philanthropy are described more fully later, but in brief he allowed public access to his gardens; he provided sports facilities for local people, including bowling greens and tennis courts; he and his wife bought Burton Wood and gave it to the National Trust; Mrs Bulley ensured that local miners and their families did not go hungry during the coal strike of 1926. Ken Hulme has recorded the story of the man who twice burgled Mickwell Brow: it was found that he lived in a poor cottage with no bath, so Mrs Bulley invited him to use the bathroom at Mickwell Brow once a week.

The houses of the gentry provided a good deal of employment in an age when domestic service was a common occupation. Any household that could afford it, even in the lower middle class, would employ a servant. Service in a well-run household was highly prized. Sarah Brazenell, whose husband was the signalman at Parkgate station, and who kept a lodging house in Parkgate, had been trained in domestic service, and her niece has written:

> *My mother and Aunt Sarah went into service at the customary age of eleven. It was an early form of domestic training. They lived with graciousness, beauty and high standards. This meant that once married, rearing children and running their own homes, their standards were automatically set and very high. This was reflected in my generation. I knew my place, I was absolutely secure, and the daily, weekly, seasonal routine set me on the path of life.*

The census lists give some idea of the large households, but we can only be sure that smaller households employed servants if they were living-in at the time of the census. One of the largest establishments in 1871 was Denna Hall in Ness, where a staff of six resident servants supported one lone lady, Mrs Barbara Stanley, whose late husband Charles had owned the nearby coal mine. Mrs Stanley had a butler, cook, lady's maid, laundry maid, housemaid, kitchen maid and a page. She, like the other owners of

SERVANTS REGISTER OFFICE.

WORK OF EVERY DISCRIPTON.

HOURS:- 9 A.M. - 4 P.M.
EVERY WEEK DAY EXCEPTING
WEDNESDAY & SATURDAY
9 A.M. - 1 P.M.

Madam T. Cottrell,
Ashcroft,
Flag Lane,
off Mellock Lane,
Little Neston.

Opposite H. Norman & Son.

Fig. 10 Advertisements like this for domestic servants were common until the late 1940s.

large houses, would have employed other, non-resident, staff such as gardeners, grooms and a coachman. Other householders who are shown in the 1871 census to have four or more resident staff were Henry Ward, shipowner, living at Woodpark; Duncan Graham, merchant, at the Lydiate; Margaret Forwood at Thornton Manor; William Gorst, cotton broker, at Rocklands in Thornton Hough; Owen Jones, timber merchant, at Stanacres, also in Thornton Hough; Samuel Radford, corn merchant and owner of Willaston mill, at Raby House; Edward Sellers, brewer, at Moorside House; Robert Beausire, merchant, at Moorside; Edmund Hett, merchant, at Leighton Cottage; Theodore Rathbone, landowner, at Backwood Hall; and Elizabeth Lyon at the house below Neston church. There would undoubtedly have been a large staff at Hinderton Hall, had the family been in residence on census night, but as it was, the butler had been left with a skeleton staff. To this list may be added two commercial establishments – the Union Hotel and Mostyn House School.

There were numbers of other families who had between one and three resident servants each, together with, in total, at least 135 domestic servants working from their own homes, as well as several charwomen and laundresses. However, the employment in the large households did not always go to local people. Gentlefolk had often moved to the Neston area from elsewhere, bringing their staff with them. The Bushells' butler at Hinderton Hall in 1871 was Swiss, and Edmund Hett's butler had been born in Africa, and was black – a nine days' wonder in Neston.

In 1907, Lionel Barber, a merchant trading between Liverpool and South America, moved into one of the first two big houses to be built in Hinderton Road, to be known by some as "Quality Street". His daughter remembers that

> *we had maids, mostly from Wales. We had someone to come in and do the washing, a cook, a housemaid, a groom and a part-time gardener.*

Miss Barber has vivid memories of her father's horse:

> *We had a horse and trap. My father asked Mr Cosgrove the vet to choose a horse for us. My mother met my father one day at the station and they rushed to see the horse which was in a stable behind the Brewer's Arms. The stableman told them to watch out for the horse's heels as it kicked out. He said that in his opinion the vet was drunk when he chose it and so was the horse!*
>
> *I can just remember the coronation of George V* [in June 1911]. *I would be about four. We went in the trap to Neston and met a brass band by the church. Rufus, the horse, whipped round and we galloped home and that's all we saw of the coronation celebrations. It was not dangerous as there was nothing to bump into. He was so wild that father took him for a gallop along the shore on a Saturday, and a long twelve-mile trot on a Sunday. He was all right for mother on Monday and Tuesday but the effect had worn off by Wednesday. Rufus eventually broke the trap and was sold to the Army as a remount.*

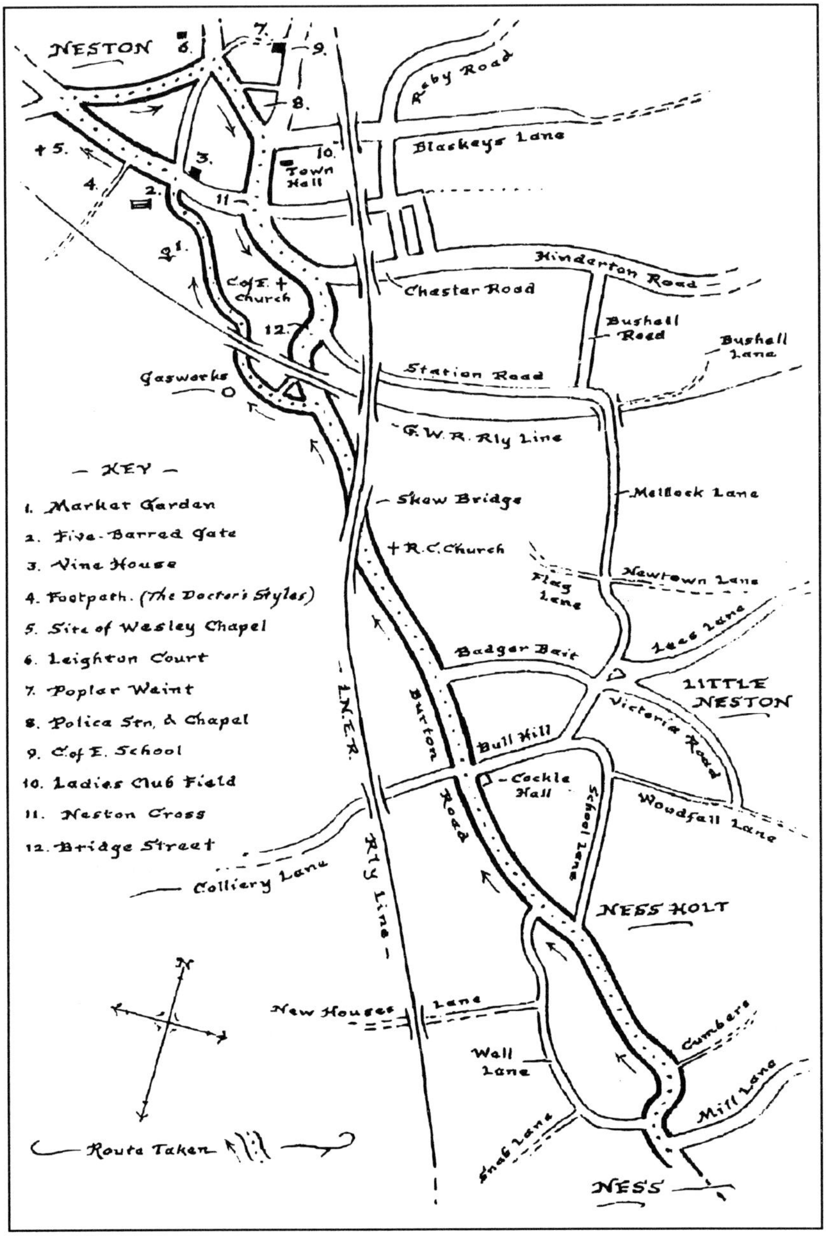

Fig. 11 *"A visit to Neston was quite an event."* The route from Ness to Neston as it was described by Mrs Swanwick.

To end the chapter, this is the lyrical description of Neston in the 1890s written by Mrs Elizabeth Swanwick when she was 80.

> **When we came from Chester in the 1890s to live in Ness, the countryside was a source of interest and delight. A visit to Neston was quite an event. From Ness Holt we walked along Burton Road, past the Colliery Lane end and Cockle Hall cottages, past the Catholic church surrounded by chestnut trees and under the skew bridge which carries the LNER line. The winds met here and could blow folk off their feet. From the bottom of Bridge Street there are two ways of entering Neston: straight on or by taking the left turning into Church Lane. Following the Church Lane route, there were some sandstone houses, terraced cottages, the gasworks and gasometer. Under a low bridge carrying the GWR line, one often came across tiny freshwater springs and a profusion of wild flowers and ferns growing on the moist grassy banks. Then on the right one passed the churchyard wall and on the left, acres of fertile land, set with vegetables and flowers cultivated by two partners who ran a flourishing market garden. At the end of Church Lane we would linger awhile by the five-barred gate and admire the scene, of cattle grazing in the meadows and a flight of seagulls in the wake of horse and ploughman as they furrowed the field. The distant views of the Welsh hills and the River Dee were magnificent, especially when the sun was setting and the glowing colours were reflected in the water.**
>
> **In Parkgate Road with its fine Georgian houses, we would see Vine House with its wall sundial. Up its cobbled side entrance there were two rooms set aside for the doctor's surgery. Down on the left was a footpath to the Neston Steam Laundry and the Old Quay farmlands.**
>
> **Further down, past two tiny cottages with cobbled frontages was the chapel where John Wesley used to preach. Turning sharp right up Buggen Lane, there was one of the largest houses in the district, known as Leighton Court, owned by a wealthy gentleman, a Mr Whineray, who also kept a pack of hounds. During the hunting season it was a wonderful sight to see the colourful garb of the huntsmen with the hounds, passing through the village on their way to outlying fields after their quarry.**
>
> **Turning right, one would pass Poplar Weint, three public houses, a Wesleyan chapel, the police station and the lock-up. Justices of the Peace held a court once a month and tried minor offences. When there were no cases to answer the sergeant used to present a pair of white gloves to the chief magistrate. In the High Street we passed the Town Hall, an impressive building of which Neston was justly proud,**

Fig. 12 Mrs Swanwick would have been familiar with this house, next to Bridson's yard at the bottom of Bridge Street, Neston.

as no other village in the Hundred of Wirral possessed one. Here local dignitaries governed public affairs. At that time Mr John Caleb Lloyd was the chairman, affectionately known as Old Colonel Lloyd. The High Street would be full of busy shoppers, horse-drawn vehicles, pony traps, carts and cyclists. As well as butchers, bakers and grocers, there was a tailor, shoemender, saddler and shoeing smith. Prices were competitive as money was scarce. There was a plentiful supply of cockles, shrimps, flatfish and salmon when in season. Nestonians were hardworking and industrious, with an innate sense of humour as they exchanged greetings in their own unique dialect: "Ow go, owd un?", "Or reet, youse".

There was a good community spirit, and the most eagerly awaited event of the year was the Ladies' Club Day, held on the first Thursday in June. A small weekly sum secured free medical services for members. The ladies walked from the school in Liverpool Road carrying flowered staffs and headed by band and banners, to the parish church. The children had a holiday from school and a field was set aside down Raby Road for Pat Collins' Amusements. The men also had their day. On Whit bank holiday members of the Grand Order of Shepherds marched, carrying shepherds' crooks, with field sports afterwards including a game of quoits.

Fig. 13 Maypole dancers in Neston in 1898. May Day, and the crowning of the May Queen, was another celebratory event.

The parish church stands almost central to the village. In the graveyard, to those who will pause and listen, the tombstones speak of inhabitants who by their strength lived well over four score years, some attaining a century or more. The Sabbath day was rigorously kept as a day of rest.

At Neston Cross, where a drinking fountain stood in the middle of the crossroads, was the old vicarage, with its wide flagged entrance surrounded by trees, and three public houses, the Brown Horse, White Horse and Greenland Fishery, which made travellers sure of a meal of bread and cheese and a drink of ale. Down Bridge Street were tall houses with high steps, iron railings and cobbled frontages.

This is a short journey through Neston, truly a good place to live with its clean air and excellent drinking water. Scenes change, nothing stands still and old folk must move along with the times, but now and again it is pleasant to recall a leisurely way of life.

SOURCES

This chapter was written by Geoffrey Place.

For the sale of the Mostyn estate, see G. W. Place, *The Rise and Fall of Parkgate, passenger port for Ireland* (PhD thesis, Liverpool University 1990). The *Liverpool Albion*'s report on the sale was quoted by the *Chester Chronicle* (1 June 1849).

The population statistics in Figures 3 and 4 were compiled by David Morris.

The account of Neston's rowdiness owes much to the reports in the *Chester Chronicle* and the recollections of Bill Smith and Kate Ryder. The reprimand of the two police officers for the illegal use of firearms is in the Police Enrolment Book (Cheshire Record Office, CJP 7/2, 3).

We are grateful to Stuart Carter for his observations on the Neston dialect, and to David Scott for the nicknames.

For memories of hard times, the recollections of Mrs Saladine, Molly Jones, Bella Anyon and Flo Dodd have been most useful.

The story about the burglar at Mickwell Brow is told in J. K. Hulme, *Ness Gardens, Bulley's beginnings to the present day* (1987).

The quotation about the benefits of domestic service is by Kate Ryder.

The uncertain temperament of her father's horse was remembered by Miss Joyce Barber.

We are grateful to Miss M. Roberts and Miss R. Roberts for permission to use the memoir of Elizabeth Swanwick.

CHAPTER TWO

THE DAILY BREAD: FARMING AND FISHING

Until the Second World War, agriculture provided the background to all life in the Neston district. Although Neston itself was not an agricultural town, sheep and cattle were from time to time driven through the streets, usually to the slaughterhouses of the butchers, and there are accounts of animals escaping and running into the shops. The surrounding villages, however, were still dominated by their farms and the large estates of the landed gentry. They were serviced by local tradesmen, such as the blacksmiths and wheelwrights, threshing contractors and millers. The harvest of the sea, too, was an important feature of the local economy. Both men and women were employed in Parkgate's fishing industry, and for a time exported large quantities of shellfish by train to many other parts of the country.

AGRICULTURE

In 1840 the eight townships of the parish of Neston were dominated by the estates of three great landowning families: these were the Mostyn family of North Wales, the Earl of Shrewsbury, and the Stanleys of Hooton.

The Mostyn estate owned nearly all of Great Neston and Leighton, including the whole village of Parkgate, as well as over 60% of Thornton Hough. The Earl of Shrewsbury owned the whole of Raby, 67% of Little Neston and an estate in Thornton Hough. The Stanley family controlled all of Ledsham and most of Ness.

Only one township in the parish was free from the influence of a major landowner. This was Willaston, where the manor had been broken up in the seventeenth century. In 1840 the largest landowners in Willaston were the Bennetts of Willaston Hall and John Lyon Winder, heir to the Lyons of Ashfield Hall. Between them they owned 51% of the land in Willaston.

When Sir Thomas Mostyn died unmarried in 1831, the male line of his family came to an end. The heir in 1840 was his nephew, Edward Lloyd Mostyn, whose father, Sir Edward Lloyd, had been made the first Baron

Mostyn. The Mostyn estate was heavily mortgaged – for £100,000 by 1843. In the same year, an Enclosure Act had been obtained for another Mostyn estate at Llandudno Bay, and the decision to create a new resort on this land coincided with the need to pay off the burden of debt. The Mostyns' extensive Cheshire estates, including 1,500 acres in the parish of Neston, were sold by auction in 1849, and the land was divided among many owners.

The Shrewsbury lands in Neston remained intact throughout the nineteenth century, and were sold in 1911–13. William Lever bought the Raby estate with Thornton Manor in 1911, and his descendants still own it today. The Little Neston estate was auctioned and broken up in 1913.

The Stanley estate, like that of the Mostyns, became heavily encumbered with debt. Sir Thomas Stanley of Hooton, whose brother Charles owned the colliery at Ness, died in 1841, leaving three sons, each of whom, in turn, inherited the baronetcy, which died with them. The eldest son, Sir William Stanley, died in 1863, but it had been his brother Rowland who inherited the Ledsham and Ness estates. Rowland had adopted the surname of his maternal grandmother, Errington. Sir Rowland Errington died in 1875, to be succeeded by his brother John, who had also added Errington to his surname. Sir John died in 1895, and the Ness estate was sold at about that time. The Ledsham estate, however, was inherited by the son of Sir Thomas Stanley's daughter Maria, who had married Sir Richard Williams-Bulkeley. Her son Richard sold the Ledsham estate to Cheshire County Council in 1908.

In the 1840s there were only a few large farms. In all the eight townships, there were eight farms larger than 200 acres, the biggest being Joseph Simcock's 267-acre farm at Leighton. There were 26 farms between 100 and 200 acres, and 33 farms between 40 and 100 acres. The proportion of arable land to grassland was much the same in each township: one-third was arable, to two-thirds pasture or meadow. Dairy farming, therefore, was the predominant form of agriculture, although on some farms the grass maintained quite a number of sheep. When New Hall Farm in Thornton Hough – one of the largest farms, at 255 acres – was sold in 1857, the auction advertisement listed 36 heifers, eight horses, poultry, much machinery, hay, oats, vetches, potatoes and swedes. At Leighton Hall FarmLeighton , the largest in the parish, there was a sale in 1862 of 24 cattle, 280 sheep, and six horses. Too great a reliance on cattle could be disastrous when cattle plague (rinderpest) struck the country. In 1866 one of the local landed gentry, Duncan Graham, offered a sheep for every cow that had to be slaughtered during the prevailing cattle plague.

According to the 1851 census returns, farming then occupied a quarter of the adult population of Neston parish. By that time the annual hiring fairs, at which agricultural labourers and other servants were engaged to work for the next twelve months, had died out. In 1826 the *Chester Chronicle* had reported disapprovingly:

> *It is with deep concern we state that the scene exhibited at Neston on Sunday last has completely disappointed our expectations. A considerable number of farmers and labourers assembled in the forenoon, when the usual bartering for labour on the one hand, and wages on the other, took place. A scene of drunkenness, the usual concomitant of this disgraceful practice at Neston, followed, which was succeeded by general fighting through the town.*

Before we come to four chosen examples of local agriculture, it is worth looking at a common feature of the landscape — the marl pit.

There are said to be more ponds in Cheshire than in the rest of England, and most of them were dug deliberately as marl pits. There are still hundreds of these pits in Wirral, evidence of this ancient method of fertilizing the soil. There are twenty marl pits on the Ashfield estate, near Neston, alone. Marl is a calcium-rich deposit, formed of ground seashells, commonly found in pockets beneath the Cheshire clay. When the marl was strewn over the fields, the lime would improve the yield of the field for several years. Marl pits were usually dug with three vertical sides and one sloping side to permit a cart to enter and leave the pit. In some localities a marl pit could be seen in almost every field, while elsewhere they might be dug in a group together, as at Marehall Lane in Little Neston.

Marl digging was labour-intensive and expensive. The teams of diggers used to supplement their income by performing songs and dances to solicit gifts from passers-by. Marl was still quite commonly dug in the early decades of the nineteenth century, until the railways began to distribute cheaper means of fertilizing the soil. At the colliery at Little Neston there were two lime kilns, and even before the railway era it is probable that the coal sloops would bring limestone as ballast to Denhall Quay, where it was reduced to powder in the kilns, fuelled by the nearby coal.

Farming in Raby

Raby has always been an estate village, owned by the Earls of Shrewsbury until 1911, when it was bought by William Lever, and it remains a part of the Leverhulme estate to this day. In 1840 the fields of farmers still tended to be scattered throughout the township, as they had been in medieval times to share out good and bad land, while two fields, Willow Brow and Grass Ground, were still divided into unfenced strips allocated to different farmers. The tendency everywhere in the nineteenth century was to amalgamate fields to make compact farms, and in the process the farms often grew larger.

Holdings	1841	1911
200-265 acres	0	3
100-199 "	7	5
50-99 "	2	1
25-49 "	3	3
2-24 "	12	10
Total over 1 acre	24	22

Fig. 14 A comparison of the acreages of Raby's farms between 1841 and 1911 shows how the sizes were changing.

Of the 31 heads of household recorded in the Raby of 1841, fourteen were farmers with more than eighteen acres, and another seven held smaller amounts of land. Only two were agricultural labourers without land, and the rest were made up of the publican, the miller, the blacksmith, two plasterers and a gamekeeper. As well as their families and farm servants, there were lodgers, including foresters, carters and the village teacher, making 190 inhabitants of the village.

We know something of the working of the estate from the documents of the Langley family. Charles Langley's tenancy agreement for Willow Brow Farm in 1871 required that 35 of his 75 acres were to be kept as pasture and that he had to obtain the landlord's consent before ploughing any pasture land. He had to preserve the hedges and plant new ones when required, clean ditches, and preserve timber, game and fish for the use of the landlord. Charles Langley's widow and son moved to Thornton Grange Farm in the 1890s, but the family returned to Willow Brow in 1933. The farm was then 67% arable and 23% pasture. Letters from this period show that the estate was corresponding with its tenants on such matters as the upkeep of hedges and fences, the shooting rights of landlord and tenant, the tenants' wedding present when Philip Lever married Miss Margaret Moon in 1937, and the retirement in 1938 of the agent, Frank Clarke, after 30 years in office.

Raby, alone among the townships of the ancient Neston parish, still retains the air of the agricultural village that it has always borne. There are still farmhouses in the centre of the village, it still has authentic mud on the roads. And the map on the next page, which shows the farmhouses as they were in the middle of the nineteenth century, has much the same plan as the village of today.

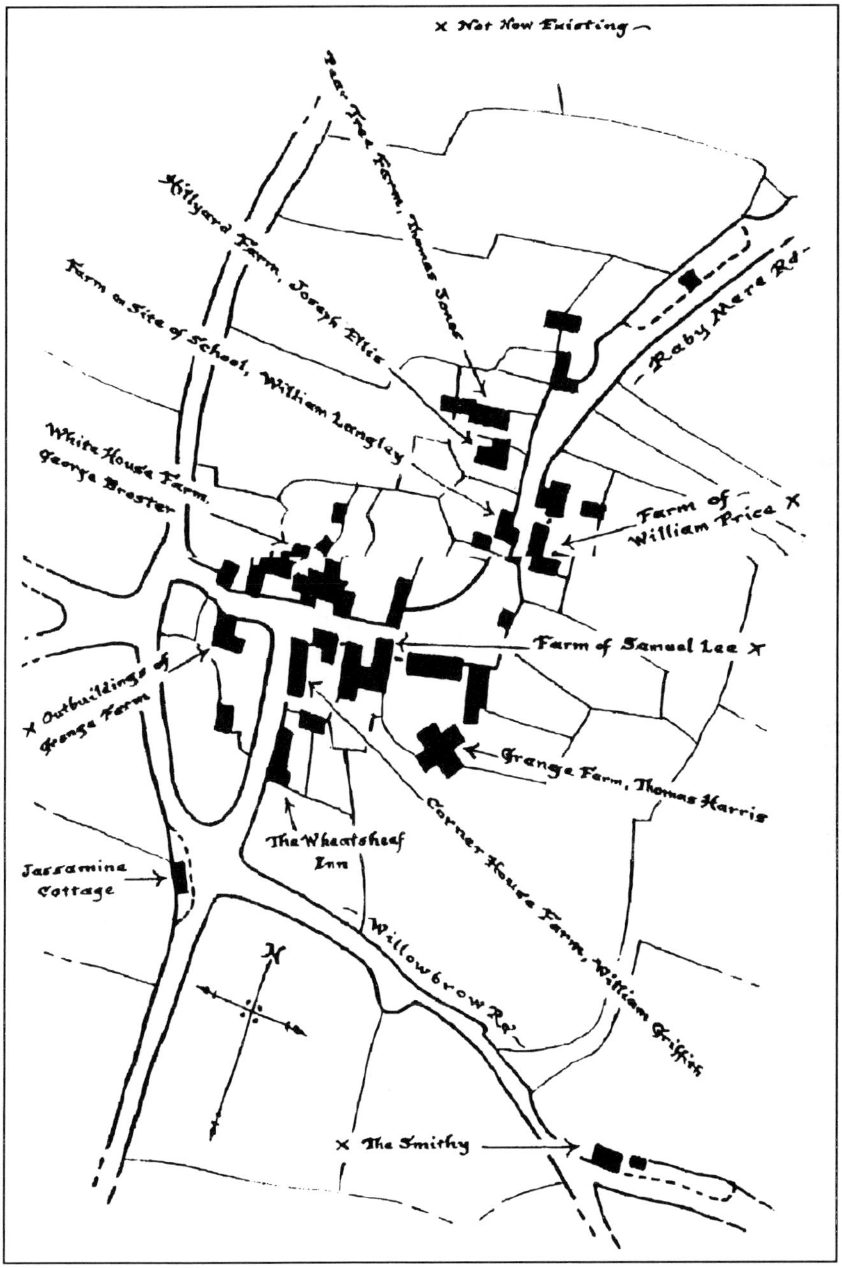

Fig. 15 Raby farms and farmers in the 1840s (drawn from the 1843 tithe map).

The atmosphere of farming in Raby has been vividly captured in this description by John Eastwood of threshing:

> **And so to the farm, with its friendly barns, clucking hens on the midden, and sound of milk squirting pleasantly into the white pails in the shippen. The threshing machine has already arrived and is in position, the tractor gently chugging and the men standing about, smoking Woodbines, glad to be doing nothing in the sunshine, shielded from the wind by the unthreshed wheat in the big red Dutch barn.**
>
> **As I guessed, Farmer Randles** [of White House Farm] **appoints me to the most unpleasant job of the day. Bagging chaff is a mucky, boring job, but at least it involves a good deal of that most delightful of agricultural pursuits, doing nothing.**
>
> **The threshing machine is an enormous rattling monster, spewing out grain at one end, baled straw (via the attached baler) at the other. The chaff theoretically comes out through two chutes in the side of the machine: in actual fact it spurts and showers from a thousand and one different crannies and leaks. However, the bulk of it comes out via the chutes, and here I take up my position as the big belt begins to revolve and the first sheaves are thrown down to the layer on top of the machine.**
>
> **My head narrowly escaping decapitation from the whirling belt I stand amidst the flying chaff with smarting eyes, waiting until one sack is filled; then slam down the lever on the machine so that the flow is diverted down the other chute into the second bag. Unhook the first bag, hump it over my shoulder, and wander across the muddy stackyard in the sunlight. Up a long ricketty ladder, the end of the huge sack bumping on my heels, to a dark, cobwebby loft where a low bay has been erected of baled straw. Empty the chaff from the bag, and briefly survey from the top of the ladder the familiar wide sweep of mid-Wirral countryside, green and silver and blue, a cloud of white gulls following a tractor as it draws a clean brown line across the old stubble, woodpigeons flying from bare black trees ...**
>
> **Toss down the empty bag, follow it down the ladder, and wander back through the hens to the roaring, rattling, insatiable machine. Then once again the limited view of insanely jigging pistons and pulleys, the dancing, whirling chaff, incessant noises, and straw all over the place.**
>
> **If anything goes wrong with my end of the machine, I call the Devil in charge. He is in the tradition of those threshing-machine**

attendants in Hardy's Tess — black-avised, greasy, unshaven, without speech. He answers nothing to my light conversation, save only a gruff "Ah!" to a direct question. His whole life is the Machine; he is the custodian and doctor, infallible on its many breakdowns, caring nothing save its tending.

Fig. 16 Thatched cottage, Raby, in the early 1900s. Once known as the Crow's Foot Inn, it now serves as a chicken house for White House Farm.

Suddenly the farmer's wife appears with a mug of steaming tea, and we know it is time for "baggins". Work stops like magic and we all crowd into an empty bay, lean and sit on bales of straw. The four regular farmworkers here are quiet, pleasant men; those who travel with the machine are tough fellows, with hoarse voices and wicked, inflamed eyes.

Work resumes, and half-an-hour later the thresher breaks down. "Bloody droom's stoock!" grunts the Chief Devil, which is the longest coherent statement he has yet made in my hearing. He and the Second Devil fling a few oaths at one another and go to work. Ten minutes later the machine starts up again with a clattering roar.

All day we toil, while the level of sheaves in the bay grows lower and lower. Vic, strongest pitcher in the village, is tireless: his flashing pikel hurls up sheaf after sheaf to the men on the platform, one of whom cuts the binder-twine of each sheaf while the other spreads the loosened sheaf on the revolving drum. Ever faster spills the gold-brown grain into the line of sacks at the end of the thresher, ever faster fill my sacks, while the loose chaff rises in choking clouds, leaking from every available place.

As the level of the stack grows lower and the pitcher and his mate nearer the ground, the mice and rats begin to emerge. Two cattle dogs are nosing frantically among the sheaves, imminently escaping death from the pitch-forks. The farm children have gathered, waiting eagerly with big sticks.

Mice run out, to be kicked or bludgeoned to death. Children cry with fearful delight, and a sheaf, bright with new blood, is speared by Vic's pikel and goes hurtling up to the platform. Men stamp on scurrying mice, lash out at rats. A mouse runs by my foot in a frenzy of terror, and I stamp hard, twice. Seeing a bloody pulp I feel suddenly desolate in this harsh farming world, knowing that I have wilfully killed something that once was happy in its fragile mousy life about the ricks and the old dark barns.

My sack spills over, chaff rises up into the chute and there is a grinding stoppage. The Chief Devil, with a muttered oath, stumbles through the mist of flying chaff, thrusts his arm right up the chaff-passage like a vet with a cow, and rights the inevitable blockage caused by the stopped exit. Once more the rattle continues.

The day wears on, until at last the sun has gone down in a yellow flaring blaze beyond Moel Fammau and a cold planet hangs like a white jewel in the west. The last wheatsheaf goes up to the platform; the last grain sack is carried over to the shed. I take the final load of chaff across to the loft, and the threshing machine slows down, grumbles, and is silent.

A central part of Raby's life was the Wheatsheaf Inn. John Eastwood was also the author of the following evocation of the Wheatsheaf as it was in the late 1940s:

To me the Wheatsheaf was the epitome of the country inn. Not only was it full of locals (if one includes those who walked over from Thornton Hough) but it was very ancient, half-timbered and whitewashed, with a thick dark hood of thatch enveloping the old building like a pixie's hat. It still is the same beautiful building, but

tarted up for the present-day, its rooms knocked together, pretty hanging baskets of flowers pendant below the less-ragged thatch. Not spoiled in any sense, but changed. It was pleasant in the early evening when the living was sweet to walk out to the Wheatsheaf, perhaps when winter was dying away and the ploughed earth exhaled its promise of spring. I liked to trudge through the scattered village as dusk turned to dark, boots ringing on the road, lights glowing in cottages and wood-owls hooting under the familiar stars. Round by the friendly sandstone barn, then the white wall of the inn glimmering in the darkness, the door pushed open, and the friendly glow of lamplight and the brusque greeting of the landlord. I'd know exactly who would be there at this time: Bert, of course, the stocky and taciturn publican-cum-farmer, dressed always in grey woollen cardigan, breeches, black leggings and boots; Ernie, who now worked on the local roads but had also worked expertly on farms, and in his heyday had been a Hunt servant for Sir Watkin Williams Wynn — Ernie sat always in a corner seat by the fire, best green pork pie hat set level across weathered forehead, dominating the conversation in his burring Shropshire voice; Bob, who preferred rabbit-trapping and the thrills and delights of poaching Lord Leverhulme's pheasants to more regular work, his cap pushed back at a rakish angle, lurcher dog crouched watchfully behind his legs; and perhaps "the gentry", standing by the bar-hatch. "The gentry" were Phil Baines, huge and florid, one-legged since Alamein, and Mr Kelly, Master of the Royal Rock Beagles. They drank whisky, top-shelf stuff for top-shelf people, whereas those who sat round the fire drank pints of black mild ale, costing about one shilling a pint.

The talk would be of farming, of the price of geese or pigs, of the wicked price of ale and baccy, of this afternoon's meet of the Beagles outside the Wheatsheaf, of how Phil Baines and Mr Kelly dug out a fox from a raddle-bank in a wood near Willaston, of how Bob shot a woodcock yesterday, "a terrible straight-flyin' bird" — talk slow and leisured, for the most part as old in character as the inn itself.

About seven o'clock the room would begin to fill. Men, greatcoated, cloth-capped, in their best shiny blue suits of serge, this being Saturday night, stamping in out of the cold evening, shouting greetings, calling for beer. Just one woman, a buxom peroxided wife, who knew and was known by everybody.

The survey of farming in Raby is concluded by a portrait of one of its inhabitants, Albert Shakeshaft. All his life he worked at White House

Farm, where a school exercise book in his handwriting is still kept. In this book he wrote, at the age of 10 or 11,

My own life. I was born on the 9th of February 1881. My parents were then living at Tarporley a pretty little Cheshire village.

When I was a very little boy we came to reside at Thornton Hough. At the age of five I was sent to school. I am now in standard six. I have always tried to be a credit to myself, the school, my teacher and to be kind and honest. Any boy who does that has nothing to fear. My school days will soon be over. I hardly know what I should like to be. As I grow older I hope I may have health, strength, kind friends and a fair share of the world's goods and pleasures and few troubles and sorrows.

Fig. 17 Albert Shakeshaft of Raby, *c.*1900.

My home. I live in a pretty little cottage in the village of Raby. We have a small flower garden in the front. There is a little land at the back on which we grow a few vegetables. There are two good sized

rooms and a small scullery on the ground floor. Up-stairs are three bed-rooms. The house is not a very healthy one. It is damp, dark and badly draining. We shall get out of it as soon as we can obtain another house. Our family is only a small one and consists of my parents, sister and myself. Father works on a farm and has to be up very early.

The house he describes appears to be Jassamine Cottage, in which, despite the unhealthy conditions he mentions, he lived for the rest of his life.

A *"crafty old couple"* who lived next to the old smithy used to be short-tempered with the village children. One day Albert Shakeshaft put a live duck down their chimney to scare them, and they gave the children no further trouble.

Albert became an expert ploughman and took part in the ploughing matches which were a feature of the rural calendar. The farm wages book for 1942 records that his standard wage was then £3 a week, with overtime paid at 1s. 3d. an hour. He was one of six principal workers at White House Farm, not counting the farmer's family. He went to market once a week and had to rise at 5 a.m. He was a committee member of the Raby Men's Club, which met in the old schoolroom to play billiards. He never married, but was visited by two women friends, between whom there was some hostility. Albert died in 1945, aged 65, and was buried in the churchyard of All Saints, Thornton Hough.

Smallholdings in Ledsham

This estate, long held by the Stanley family, was sold by auction in Chester in August 1908. Empowered by the Smallholdings Act, Cheshire County Council bought the 800-acre estate. A smallholding was supposed under normal circumstances to be no more than 60 acres, and the intention was to give a chance to people already experienced on the land, such as former farm bailiffs or farm labourers who had saved some money, to rent their own land. Before the sale there had been five or six farms on the Ledsham estate, the largest being some 300 acres, and this land was split into 33 smallholdings. Of these, 26 were dairy smallholdings of various sizes, the largest being 50 acres and the average 29 acres. There were also six market gardens of about five acres each, and five allotments of one or two acres.

Of the six former tenants named at the time, four remained in their old houses, and twenty new houses were built by the county council. They were three-bedroomed houses, four detached and sixteen semis, and some carry a date tablet marked "C.C.C. 1908". Their outbuildings included dairy, shippon, piggery, stabling, granary and cart shed.

Fig. 18 A pair of Cheshire County Council's smallholdings in Ledsham, as they appear today.

The rents were designed to pay back the capital and management charges over 80 years for the land and 60 years for the buildings. The Ledsham estate was the first of several purchases made by the county council over the next 24 years, resulting in some 280 smallholdings which Cheshire still administers.

Little Neston

Whereas the agriculture in Raby and Ledsham is still very much alive, the farms of Little Neston are almost entirely a memory, stirred by road names like Ivy Farm Drive and Rock Farm Drive, by buildings like Rose Farm Garage, and by an inscription on a wall in Ashtree Drive saying "Barn slated 1890".

At the time that the Talbot estate in Little Neston belonging to the family of the Earl of Shrewsbury was sold in 1913, there were four large farms: White House Farm with 113 acres, Ivy Farm with 93 acres, Rock Farm with 73 acres and Rose Farm with 66 acres. Three smaller farms were Mellock Farm with 10 acres, Ashtree Farm and Lees Lane Farm.

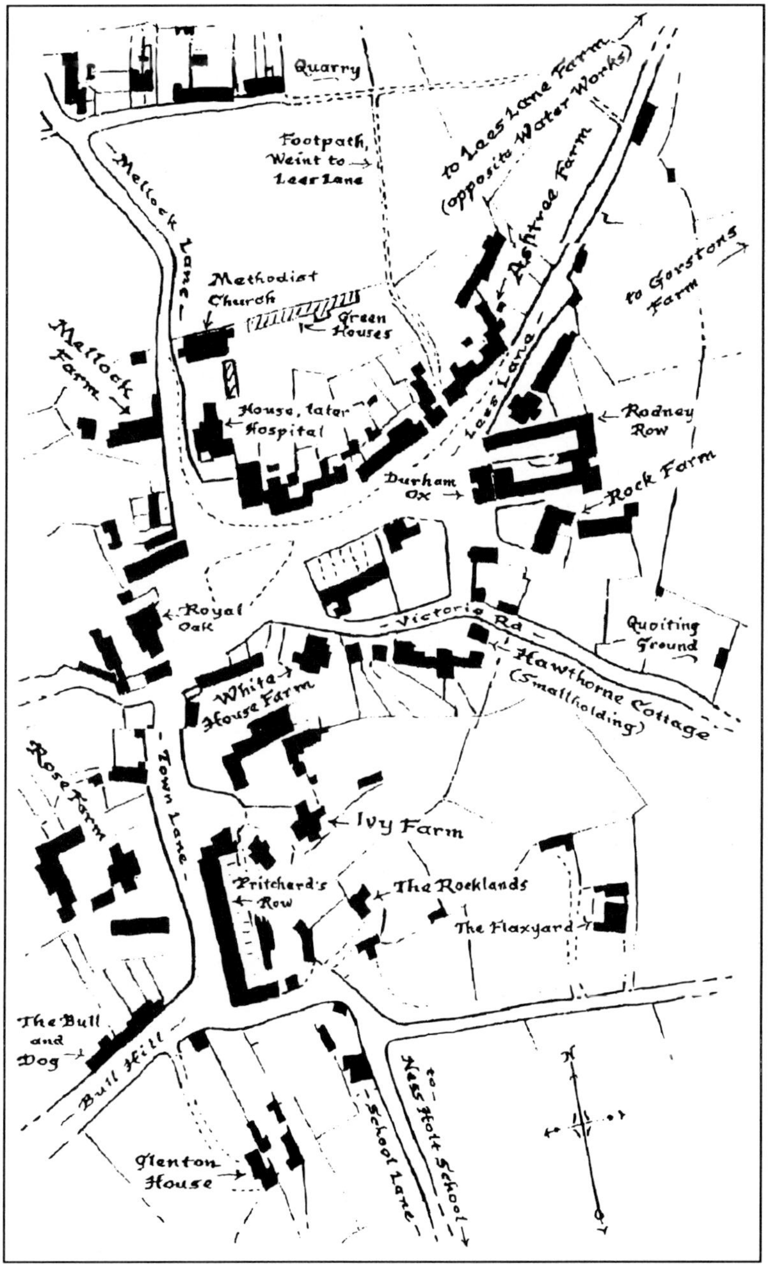

Fig. 19 Farms in Little Neston (adapted from Lord Talbot's estate map of 1913).

In the case of Rose Farm, a garage now stands on the site of the farmhouse, and its land is now covered by Thirlmere and Coniston Roads and Rose Gardens. At the corner of the field by Burton Road there was a marl pit called Parr's Pit, which had filled with water, and in cold winters people skated on it. The farm's L-shaped outbuildings were typical of those found locally: there was a stable with three stalls, shippons for eighteen cows, piggeries, a potato store and a mixing house provided with horse power. This would have been a horse "gin", or engine, where a horse walked continually in a circle to turn a wheel and so drive the machinery. There was also a large sandstone trough in the yard and a Dutch barn. Shops now cover the site of the orchard. In 1913 Joseph Royden held the farm, but in the 1920s it was occupied by the Dodd family. They had shire horses for heavy work like ploughing, and a pony and trap to deliver milk.

Fig. 20 A ploughing match, off Lees Lane, Little Neston.

Almost opposite Rose Farm was Ivy Farm, which was run by the Scott family. George Scott had come from Northumberland in 1837 to farm at Denhall, and his son Thomas took over what was then called Sutton's Farm in Little Neston in 1876. His son Robert renamed the farm Ivy Farm when he married Bertha Swift in 1901. They were able to buy the farm in 1913 for £3,300. Their land is now covered by the houses of West Vale, West Drive and Homecroft. One of their farm workers was Tom Jones, who lived in Pritchard's Row. The story goes that when he got up in the morning he would let his dog out of the house, and while Tom was dressing, the dog would run down Bull Hill and Colliery Lane (now Marshlands Road), sort out the cows for milking, and have them ready for his master at the field gate.

Next to Ivy Farm, on the south side of the Green, was White House Farm. Its shippons are now converted to houses looking on to the Green, and the bull pen and pig sties were on the site of the first and second shops in Town Lane. Before the buildings were converted into shops, the Town Lane side was just a blank brick wall. In summer men used to sit against this wall in the warmth of the evening sun. There was a pinfold on the Green in front of White House Farm, where stray animals were kept until their owners reclaimed them. In the 1930s the Scotts of Ivy Farm bought White House Farm and sold their original farmhouse to a solicitor.

Fig. 21 The Green, Little Neston, and White House Farm. The old Royal Oak (thatched gable on right) burned down in 1901.

Rock Farm occupied the hill behind the Green, and some of its land is still farmed by the University of Liverpool's veterinary research station, while the rest is covered by Stone Bank Drive and the Rock Farm estate. Rock Farm was run by the Jones family since at least 1881. Until the 1920s the farmhouse was Rock Farm Cottage, which stands at the top corner of the Green. The family continued to develop the farm buildings until 1936.

Of the smaller farms, Mellock Farm stood opposite Little Neston Methodist Church. Its land is now covered by Talbot Avenue. In 1913 the farmer was Edward Williams, who sent his milk by train to the Royal Liverpool Children's Hospital in Heswall. When Neston cottage hospital was established just across the road from the farm, they too asked to be supplied with milk, but the farmer did not have enough cows, though he did supply the occasional jug of milk in emergencies.

There were also two small farms in Lees Lane: one of them, Ashtree Farm, is commemorated in Ashtree Drive; the other, Lees Lane Farm, was not part of the Talbot estate, but belonged to Lord Leverhulme. In the 1920s Reginald Dodd was the farmer, paying an annual rent of £70.

Fig. 22 Lees Lane Farm, Little Neston, in the early 1900s. It stood on the high ground opposite the site of the present waterworks.

There were two further smallholdings in Little Neston. Generations of the Woodward family lived at Gorstons, an early longhouse cottage near the site of the present reservoir. One local resident used to say *"people come up here and say 'What a lovely view', but you can't fill your belly on a view"*. Early potatoes were grown at Hawthorn Cottage in Victoria Road. The sale of the crop in early June, which is unusual for the district, paid for the family's holiday later in the month.

The farmers of the district kept dairy cattle for milk, cream and butter products. They were not making cheese in the twentieth century, although they may have done so earlier. We know from farm inventories that Mrs Langley was making cheese at Grange Farm, Thornton Hough, in 1891, but no cheese was being made at two Raby farms, Willow Brow and White House, in the 1930s. Milk was sometimes delivered in bottles, but some households preferred to keep a milk can, which was filled from a tankard, or churn, carried on the float. Beef cattle, ready for slaughter at 18 to 24 months, were often sent to the market near the Northgate in Chester, or to Hooton Smithfield, where the station car park is now. Cattle were moved on the hoof, in a farmer's trailer or by a haulage firm. There was a cattle pen at Neston (South) Station.

When sheep were shorn, the wool was put into sacks for selling at the Linenhall Street stables in Chester, or directly to wool merchants. All kinds of poultry — chickens, ducks, geese, guinea-fowl and bantams — were kept for eggs or the table, and locally killed poultry was much in demand at Christmas.

The corn crops — wheat, oats and barley — were stored in the barns after harvesting until the threshing contractors, Bridson's or Gray's, began work in November. The grain was usually bagged and kept for winter feed, and the straw was used for cattle bedding.

Fig. 23 Harvesting in Little Neston with a self-binding reaper.

Farm workers were usually specialists. Horsemen ploughed, rolled, scuffled and reaped, while cowmen milked and tended the cattle. Shepherds were employed to look after large flocks of sheep, but smaller flocks were usually looked after by the farmer.

THE MILL AT WILLASTON

Throughout the nineteenth century, Willaston was dominated, physically and sometimes economically, by Willaston mill. This corn mill was driven solely by the power of the wind until 1860, when a steam engine was added. In that year the mill was bought by Samuel Radford, whose father had started the family business of corn merchants in Liverpool, where they owned the Albert mill.

For some twenty years Willaston mill was very prosperous; powered by both steam and wind, it no longer served the local farmers only, but ground grain imported by the parent company. In 1867 Raby House was built in Benty Heath Lane, probably by Samuel Radford, who was living there at the time of the 1871 census. But a crisis of some kind overtook the family business. In 1879 Samuel's son, Samuel Leigh Radford, took out a mortgage on Willaston mill, but could not pay the interest, and the lenders foreclosed. The corn mill passed to other hands, although the Radford firm continued in Liverpool until it failed in 1903.

The following portrait of Willaston mill was written by Leslie Edwards from the recollections of his grandfather, the engineer of that first 1860 steam engine. (Unfortunately we have not been able to find any record of the loss of the Radfords' two ships named here.)

> **This is some of the history of the old mill at Willaston told to me by my father, George Edwards, born at No.1 Mill Cottages in the year 1868, and also by his father, John Edwards, my grandfather, who I unfortunately never knew.**
>
> **My grandfather came with his wife to live at Mill Cottages in the year 1860. His job was to look after a steam engine that had just been installed in the mill for the purpose (of course) of milling wheat into flour and the other products produced from such an operation. My grandfather came to Willaston Mill from Wrockwardine in Shropshire, where he did his training in steam engineering, which at that time was a young industry.**
>
> **At the time my grandfather came to work at the mill, it was owned by some people named Radford. They were very kind and generous, and especially to those who worked in the mill. At Christmas the mill was closed for a week, and the Radfords gave parties for the workers, their wives and children, with gifts for them all, gifts of geese and**

Fig. 24 Erected in 1800 to replace a previous peg mill, Willaston mill, seen here shorn of its sails, was, and remains, an imposing building in the landscape. It is 80 feet in height, with a "Kentish cap", and has five storeys The millers would have adjusted the sails from the platform.

meat, both pork and beef for the wives to cook for Christmas dinner. This was, of course, very well received by the workers, whose pay was round about 14s. per week. My grandfather was the highest paid, and his wage was 24 bob a week for a twelve-hour day from 6 a.m. until 6 p.m. He had to be there at 5.30 a.m. to see the engine was all ready for starting up.

After the steam power came to the mill the windmill was still used, so that they had a very efficient mill with a high production rate. In fact it was in its heyday one of the best equipped mills to be found in Great Britain, and also one of the biggest of its kind. The mill itself is 110 feet high, and apart from that it stands on very high ground. The whole top of the mill is made so that it could be turned round to put the sails into the wind, no matter which way it might be blowing. The sails could also be feathered (I think this is the right word), so that if a gale was blowing only the edge of the sails would be facing the wind, so the wind would not have as much purchase and hence not send the sails round too quickly.

The shaft from the sails to the driving mechanism to the mill stones is massive and I am sure it is at least one foot in diameter, tapering at both ends, with the shaft that actually drove the stones made of a solid oak beam about 20 feet long, the shaft on which the sails were fixed being of either iron or steel. Also in the roof of the mill was a brake to hold the sails, once they had been set in the right position. There was also a hoist there, with a chain reaching from the top floor of the mill to the bottom for hauling sacks of grain up for milling.

The steam engine had one large cylinder with a massive flywheel, 30 feet in diameter, only half of which was visible, the other half running under the ground or floor of the engine house in a kind of shaft, about two inches clearance either side. The stones driven by the engine were on the ground floor of the mill, and were driven by a shaft going under the floor from the engine house to the stones. The engine house was built as a lean-to on the outside of the tower.

Shortly after my grandfather came to the mill, a man by the name of William Coathup was sent to William Fowler's of Leeds, to bring back a traction engine to haul the grain from Birkenhead docks to the mill and the flour back to Birkenhead, as well as other places. There were two other men with him on his way home, one as fireman, and the other poor man had to walk in front of the engine waving a red flag, which was the law in those far away days.

The day the engine was due back in Willaston was a red letter day for the villagers, all getting a half-day holiday, with great merry-making,

all the people who were able walking to the junction of Hadlow Road and the Chester High Road to meet it and escort it back to the old mill with flags waving and cheers all the way, with much speculation as to how it would get round the corners and up the mill hill, but the driver and his mates managed it with flying colours, and all the doubting Thomases had their minds put at rest. It was, I believe, the first traction engine to work in the whole county of Cheshire, and after its life at the mill I believe a man by the name of Bridson of Neston bought it and used it for years for threshing corn on the farms in the Wirral, and his son and grandson after him. William Coathup went to drive the engine for Mr Bridson, and did so for very many years after. He was a grand old gentleman, and I can just remember a tall, handsome old man with a long white beard.

There was also another type of engine kept at the mill. It was similar to a traction engine, only it could not move under its own power and had to be drawn by horses to wherever it had work to do; it was called a portable. I believe they were used for threshing, sawing and driving other machinery, and also for lifting heavy objects by means of a cable round the drum running through a set of blocks fixed to a tripod. This old engine was still under a cart shed in the mill yard when I was a boy, and I and other boys born at the Mill Cottages used to play for hours on it, as one may imagine. During the 1914–18 War it was cut up, along with the old engine that drove the steam mill, the boilers and all other metal forming the vital parts of the machinery, and sold as scrap by Mr Catto, who then owned the mill and lived at Willaston House — the big house right opposite the mill.

About (as near as I can tell) ten years after my grandfather went to work at the mill, Mr Radford had some very bad luck. He owned two sailing ships, both engaged in hauling grain from Russia to Birkenhead, supplying the life blood of the old mill, and he lost them both in a gale on their way back loaded with grain from Russia. This disaster broke Mr Radford, and it was really the beginning of the end, as far as the mill was concerned, although it went on working for about twenty years after, though never on the same scale. Mr Radford had to cut his losses and sell the whole business. It was a very sad blow for the working class people of the village, for about 50 people were employed either directly or indirectly in the running of the mill, and besides that the Radford family were such kind and considerate employers, not only to those who worked for them but also to the old and sick of the village. The two ships, by the way, were called the *Helen Radford* and the *Marion Radford*.

The next family to take the mill over was named Hawkins, but by this time it was becoming uneconomic to cart grain from the Birkenhead docks and haul it back again, and the mill had to rely more and more on milling for the local farmers, until finally Mr Hawkins had to give it up. I should think that this would be around 1888. Mr Hawkins built himself a farmhouse and outbuildings and started farming the place which is now known as Seidloom Farm and is just by where Hadlow Road Station used to be.

After Mr Hawkins's days at the mill, a man by the name of James K. Catto came to live at Willaston House. He bought the mill, the mill yard and mill cottages and all the surrounding fields. He rented the mill to Mr Jack Hale, and put in the basement a gas engine to work some of the mill machinery. Mr Hale farmed the Church Farm in Willaston and also sold animal foodstuffs.

The mill ceased to function as a mill about 1930, and Mr Catto had the sails sawn off because they were becoming unsafe. A firm by the name of Charles Gray, of the Mill, Leighton Road, Neston, got the job of taking them off. Mr Gray kept several traction engines and steam rollers, and used the traction engines for threshing all round the Wirral for very many years, and the rollers for road making and repairing.

In the mill yard there was, as you went through the mill yard gate, first a bakery, then a cottage, then stables to hold about six horses, with hay lofts above them, a cart shed and lastly two more cottages, all one long building. But today, of course, it is all altered, the bakery, stables and cart shed being converted into houses.

In the days when Mr Radford owned the mill, all the workers' wives from the village could take their bread there to be baked in the back oven. My father told me that after the harvest a lot of women and children of the village would go gleaning, thresh what corn they got, and take it to the mill to be made into flour, and then get it made into bread as and when needed. The bakery was later done away with and made into a laundry, where any woman out of the village could take the week's washing to be done. But after Mr Catto came, this was brought to an end, and only his family's and their servants' washing was done there, but by then nearly all had their own boilers, so it made no difference.

There were, as may be supposed, some characters who worked at the mill in my grandfather's time that my father told me of. One was John Colley, who lived in a cottage in the mill yard. If a gale started in the night he would get up out of his bed and go into the mill and

Fig. 25 An old cottage in Neston Road, Willaston, in 1908 (now demolished).

pray to God to keep the mill safe. He must have loved the mill and his work there.

Another man there, whose name was William Derbyshire, was a giant standing 6 ft 10 in. tall and weighing well over 20 stone. He could jump up and kick the ceiling of the cottage where I was born. He used to do this of a Christmas, first removing his shoes, and the ceiling would be about 10 ft high. One day for a bet he said he could carry 6 cwt on his back. A special sack was made to hold it, and one Sunday morning after Church all the men out of the village and his workmates came to see him do it. He not only carried 6 cwt, he carried 36 score pounds of flour, which by my sums is 6 cwt 48 lb. He carried this weight the width of one of the buildings and back, which was 22 yards. His own weight, plus the weight of the flour, left the impression of the hobnails in the boots he wore in the floorboards. My father took me into the mill to see the prints when I was a boy, and although this had taken place about forty years before I was born (which was 1910), each step he'd taken could be distinctly seen. In spite of all his size and strength, poor William Derbyshire passed

away when 41 years of age, and was laid to rest in Eastham churchyard.

Yet another character was there when my grandfather worked there. He was a man named Thomas Cush [real name Smith]. **Thomas was a very different character from William Derbyshire: where he was a kind and gentle giant, Tom was tough and hard. He was not intelligent enough to keep a job, but would earn a few bob a week running errands for the men working at the mill and catching rabbits. He was about 5 ft 10 in. tall, but with a tremendous chest and shoulders and very strong, as you may imagine. Tom was nearly always in trouble with the police. If he needed a new shirt or socks he would pinch them off a clothes line or go and pinch apples or spuds out of a field or garden, but he never did any serious crime but once, as you will see. In the winter my grandfather used to let him sleep by the boilers, where he was snug and warm, but in the summer he would sleep out anywhere.**

One day, Tom was in Neston and his wardrobe must have needed replenishing, for he stole some shirts and long johns off a line of washing, and unfortunately for Tom the good lady of the house caught him in the act. But of course Tom made off with the spoils. On the next Saturday, my grandfather and other men from the mill went to the Red Lion in Willaston for a pint of ale after work finished at 2 o'clock. When they got there Tom was in, for he liked his pint, did Tom. They had not been there long when in walked a police sergeant and two constables looking for Thomas for pinching the clothes off the line in Neston. The sergeant said "I charge every man in this house to assist in the arrest of Thomas Cush in the name of the Queen". With that a fierce tussle took place, for Tom was so strong that no one policeman could take him. Finally they got Tom pinned to the floor, put the handcuffs on him and started to walk to Neston Police Station. When, however, they got to Hanns Hall Farm, Tom decided it was far enough, smashed the handcuffs and chased the policemen over the fields, but luckily for them never caught them.

Another day Tom must have fancied some eggs for tea, for he broke into a farmer's new shed and stole all the eggs. The farmer saw him, and this time Tom was arrested and sent to prison. When he came out he had it in for the farmer, and one day he got to know that the farmer was going to Birkenhead by pony and trap. Tom walked to Storeton Quarry and waited there until he saw the farmer coming back. The farmer panicked, knowing what Tom could do to him if he once laid hands on him, so he pulled up, jumped out of the trap and ran for help to the Traveller's Rest. Tom got the pony and trap, took the pony

out of the shafts and threw the trap over the wall and into the quarry, where it of course smashed to pieces. This was, of course, a very serious offence, and police in the whole area were looking for Tom. One day a young policeman saw Tom on the Birkenhead side of the Clatterbridge Road. Tom went for him and the policeman pulled a gun and shot Tom and wounded him. [This was in 1880. The policeman was John Dillon, who had fired over the heads of some Neston miners the year before. He was dismissed from the police.] **He later emigrated to Australia where he one day ran amok, shot two or three people and then himself. Maybe Tom's death played on the poor man's mind, but if Tom had got hold of him he would have undoubtedly severely hurt him, so what could the poor man do? Tom was laid to rest in Bebington churchyard.**

Fig. 26 The annual Shepherds Club procession passing Church Farm, Willaston, in July 1908.

At one time the tower of the mill was whitewashed and the windows, doors and stage tarred black every year in time for the Shepherds Club Day which took place on the first Thursday in July. I can well remember Willaston Shepherds Club. It finished about 1929 I think. All the members used to walk with a large banner behind a hired

band, with all the usual entertainment that goes with such an affair, roundabouts, coconut shies, etc.

The mill tower that stands today was built in 1800 I believe, and has stood there looking out over the Cheshire Plain during the reigns of seven kings and two queens, in good times and bad.

And last, inscribed on one of the hoppers in the mill were two verses my father pointed out to me when I was a boy, and they have stayed in my mind ever since. The first one was

"God's providence is mine inheritance, God bless this Mill."

I have always thought that whoever wrote it must have felt very secure in his life and work there. You cannot imagine anyone asking God to bless his place of work today, unless he was a vicar.

The second verse went like this:

"A.P. is my name
Old England is my nation
Willaston is my dwelling place
Christ is my salvation
And when I'm dead and in my grave
And all my bones are rotten
The bell shall toll For some poor soul
When I am all forgotten."

I have often wondered who A.P. was (my father didn't know) and what he did, but I think I would be right to say whoever A.P. may have been he was a realist and could look life in the face and take whatever it sent along.

Of the two Neston threshing contractors mentioned in this account, the Bridsons' business is described in Chapter Eight, because their steam engines were also used for tar spraying.

The other owners of steam engines were the Gray family. Wolton Gray had, by the time he died in 1891, six threshing machines, including *Neston Lassie*. He had lived in Neston for 32 years, and in the 1870s had his threshing machine and timber business in High Street, at the corner on the south side of Raby Road, dealing frequently with Liverpool boat builders. Gray had lost his right arm in a threshing machine accident. In the early 1880s he took over the yard that had belonged to the Youds family in Cross Street, and had sheds and other buildings erected on it.

Part of the Gray family ran a similar business at the Old Mill Yard in Leighton Road. This was continued in the 1920s and 1930s by Charles Gray, with his business as haulage contractor, steam saw mill, wheelwright and smith.

Fig. 27 The windmill in Leighton Road, Neston, is the survivor of two eighteenth-century mills which stood side by side. Its partner was severely damaged by a storm in 1822, but this mill ground corn until *c.*1885. It is much smaller than Willaston's mill.

FISHING

Before about 1820, Parkgate was not a fishing village, although there were fish there. With few exceptions, the men employed at sea described themselves as mariners, though they may have fished between voyages, and men with other occupations, such as publicans, are known to have fished to supplement their incomes. The fish recorded at Parkgate then were usually herrings: in 1797, *"a plentiful supply of herrings caught near Parkgate were sold in Chester at 1/- per hundred"*. And in 1809, *"the herring fishery at Parkgate has been uncommonly productive this year. Several thousand have been sold every day this week at Chester"*. Until 1809 there was a herring house in Parkgate at which the fish were cured, either smoked to become "red herring" or salted to become "white herring".

By 1820, however, the position had changed. A bounty paid to boats engaged in herring fishery was discontinued; the shipping had ceased to visit Parkgate by 1815, so that mariners would have to look to Liverpool for ships; and the end of the Napoleonic Wars brought many unemployed men home. In 1829 when a storm wrecked many fishermen's boats, it was stated that *"all the seafaring men belonging to Parkgate have been at one time or another in the service of the Navy, and fought and bled in defending the liberties of their country".*

Parkgate therefore became much more of a fishing village after 1815, though not for herring. Herring prefer cold water, and the shoals had moved towards the Isle of Man. Fishing in or near the mouth of the estuary was for those creatures that prefer warmer water: shrimps, cockles, mussels, and flatfish like plaice, flukes, dabs, soles and sometimes rays. The problem during the first half of the nineteenth century was the disposal of the catch. There was a limit to the quantities saleable locally, and the catch had to be carried, often on foot, to Chester or Birkenhead. Mrs Catherine Whitehead, born in 1844, used when young to walk to Birkenhead with a huge basket of shrimps on her head.

Fig. 28 Fishermen leaving the middle slip, Parkgate.

Even after the railway came, the lack of refrigeration meant that fish had to be sold quickly. In the 1920s Mrs Fewtrell used to take fish on her bicycle and hawk them in villages such as Capenhurst. In the same period, Parkgate people would go to meet the fishing boats as they came in and buy flatfish, weighed on the sea wall at 3d. a pound, and very much alive.

In the years before the railway came, the number of fishermen was not high. Of people actually living in Parkgate, there were thirteen fishermen in 1841, twelve in 1851, and sixteen in 1861. There were others who lived in Neston. In 1871 the number of fishermen living in Parkgate had risen to 25, with seventeen living in Neston. The number of fishing boats was estimated in 1878 to be 45, and a report in 1910 said that there were 36 boats from Parkgate and Heswall.

Shrimps were often caught from "nobbies", which were shallow-draught, almost flat-bottomed, cutter-rigged vessels, designed for the shallow estuaries of the North-West. These boats pulled a 22-foot trawl, and many were built at Arnside. The Liverpool Maritime Museum has a 1:32 scale model of a Chester river nobby. Shrimps were also caught with hand nets. Besides the nobbies, which had one mast, and were favoured from about 1900, there were "jiggers" which had two masts, and "punts", which were large rowing boats used for gathering shellfish.

Fig. 29 Sacks of shellfish being unloaded at Parkgate.

Shrimps were known as "shanks" and were gathered by "shankers". At least one shanker, "Swad" Jones, used to trawl in the shallows off Parkgate with a horse and cart. Hand raking for shellfish was called "scratting". The scratters, usually women, could be heard clattering along the Parkgate Parade early in the morning. Armed with rakes up to fifteen feet long, they would follow the tide along the cockle banks, an hour later each day, collecting not only cockles but mussels and crabs. From the late 1880s they could leave their children in a crèche in the yard of the Parkgate infants' school, in a corrugated iron building called the Tin Room. The crèche was run by Miss Lyon from Ashfield House.

Occasionally there would be a glut of fish, and many non-fishermen would try their luck. This happened in 1881, when a flush of dabs, flukes and flounders appeared off Parkgate, and some eighty men and boys hunted them, often by spearing them with fish forks. The same sort of scenes are said to have taken place in the 1920s.

The coming of the railway in 1866 made a great difference to the fortunes of the local fishermen, because it enabled them to sell their catches of cockles and mussels for consumption in the industrial towns of the Midlands and North. In 1893, a total of 23,200 bags of cockles and mussels were sent from Parkgate station, and there were fears that the principal mussel beds at that time, called the Blacks, off Dawpool, would be overexploited. A resident of Parkgate, H. H. Holbrook, was a fisheries expert and had been a government minister in Canada. He was appointed to the Dee Fishery Board in 1888 and pressed for control of mussel fishing. A public meeting was held in Parkgate to discuss this proposal, but it was thinly attended by the fishermen. An order under the 1888 Fisheries Act, providing a close season for mussels, was imposed, and in 1894 some of Parkgate's fishermen were complaining that this regulation was being flouted by their own number; two men were fined for it. One of the Parkgate fishermen, Charlie Cunningham, was a "river policeman", who checked that the shellfish were not harvested too small.

Besides Holbrook, there were others of the local gentry who took an interest in the well-being of the fishermen. Reginald Haigh of Leighton Banastre chaired meetings and arranged concerts. Thomas Comber of Leighton was described at his death in 1902 thus: *"The local fishermen never had a warmer or more cordial supporter in protracted agitation for a redress of their grievances."* Holbrook arranged a series of lectures in 1895 in the old chapel on the topics of "Cockles and Mussels", "Flukes and Shrimps" and "Recent Fishing Research".

Sir Norman Hill of Leighton House, an expert on marine law, got some fishermen out of a spot of trouble in 1906. This was an occasion when the mussel harvest was poor in the Dee, and some Parkgate men went to Aberdovey. There, the locals resented their intrusion and dragged the Parkgate boats into a football field. After Hill's intervention there was no further trouble, but one bone of contention was said to be that the Parkgate mussel rakes, three feet broad, were twice the size of the Aberdovey rakes.

Similar problems had occurred before, but the other way round. In 1878 the Parkgate fishermen mustered threateningly when three men arrived by train with their boats from Morecambe Bay, intending to fish in the Dee. The matter ended peacefully when two local gentlemen agreed to buy off the interlopers.

Fig. 30 Fishing nets drying by the Watch House, Parkgate, *c*.1910. The Watch House had not yet had its walls rendered.

Fishing could be a hard and sometimes dangerous trade. The storms of the Dee estuary were much worse when the whole estuary was fully tidal, because the wind speed was faster over the water than it is over the present saltmarsh, which slows it down. Many fishing boats were damaged in a great storm in 1881, and John Wood, the landlord of the Red Lion and formerly a ship's carpenter, offered to repair them. Eight years later, 22 boats were wrecked. In 1908, seven boats were broken in pieces and a further fifteen were damaged. A benefit society had been formed for the fishermen in 1894 to provide insurance for such calamities. They had previously relied on the insurance provisions of the Shipwrecked Mariners' Society, but there had been some complaints about this. It was reported in 1902 that the membership of the Parkgate Tontine (a form of benefit club in which the last survivor scoops the jackpot) was mainly for fishermen and had a membership of over sixty.

Sometimes the loss was of human life. William Smith was only 15 when the wind carried his boat off course in 1882, and he was found dead from exposure the next morning. Lemuel Mellor was a fisherman living in Pyke's Weint in Neston, who fell out of his boat and drowned in 1900. Two other fishermen named Mellor were to drown in 1920 and 1922. As well as the hazards of accident, there was the danger of hardship caused by bad weather or a poor season, and fishing families would sometimes need support from their neighbours.

The fishermen of Parkgate were a conspicuous sight in their navy blue jerseys, often to be seen mending their nets in the open air. At one time they used to wear billycock hats (a kind of bowler) when they set sail. When well away from land they would stow the hats under their seats and put them on when they returned to land again.

The fishermen were often known by nicknames, many given ironically. "Six-foot" Smith was a small man, while "Bad-luck" was the most successful. Other names were "Spurner" (real name Jack Smith; over a hundred people walked in his funeral procession in 1925), "Why-why", "Slen" and "Geddy".

After the First World War, trainloads of shellfish continued to leave Parkgate station, while visitors came in large numbers to Parkgate to enjoy its famous shrimp teas. Usually the shrimps were sold plain boiled and peeled, but the Dee Shellfish Company, started in 1929 and operating next to the Boat House, investigated ways of preserving them so that they could be sent by post. Cockles could be sterilized and shrimps were potted in butter and spices. The company ceased trading in 1931.

Mussels, by contrast, were eaten raw, and for this reason there were persistent fears that they might be polluted by sewage in the Dee. After 1911 the mussels were mostly harvested from the Salisbury Gut, near the mouth of the estuary and well away from any outfall. Nevertheless, there were fears in 1927 that the Ministry of Health might close the Dee mussel fishery, a serious threat to the local economy, for the 1921 census listed 53 fishermen in Neston and Parkgate, and in 1911 49 were listed. Not all these were necessarily working fishermen, as it was estimated that in the 1930s there were some 30 fishermen working from Parkgate. In the River Conwy, cleansing tanks had been established in which the mussels could cleanse themselves before being bagged, and a meeting was called in Parkgate to discuss the possibility of establishing a cleansing station in the Dee. The fishermen were against it, partly because they refused to believe their mussels were a danger to health, and partly no doubt because they foresaw where the cost would fall.

A. G. Grenfell offered the use of his swimming bath in the winter, but later withdrew the offer. The threat became serious in 1935, when the cities of Birmingham, Leeds and Bradford all banned the sale of shellfish from the Dee. Dr Yeoman, the Medical Officer of Health for Neston, sympathized with the fishermen because he could not find any evidence that mussels actually caused illness, although they certainly contained large numbers of *bacteria coli*. The councils of Neston, Wirral and Hoylake agreed to discuss the establishment of a cleansing station, but nothing was done.

A few Parkgate fishermen had fished for salmon, but this required a licence, and the salmon were normally in the main current of the river, on the Welsh side. In 1926 a Parkgate fisherman was refused a licence for a draft net to catch salmon, and complained to his Member of Parliament that the Dee Board of Conservators favoured the Flintshire fishermen. An inspector was required to report on the situation, but he concluded that the 30 licences allowed by law were being allotted fairly. Of course, not everybody bothered about a licence. Some salmon poachers would spear the fish with a pikel, or pitchfork.

The rapid changes which took place in the Dee estuary, which were to bring the Parkgate fishing industry to a close, were entirely caused by man's interference with nature. It is not true to say that the estuary silted up naturally. Until 1737 the mainstream of the river had run along the Wirral shore, thus allowing Parkgate to be used as a passenger port for Ireland. In 1737 the river was turned into an artificial channel, the New Cut, between Chester and Connah's Quay, and the water then crossed the estuary to resume its original course at Parkgate. But gradually the River Dee Company persuaded the river, by blasting rocks and building training walls, to remain on the Welsh side. Meanwhile the land inside the loop of the New Cut was slowly reclaimed, slice by slice, from the tidal estuary, which is why it is called Sealand. This reclamation was not completed until 1916. Each slice of reclaimed land meant that the tide came in a shorter distance and therefore the receding tide had less scouring power, taking less silt with it. Finally, spartina grass was planted on the sandbanks by the John Summers steelworks in order to bind them together. The plants were supposed to be infertile when planted in 1927, but they soon proved to be very fertile, and spread rapidly. The roots collected mud and silt, and there followed a rapid rise in the floor of the estuary.

It was a combination of these causes which brought about the saltmarsh, but it is also said that the closure of the colliery in 1927, and the cessation of the flow of water which had been continuously pumped from the mine, also hastened the end of the water at Parkgate.

The occasional tide failed to reach Parkgate from about 1930, the outbreak of War in 1939 put an end to discussions about cleansing mussels, and after the War it was no longer possible for fishing boats to operate at Parkgate.

SOURCES

This chapter has been assembled by many hands and with the help of many voices.

For the Agriculture section, information on Raby was collected by Clive Edwards, assisted by the memories of Graham Langley, Mrs Ethelwyn Randles and Mrs Doris Wilson. We are most grateful to John Eastwood, who died in 1994, for permission to quote from his book, *Wirral Born and Bred* — a collection of articles which were first published in *The Wirral Journal*. The sections on the large estates and on Ledsham were written by Geoffrey Place. The deeds of the Ledsham estate are held by the Treasurer's Department of Cheshire County Council. The section on Little Neston was written by Edward Hilditch, who made use of the sale plan of the Talbot estate of 1913 and the memories of Jim Anyon, Mrs Hough, Helena Mealor, Walter Scott, George Tilley and Elizabeth Watts; the information on Ivy Farm came from a family history by Joan Scott. The account of Willaston mill was written by the late Leslie Edwards, and details from the mill's deeds were provided by David Morris; John Eastwood and Mrs Tilleard-Lewis gave details of the Radford family.

The section on Fishing was written by Geoffrey Place, relying on a report on shellfish by the Neston Medical Officer of Health in 1935 and information from the *Chester Chronicle*.

CHAPTER THREE

EARNING A LIVING

The effect of the Second World War was to bring about a watershed in employment opportunities for Neston, one of the reasons for ending our survey in 1940. Coal mining had already ceased, fishing did not revive after the War, and agriculture was to take on a new face. However, during our hundred years, employment was available in a range of industries and businesses, large and small. They included a colliery and a cable works; building firms; laundries; a plough works; Arthur Bulley's gardens at Ness; a fine arts studio; and a variety of retail shops and services to provide for a growing population.

George Tilley, a Nestonian born and bred, has given the following account of his early life:

> **I was born at 14 Eldon Terrace in 1903. My mother later changed houses with the people in Number 4 Eldon Terrace because it had three bedrooms and we were an extra-large family.**
>
> **At the end of the First World War my father retired from the colliery, suffering from miners' blindness caused by being underground so long. There was no machinery in the mines: the coal had to be got with a pick. He was paid by results. He cut the coal and his brother filled the boxes, which held 10 cwt of coal. They came home with 21 shillings a week for the two of them. They worked a six-day week, 48 hours a week.**
>
> **I went to the church school at the top of Neston. When I was eight I got a part-time job working for Harry Peers. He farmed the land where the council houses are now. I took out the milk along Raby Road, Raby Park and Blackey's Lane. I got sevenpence-ha'penny a week, and I left the money to accumulate for four weeks. Half-a-crown bought a whole hundredweight of potatoes, so I kept the family in potatoes.**
>
> **In 1914, when I was eleven, I was taken from school to work at Swift's the butcher. I was in Standard 6, and the schoolmaster Mr Warren was in charge of Standards 6 and 7. I would have only had Standard 7 for the next three years, had I stayed.**

Swift's the butcher had a slaughterhouse behind where the National Westminster Bank is now. I was slaughtering before I was 14. We got cattle each Monday. The boss went on the 7.50 train to Hooton. I went on the 11.40 train. The cattle market at Hooton was by the station, where the car park is now. I had to bring the cattle back from Hooton to Neston. Often there were 35–40 sheep; I walked in front and the sheepdog followed behind. The four and a half miles took one and a half to two hours. If the boss could not get what he wanted at Hooton, he went to Greasby market. I had to drive bullocks back from Greasby, and it was late by the time I got back. I went by bike after I came back from Hooton.

The boss also bought Scotch bullocks from the Gladstones in Burton. He bought two or three at a time, only when they were fat, and I had to herd them to Neston.

The day after War was declared in 1914, all the young men in the district lined up at Neston Cross and marched to Neston station (the bottom one) and went to Birkenhead to the recruiting office. Every eligible fellow went. Only the unfits came back; those enlisted went mainly in the Cheshire Regiment.

Farmers were short of workers, and they came round and picked out lads. I went to Haddon Hall Farm, by Ness Gardens. Jimmy Grundy was the farmer, and he paid me 2s. 6d. a day and as many potatoes as you could carry home. It was a long way to carry the potatoes home, so I got my father to meet me half way.

During the War there was a rumour about an escaper, Jack Anyon. They said he had escaped from the Germans, and was coming home on a certain train. All Neston turned out to meet him, but he did not come. He came back later in the War.

My brother Albert was called up in 1917. He had little training, as he was sent to France a month later. Within a month he was captured. He walked through France, and ended up in Munster down the mine. He was there to the end of the War. He lived on black bread and sauerkraut, and came back a skeleton. We met him at Neston station; the whole village turned out to meet him. Mother had had a telegram during the War to say he was missing, presumed prisoner, and not one word except a telegram to say he was coming back. Albert was the oldest, so mother's favourite. We had a big party, the sky the limit.

From Swift's, three joined the army — Pemberton Swift, Frank Crawley and Tich Minshull. All three were killed.

During the War Swift's did not replace the people in the army, so I went on farms killing pigs. The first one was for Johnny Dodd, who had a farm in School Lane, Little Neston. I was 14, and was paid 10s. for it on the Friday after it was cut up.

The end of the War was on a Monday morning at 11 a.m. on 11th November 1918. There was a telegram posted up in the Post Office [opposite the Greenland Fishery, by Jackson's tower]. **Swift's always had bunting for Ladies' Club Day, so before I went to Hooton I had to put up the bunting. There were trees where Tesco's is now, and I put the bunting from lamp posts and trees across to the shops. I dressed the place up before I went to the station.**

After the War there was influenza. It spread round the district, as everyone was in poor condition. They did not have the medicines to combat it. A lot died.

The miners had pig sties, and I got jobs from various miners in New Street. I killed the pig in the sty and dragged it into the kitchen. There was a grid in the middle of the kitchen floor. I scalded it and got the bristles off. I dressed it in the back kitchen and hung it up for two or three days afterwards. The miners had the bacon, and they sold the ham to the toffs in Hinderton Road to buy another pig.

The Swifts had four daughters, and they were brought up on goat's milk. When the nannies were breeding there were some billy-goats born. I killed them at six months and got 6d. per goat for dressing them.

Harry Peers's father had Brook House [100 yards from the Five Ways junction, on the road towards Thornton Hough]. **He produced lambs, and Harry Peers and Tom Swift went into the field to choose young lambs for Easter. They were £3 a head. When killed and dressed they were sold at 25s. a quarter, regardless of weight. They were sold to the toffs for Easter Sunday.**

When I was 18 I went home one Friday and was told that I was finishing at Swift's and going down the coal mine, as it paid more. I was down the pit until I was 24, when they brought me up to work in Neston station yard as a coal agent for Wirral Colliery. I worked till 1926, till just after the General Strike. Down the mine I worked as a rope rider. On the coal face there was one miner to every ten yards. As they drove in they got away from the engine and ropes. I had to take away full boxes and give miners empty ones. Each drawer filled 30 boxes a day, and each box held 10 cwt. The seam was the two-foot one, and underneath was 10" to 12" of fireclay, which was valuable. It

could have been used to make tiles, but it was never brought to the surface. Its value was only realized after the pit closed.

After the miners had cleared a length, the night shift brought in what was called the "iron man" to get the fireclay out. It was a wheel with scoops, and it went in one yard under the seam. If the fireclay had not been taken out, there would have been no space for the coal to expand and burst.

The miner did the drilling, and the lad who was the drawer filled the tubs and passed them on to me. I changed a full tub for an empty one.

My brother worked at the bakehouse belonging to Billy Evans in Liverpool Road. I got a job as a van driver for this firm. After I had been there some time, the boss asked if I would have a spell in the bakehouse so I would be able to take the place of anyone who was ill. So I learned bakery.

In 1935 I got a job as a van driver with Benson's the greengrocer. He wanted someone who knew the district. I got £3 a week at the bakery; he offered me £3 10s. I worked there till I joined the RAF.

COAL MINING

Commercial mining activity in Neston parish began in 1757, centred initially on Ness Colliery but later dividing, with a separate concern in Little Neston. Coal was mined for almost a hundred years until about 1855, when activity ceased. A new company with different owners was formed in 1874, and mining then continued in Little Neston until 1927.

At first, the colliery was sited in the area which straddled the boundary between Little Neston and Ness, the coal pier from which the coal was loaded onto ships being slightly on the Ness side of the actual boundary. This small outlier of the North Wales coalfield was worked as one enterprise, known as Ness (or sometimes Denna) Colliery, and owned by the Stanleys who lived in Denna Hall. Royalties were paid to the Massey-Stanleys of Hooton as landowners in Ness, and the Earl of Shrewsbury, the Cottinghams and a minor landowner in Little Neston. The amount of coal extracted in the eighteenth century appears to have been between 10,000 and 20,000 tons a year.

Disputes about boundaries and royalty payments had started early in the life of the colliery, and when the proprietors' lease for mining in Little Neston expired in 1819, each township was mined separately — Ness by the Stanleys and Little Neston by the Cottinghams. Boundary disputes continued, culminating in two successful lawsuits in 1821 and 1822 by Thomas Cottingham against Sir Thomas Stanley for trespass.

Fig. 31 The colliery quay, built in the 1760s, was last used for coal in the early 1850s. William Lawton, seen here, lived in a cottage built on it. Later the cottage was the home of Fred Jones, a wildfowler and maker of punt guns.

In Ness, where three seams (two-foot, five-foot and seven-foot) were worked, the search for coal became increasingly desperate. In 1852 it was advertised for letting *"with good shipping pier"*. There was a last, unsuccessful attempt to find the two-foot seam in 1854. A sale of equipment was held in 1855 and the mine was closed.

The situation appears to have been little better in the Cottingham colliery in Little Neston, where the five-foot, six-foot and seven-foot seams had been worked from pits on both sides of Colliery Lane (now Marshlands Road). The Cottingham estate was offered for sale in 1851. The last-known mining activity took place in 1852.

At the time of the 1841 census, 94 colliers were living within the parish of Neston, with 38 in Ness, 34 in Little Neston and 22 in Great Neston. No-one was described as manager, but James Gregory was listed as coal agent, and George Jackson as colliery agent. In 1851, the census returns described James Gregory as a colliery proprietor employing 120 men, and his son Peter, aged 18, was the colliery clerk and bookkeeper. There was a coal sloop, the *Mary*, at the colliery quay on the night of the census, and two crewmen were listed. Children were rarely employed in Neston, but the colliery was an exception, there being seven boys under 14 working there. The youngest two were 9 years old – one a coal miner, the other a coal carrier. Nearly all the workers at the mine were born locally, although eleven were born in Wales and five in Lancashire. Later in the century, many of the miners came from outside the district.

For a few years the Anglican Smelting and Coal Company occupied the Little Neston site, with the smelting works on the north side of Colliery Lane. This business did not prosper, and its machinery was sold in 1866. In the 1861 census returns, therefore, only two coal-miners were listed, and in 1871 two elderly men called themselves colliers. But ten years later there would be 146 men employed at the mine, four-fifths of whom came from outside Neston.

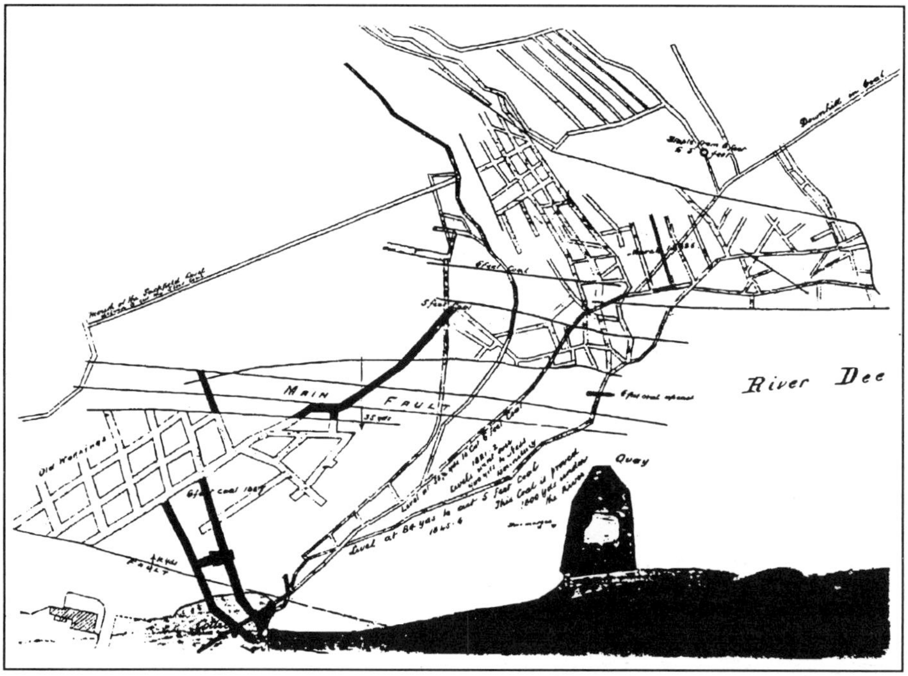

Fig. 32 This drawing of the colliery workings, made before 1855, shows how the galleries ran out under the river. The dark strip at the bottom is the bank, with an earth quay (not the stone colliery quay) jutting from it.

The question of reopening the mine workings was raised in 1869 at a Parliamentary Enquiry. Evidence was given by a mining engineer, Thomas Cottingham, whose father had owned the Little Neston mine. He said *"The reason why Ness Colliery was given up was, I believe, it was presumed to be exhausted as far as regards the 2 feet, the 7 feet coal and the 5 feet."* He also said that Stanley's mine did not survive the lawsuits of 1822. He believed that there were large supplies of coal underneath the old workings.

Eventually, a fresh start to mining coal at Neston was made when a new shaft was sunk in 1874.

In April of that year, Charles Mott of Birkenhead made an agreement with the trustees of the Earl of Shrewsbury to lease two-thirds of what were called *"the wastelands of Little Neston which lie under the estuary of the River Dee, an area of about 1,000 acres"*. Mott obtained the right to sink whatever shafts were necessary to mine cannel coal or ironstone or fireclay.

Transport of coal was provided for by an agreement with the London and North Western and the Great Western Railways to build a branch siding to convey coal from the pits.

A few months later another agreement was made whereby John Biggs, a merchant, formed the Neston Colliery Company to buy out Mott's rights in the earlier agreement.

Fig. 33 The newly opened workings of the Neston Colliery Company, as painted by Arthur Suker in 1875. The extensive shingle foreshore can be clearly seen.

Evidence on the progress of the company is fragmentary. Planning permission for colliers' houses in New Street was given in 1875. This would allow the company to increase its labour force. The lease of April

1874 was for three-fifths of the land. The remaining two-fifths were held by Cynric Lloyd, who became bankrupt in 1876. There is a series of letters in the archives of the Duke of Norfolk advising the Duke about making a bid for the lease. A letter dated 30 April 1876 quotes Mr Mott as saying that *"his company did not expect to make sales to any amount for eighteen months"*. The following day, another letter drew attention to a different problem: *"I am sorry that the coal boring has not been successful, but suppose the company had good grounds for trial in that place. As it is a company we may assume it is pretty sure ... it is wonderful what rascality there is in boring."*

The Duke of Norfolk failed to buy the rights, as they were sold for £7,500 to the brother of the vendor, Colonel Lloyd.

The first manager of the colliery was William Hampson, who moved from the Wigan district to Neston in 1874. He stayed at the colliery for six years. His brother Henry Hampson also came, and was engaged in tunnelling work, at which he proved to be an expert. He also bored artesian wells, including the one at Mostyn House School in Parkgate. James Platt, from Bickerstaffe, Lancashire, was appointed manager in 1880, on Hampson's departure, and stayed until 1910.

Fig. 34 Workmen at the colliery. On the left is Ellis Roberts, the engineman, familiarly known as "Peg Leg" after he had lost his leg as the result of an accident in the mine.

Another person to move into the district was Ellis Roberts, a native of Whitchurch. The work of sinking the shaft was in its early stages when the sides caved in, burying Mr Roberts and several others. Fortunately no-one was killed, but he had to have his leg amputated. The first operation was not successful, as gangrene developed, and more of his leg was removed in two further operations. It was now so badly damaged that a normal artificial limb could not be fitted, and the colliery carpenter made him a special leg. He worked as an engineman on the surface until he retired.

Another accident occurred in May 1876, when some brickwork at the pit head gave way and one of the sheer-poles supporting the head gear broke. A labourer, Hughes, was killed, and Isaac Fisher, a foreman, was seriously injured and died later.

The new mine attracted workers into the district. The 1881 census shows 147 colliery workers, of whom 64 were born in Wales (usually Flintshire), 30 in Lancashire (often Wigan), and 33 from Neston parish.

While the census figures give details for 1881, they cannot give the fluctuations either side of that date. In November 1877, the *Chester Chronicle* reported flooding from old workings. The water rose 80 yards, but nobody was hurt. On 12 January 1878 the paper stated that 180 colliers with no work because of the flooding had left to seek work elsewhere. Other floods in April 1882 drowned nine pit ponies.

In September 1884 the miners went on strike for higher wages. The colliery closed and many men left the area to work in Wigan. Ten days later the Neston Colliery Company held an extraordinary shareholders' meeting. The following resolution was passed: *"That it has been proved to the satisfaction of the meeting that by reason of its liabilities the Company cannot continue in business and that it is advisable to wind up the same."* It was a voluntary liquidation, and the process took nearly two years, with the final meeting on 13 July 1886.

A new company called the Wirral Colliery Company was set up, and this proved to be the longest surviving company working the site. In 1892 W. Fairlie wrote a paper on the geology of Wirral, in which he stated that the Wirral Colliery Company was mining about 100,000 tons of coal a year. Underground workings of five-foot and six-foot seams extended in a north-westerly direction 1¾ miles under the Dee, and the seven-foot workings were more than 1½ miles under the sea. He also referred to the problems of water from the River Dee flooding the workings. This had only affected the six-foot coal. He went on to say *"At the present time there is no difficulty with water, which is well under command, the company having erected not long ago a very large pumping plant. The mine water is very salt."*

The company would have been helped financially by a rise in the average price of coal, from 5s. 2d. at the pit-head in 1886 to 8s. 2d. by 1890. Prices fell again, to 6s. 5d. by 1895, when the colliers' wages were reduced by 15% because of depressed trade.

By the turn of the century trade had recovered significantly, and the period 1900–10 saw the colliery employing between 160 and 200 workers. At first only the seven-foot seam was worked, but in 1906 the six-foot seam was reopened, and production was estimated at 45–50,000 tons.

In 1911 the company went bankrupt. Figure 34 shows how employment fell from 180 in 1910 to 49 in 1911, possibly because the first national coal strike occurred in that year. A new company was established, and by 1913 employment had recovered to 187. This company did not last long, being replaced by the Wirral Colliery (1915) Ltd.

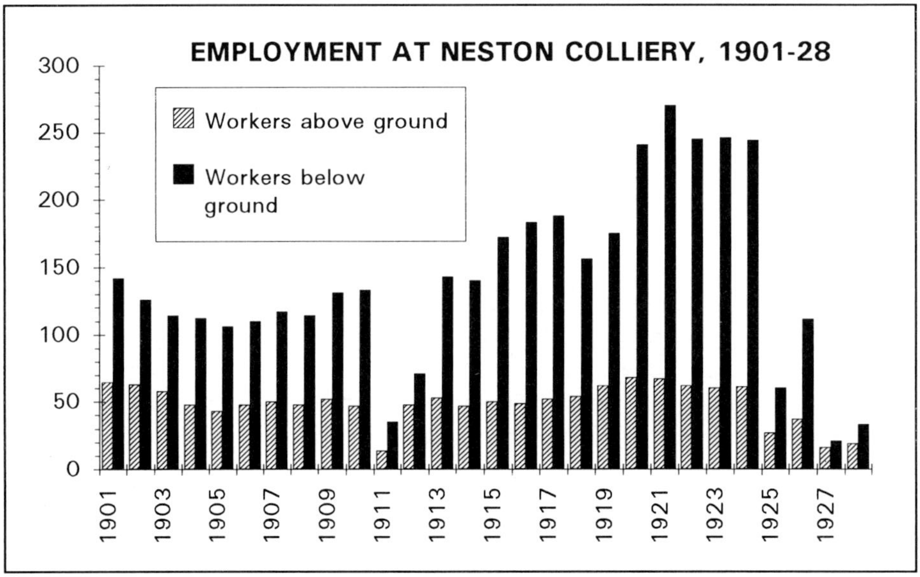

Fig. 35 Employment at the colliery at Neston, 1901–28.

The outbreak of war in 1914 led to many miners enlisting in the armed forces. To maintain coal supplies the Government built up a system of controls which led to the virtual nationalization of the industry by 1918.

Wartime shortage of labour is mentioned in this account given by Harry Sowden, of an accident which took place on 10 July 1916. He was aged 14,

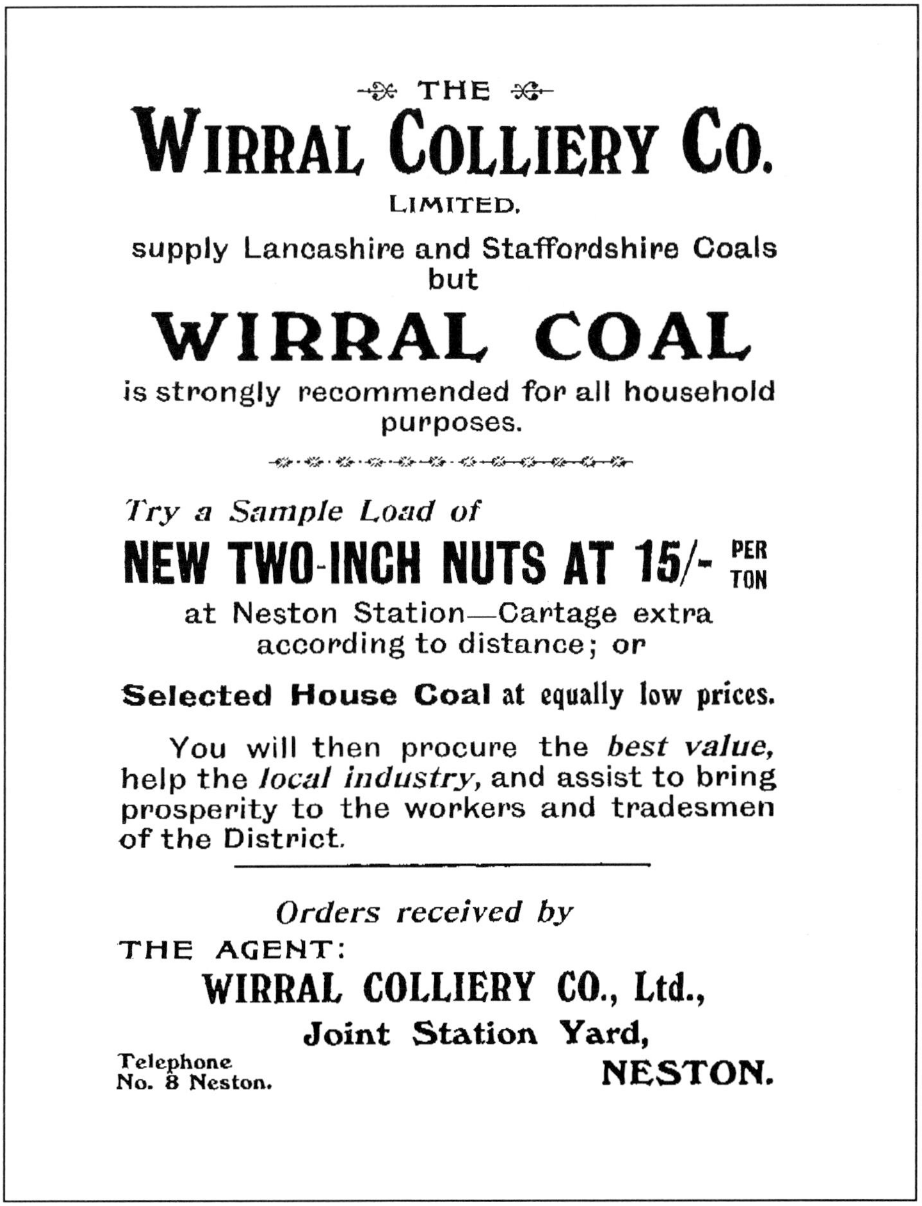

Fig. 36 An advertisement for local coal, as it appeared in the Neston parish magazine for October 1913.

and worked in the seven-foot seam, which was reached by a steep incline called the seven-foot slant.

> *Full boxes went up and empty ones down by means of an endless rope driven by a steam engine. The steam came from the boilers on the surface. Jimmy Hollis was the engine driver. I was responsible for relighting any lamps which went out. They were hooked on a box, four or five at a time, to take to the men below. Jim Wilcox was in charge of the section below, and I had a battery at the top of the slant to light the lamps. I went down with some lamps, and Jim Wilcox told me to take his lamp and relight it. He said I would be all right holding on to the chain. He gave me his lamp, and I set off in the dark. Half way up the slant the rope broke. Trucks came at a rate – full and empties whizzed past, the roof crashed down. I hid at the side, and the trucks missed me. I heard Jim Wilcox shout, "Are you there, Harry?" He did not expect to find me alive. I was not hurt, but scared stiff, and I would not go underground again. I was offered a job on the surface as a stoker, agreed provided I got a man's wage instead of a boy's. They agreed because of the shortage of men during the War.*

A War Relief Fund was set up from contributions from wages. £144 15s. was collected, and this was used for the benefit of men from the colliery who had served in the armed forces, and their dependants. In 1927 the administration of the fund was continued by the Neston and District Council of Social Service.

Boom conditions for the coal industry continued for a short time after the War, but coal faced competition from other fuels, such as oil, and export markets declined. In the face of this decline, the coal industry became the centre of some serious industrial disputes.

In 1919 the Miners' Federation demanded a six-hour day, a 30% increase in pay, and nationalization of the mines. The Government appointed the Sankey Commission, which recommended that the principle of state ownership should be accepted. The Government still controlled the mines from wartime, and as it showed no sign of nationalizing them, the miners staged a strike for seven days in September 1919. In the final months of 1920 the demand for coal was starting to fall, and in order to avoid losses the Government decided to speed up the return of the mines to their private owners.

The private companies decided that the only way they could avoid losses was to reduce the miners' pay. Miners protested and refused the new terms. In March 1921, when the mines passed out of Government control, the miners were locked out by the owners. Neston miners also stopped work, and they were joined by the pump men. Ten management staff had to man the pumps, to prevent the workings being destroyed. The pit ponies were brought out before the miners stopped work.

Nationally the miners sought help from other unions, but this was refused, and they were left on their own. The strike was a long one, and on 12 June a sports day was held on the Comrades Field, next to Neston parish church, in aid of a fund for the children of miners. The event had been suggested by the mine manager, Mr J. Williams, and the company lent pit ponies for a "Derby".

The strike ended in July 1921, when the miners were forced to accept the owners' terms. Wage rates were reduced, and the national system was replaced by local ones, which varied by as much as 50%. Disagreements led to another strike at Neston briefly in December 1921. The coal was sold at North Wales rates, but the men were paid at Lancashire and Cheshire rates, and the company wanted the men to accept the North Wales rate.

Numbers employed at the colliery increased rapidly after the War. The greatest number was 337 in 1921, compared with 196 in 1913. Output in 1924 was 60,000 tons, which suggests that productivity was falling, as many more workers were needed to produce a small extra output. Nationally the post-war boom had ended, and by August 1922 there was short-time working; a month later there were rumours that the colliery was going to close. Such rumours were not correct, but they reflected increasing difficulties.

The situation deteriorated in 1924, and on 13 December the company gave fourteen days' notice to 300 of its employees. However, it said that absenteeism of up to 60 men per shift was the reason for its decision.

By the time the notice had expired, the company had changed its mind. Instead, unprofitable seams were closed and the work-force was reduced by about a hundred men.

In April 1925 there were reports of machinery being dismantled and pit ponies brought to the surface. The mine owner, Mr W. R. Davies, then decided to close the colliery, as it was losing £250 a week. He offered the men who were members of the North Wales Miners' Federation the free use of the mine and £50 a week for three months against losses. There were local negotiations on how to cover the losses, with a proposal that they should be shared equally between the mine owner, a local committee and the miners. Only the miners refused. Their spokesman, J. Thompson, said *"We could not see our way to guaranteeing the one third, neither could it be guaranteed to produce any more coal per man unless additional power were put into the pit."*

The mine continued for another year at a lower level of activity, and then national events took over. The Government had appointed the Samuel Commission to enquire into the industry in 1925, and it reported in March 1926. It proposed some long-term improvements to the industry, such as pit-head baths, but proposed an immediate cut in wages. The owners rejected reorganization of the industry and demanded not only lower wages but also longer hours. The miners refused these terms, and on 1 May 1926 they were locked out. They asked for support from other trades unions, which they quickly obtained. At midnight on 3 May a General Strike started. This ended on 11 May, when the other unions withdrew their support, leaving the miners to fight on alone.

Neston miners were on strike for six months, and there was much financial hardship. They had help from the Bulley family, who lived at what is now Ness Gardens. A. K. Bulley was a wealthy Socialist, who saw support for the miners as part of his principles. His daughter recalled in an interview:

> *My mother fed the miners' families. She worked out a careful system in co-operation with the local tradespeople. At the end, when she came to tot it up, she had spent what another woman in her position might have spent on a Rolls Royce, and, my word, she had much more satisfaction!*

Each miner and member of his family was given 5s. a week, in the form of vouchers for food.

Nationally, miners were forced back to work, and they had to accept longer hours and lower pay. Jack Jones, who was 16 at this time, said miners picked coal off the waste tips, and sold it. He also remembered Mrs Bulley bringing soup to Ness Holt school mornings and evenings. One of the older miners told him that a union man stood up on a box and said they had to go back: *"Half a loaf is better than no bread."*

Work started again after the strike, but only for a few months. The *Birkenhead News* reported in March 1927, *"Serious blow to Neston. Coal pit to be dismantled. The owners of the Neston Colliery have decided definitely to close and dismantle the pit ..."*

The notice read:

> *To all persons employed at the Wirral Colliery. It has now been finally decided to close the pit and dismantle it, therefore fourteen days notice expiring March 12th is hereby given to each person employed*
>
> [signed]
>
> *John Taylor, manager.*

The *News* also reported, *"Already the partial closing down of the colliery has given a serious blow to tradesmen and it is feared this final step will further depress the prosperity of the village."*

One cause of the closure was the royalties required by the local farmer, Mr Tozer, which the company could not afford. Exploration work started, to find new reserves. As Mr Millington recalled,

> *The pit was near closing and we were desperate to find a fresh seam to work. We had been told that there used to be a four-foot seam at about sixty feet, so*

with the cage half way down the shaft the men began to dig. When we broke through, hundreds of gallons of water rushed out and sent the cage spinning.

They had found a worked out seam. The mine was finally abandoned in July 1928.

Cyril Oxton was one of the last workers there, and he helped to demolish the surface buildings. *"We had to pull the head gear over, using the Lord Talbot* [a steam locomotive]. *We coupled a wire rope to the head gear, sawed through the pillars and pulled it over with the engine. There was a terrific crash."*

Fig. 37 The *Lord Talbot* engine was used to haul coal from the colliery to the sidings at Parkgate. The locomotive was new when delivered to the colliery (*c.*1880), and was sold or scrapped after its closure.

Coal mining has always been a dangerous occupation, and although we have no information of a major disaster, there were a large number of accidents. The mine accident book for 1911–27 survives, and over those sixteen years it records 530 injuries, with the largest number, 62, in 1922, when employment was at its maximum.

In all, four deaths were recorded, and there was also a case of serious injury which led to death four years later.

In June 1914 William Barnes was roofing in the King Mine, when a stone fell from the roof, killing him instantly. He left a widow and six children.

In March 1917 Richard Roberts was killed on the surface. He was helping to shunt trucks, and was walking alongside a slowly moving railway wagon, holding the brake. He slipped and fell under the wheels. His mother saw the accident, and the shock turned her hair grey by the following day.

In June 1924 Robert Evans and George Shaw went together for the 6 a.m. shift. When they got to the pit-head they were told to go home, because there had been a fall of rock, and William Jones and Tom Price had been buried. William Jones died, but Tom Price survived with an injured arm and shoulder.

Frederick Abel was killed in January 1926. He was going to turn on a compressed air tap for his father when he was hit by a stone falling from the roof. It was the custom that after a fatal accident work stopped for the rest of the day. Jack Jones confirmed the accident book's account.

A case of delayed death occurred when W. Briscoe was cut on the head and leg when coal fell on him in March 1921. He died in August 1925 of a cerebral haemorrhage, and Dr Gunn stated that *"in all probability his death was due to this accident"*.

Mr Millington said,

> *A common sight in the mine were fossilized trees. We would tunnel right through them and you could see the rings in the roof of the tunnel. The trees were made of ironstone and sometimes the whole fossilized tree would drop out of the roof like a pillar of stone. There were quite a few accidents caused that way.*

Cyril Oxton described what it was like to go down the mine:

> *We used to get to the pit at 6 a.m., go to the lamp room, produce a tally and get a lamp. That was tested by the lampman by blowing all round it. If there was a bit of gas the lamp would go out, of course. Then you would go to the pit bank, where your lamp was tested again, and you were searched for matches or cigarettes. You got in the cage, eight at a time, gates closed, signalled to the winder, and down you went. It was a queer sensation leaving the surface of the ground. When you got to the bottom your lamp was tested again and you were searched for matches. You waited five to ten minutes till you got your eyesight, and then you set off for your job, which could be three quarters of a mile away.*

And George Shaw described the working conditions:

> *When lads went down the pit they were to be a "pusher-up". They helped to push the trucks up the steep incline.* [Jack Jones also did this work.] *The face was very low and you could not put your hands on the top of the truck.*

You fitted a bow to the side so that you could push the truck without crushing your hand. The colliery blacksmith made these bows for the trucks. When you got the truck to the coal-face the roof was too low for you to load it. You had to put the truck in a hole and take the wheels off. If you were coming back to the shunt and your light went out you were in total darkness. So you put both hands on the rails and followed them down to the shunt so that you did not hit the pit props.

Fig. 38 The sidings at Neston colliery on the day that the colliery closed in 1927. William (Bill) Ashbrook is in the centre.

You put your lunch in a tin: if it was in a handkerchief the mice would get it. Pay depended on how much was produced. If they were not mining coal, but stone or fireclay, they were paid a day rate. Each miner had a bundle of tallies with his number on. At the coal-face you filled the truck and put a tally through a hole in the top. The coal went to the pit-head, and when it came out of the cage the trucks were weighed, the tally was taken off, and the weight was recorded in a book. The total was calculated at the end of the week.

When you were paid you went to the little window in the pay office and shouted out your number. [Mr Shaw's was 211.] *Your pay was in a little tin. You took the money out and put the tin in a box as you went out.*

Cyril Oxton summed up his feelings on the closure of the colliery with these words:

It was a living for a good many. We did not get a lot of money but it was always there, and it did not matter what you could do, you could always find a job there.

QUARRIES AND BUILDING

The base rock of the Wirral peninsula is sandstone, with a layer of boulder clay covering it. Great Neston, like most of the townships which made up the ancient parish, is built on an outcrop of this sandstone that provides a firm, dry location for a settlement, and also a useful building material. The overlying clay has been utilized to a lesser extent for brick manufacture. The ready availability of these materials could be an explanation for the large number of small building businesses in the area over the period covered by this book.

The Mostyns had had a quarry from before 1814 on land at the junction of Mill Street and Park Street which was still being worked in the 1870s by Johnson Houghton. There were complaints about blasting, and it was soon abandoned and left to cause a nuisance for many years, filling with water that had to be pumped out, until eventually, in 1900, it was used by the council for refuse dumping. Despite promises by the council that only "dry" refuse would be put in it, there were complaints about the smell from "wet" refuse. After it had been filled it was used as a council yard.

There was a quarry on land at Cross Street to the rear of houses in Park Street. The quarry belonged to the Youds family, and it would seem likely that its stone was used for the National school built in 1858 and the cottages in Poplar Weint. Several generations of the Youds family, most of them builders, lived in May Cottage in Mill Street from 1767 until 1886. The land that had been occupied by their quarry was later the site of Wolton Gray's timber yard, and then John Fleming's building yard.

A third quarry in this area was dug in 1912 behind the 1859 vicarage in Wood Lane for Mr Whineray of Leighton Court, and worked by the Wright brothers from Derbyshire from 1914. This was used as a tip in the 1920s and 1930s.

Quarry Road, on the route to Willaston, was the site of three quarries, including Hinderton quarry, which belonged to the Bushells and was next to the water tower, and one directly across the road which was used by the Local Board for road stone. In 1890 Lord Talbot's agent claimed ownership of this, the Flatt Heath Road quarry, demanding payment for the stone, but the Board refused to pay, saying it had been using the stone for twenty years. Hinderton quarry stone was said to be of superior quality, being particularly straight-grained. The wall at Brook House in the Parade at Parkgate is said to be made of this straight-grained but softer Hinderton stone, while the gate caps are of the Wood Lane sandstone, which has some gravel in it. There was a third quarry behind the cottages on the corner of Quarry Road and the Chester High Road.

The builders in Little Neston were also known as skilled masons. The Normans had a quarry from at least 1869, and Henry Norman's business was established in 1894, with many members of the family in the building business since that date. Their quarry was in Quarry Lane (now Newtown), where they built the sandstone cottages which still stand, as do the ones they built at the bottom of Badger Bait. The small brick semi-detached houses in Mill Street and some in Raby Road were also Normans'. Like most of the builders, they were also in the funeral-directing business.

Fig. 39 Stonemasons in 1910, including some members of the Oxton family, building The Fenns in Burton Road, Ness Holt, opposite Furrocks Lane.

The Oxtons, whose quarry was at the top of Woodfall Lane, were in business as builders in 1851. Their stone was of superior quality and was used for the houses built opposite the youth centre in Burton Road for three members of the Oxton family, including Henry Oxton, a foreman mason on the construction of Liverpool's Anglican cathedral. They also built the house in Burton Road known now as The Fenns.

The biggest builder in the area in the latter part of the last century was William Pritchard. In 1861 he was described as stone mason and builder, with sixteen men. Twenty years later he had 25 men and five boys. Pritchard's Row in Town Lane, Little Neston, is a terrace of cottages converted from stone farm buildings in the 1870s. The stone is visible to the rear of the houses, though the front is brick. The house which became the Neston War Memorial Cottage Hospital in 1920 was built by William Pritchard as his own residence, Dee View, in the early 1880s. He also built the gasworks in Church Lane, and Neston's town hall. This building, which had its foundation stone laid in September 1888, was ready for its first function in February 1889! Several shop frontages were Pritchard's work, and as a speculative project he also built The Towers in Chester High Road when his men were between jobs.

A notable Neston builder at the beginning of our period was William Quay, who had a timber yard in Raby Road (then known as Lodge Lane because of the water tank, or "lodge", situated at the top of the lane). Quay built the Wirral Union Workhouse at Clatterbridge in 1836, and some of the outbuildings at Ashfield Hall.

This same site was occupied by another builder in the 1880s — William Grocott, who in 1881 had eleven men and three boys working for him. He did a lot of small building work for the Local Board, and built the cottages near the top of Parkgate Road. He owned the disused water tank that had supplied some residents before there was a Local Board supply, and he was given permission to remove the lead pipes that fed the tank.

Two generations of the Woodward family, John and his son Albert, ran a joinery, building and later funeral-directing business in the town centre, on the site of the old brewery, where the old persons' centre now stands. John Woodward had served on the urban district council for thirty years by the time of his death in 1935. Woodward's built the terrace of three shops in Bridge Street, "Woodward's Cottages" off Bridge Street, and the shop in Bridge Street, currently a butcher's, which was built for Pearson's in the mid-1920s.

Around the turn of the century, Joseph Johnson had a decorating and plumbing business in High Street where Barnes's butcher's shop is currently situated, the shop at the Cross end of that row being run as a café by his sisters. The business used the yard at the rear of the premises, and they employed a gas engine to generate electricity for lighting the business and running the woodworking machinery. They built property in Raby Road, Parkgate and Little Neston. Just as with other local builders, it is still possible to see manhole inspection covers bearing their name.

Established in 1881, Fleming's became the most prolific of Neston builders in the first half of this century. The business was established by William Fleming, who died in 1900, leaving the business to his sons, Albert and John. They dissolved the partnership in 1912, however, and commenced their own businesses. Fleming's carried out work on Mostyn House in the 1890s, erected the "temporary" corrugated iron schoolroom in Park Street in 1892, and built the manse in Parkgate Road in 1901. The first St Michael's church in Little Neston was their work in 1914, and they did building throughout Wirral, including the Liverpool Children's Hospital in Heswall, and several large houses speculatively built in Wood Lane in the 1930s. John ran his business until the Second World War from Cross Street and Liverpool Road, and built the present engineering works in Liverpool Road for his own use. Albert was in Leighton Road, where he also had his brickworks until he went bankrupt, just before the Second World War. Known as the Neston Brick Company, it was on the site where Fairholm Avenue now stands.

Fig. 40 This brickworks in Burton Road, at the foot of Bull Hill in Little Neston, belonged *c.*1900 to W. G. Scott, who lived at Penketh House, Church Lane, Neston.

Other twentieth-century builders included Cross and Mannion in Brook Street in the 1920s; Oxton and Jackson, who built the present waterworks building, and whose yard was in West Vale; Thomas Anyon of Brook Street; and Benbow of Brook Street.

In the eighteenth and early nineteenth centuries there was a brickyard where the Clayhill industrial estate now stands. It was said by George Gleave in an 1880s *Chester Chronicle* article to have been in earlier years *"ablaze with brick kilns"*. For a few years around the turn of the century there was a brickyard at the junction of Colliery Lane (now Marshlands Road) and Burton Road, belonging to W. G. Scott.

THE CABLE WORKS AND THE LAUNDRY

Along the ancient roadway from Moorside to the Old Quay, between the town and the marshes, are a few derelict remains of the Deeside Electric Works established in 1882 by G. C. Taylor and Company. The lane, known in later years as Laundry Lane, and Old Quay Lane, was a century ago known as Muddy, Dirty or Love Lane.

George Crosland Taylor was born in 1857, son of a successful woollen goods manufacturer from Huddersfield. He entered the family business at 16, but developed more of an interest in the machinery than the product. This interest persuaded him to visit the Paris Electrical Exhibition in 1881.

Crosland, as he was known, claimed to have first encountered Neston while on a bicycle ride, stopping for refreshments at the Golden Lion Inn. On a subsequent visit he recognized the area's potential for a manufacturing industry — a good supply of water, a gasworks under construction, and labour (though he was warned by friends that Neston did not have men capable of carrying out such an undertaking, nor sufficient men for employment in the works). Crosland was only 24 at the time, living in Thornton Hough, where he opened a quarry, probably behind the farmhouse next to the present school. He built the sandstone Deeside Cottage, which still stands in Old Quay Lane, and he also built a large part of the factory of the sandstone. He had pitch laid on the surface of the lane by John Devaney.

The original idea had been to manufacture electrical machinery or lights, but instead they decided to make insulated cables. These were in demand for Post Office telegraphy signalling. The substance used for insulation was gutta-percha, a brown, leathery substance obtained, like latex, from trees (and also used for chewing-gum at this time). Employment was expected for around two hundred men. A corrugated iron shed was built on the site, about 170 feet long, to contain water tanks to cool the freshly extruded gutta-percha. An artesian well was sunk to supply the 300 gallons an hour needed for the process. No pump is needed for raising the water in an artesian well: it is forced to the surface from a deep layer of rock by hydrostatic pressure.

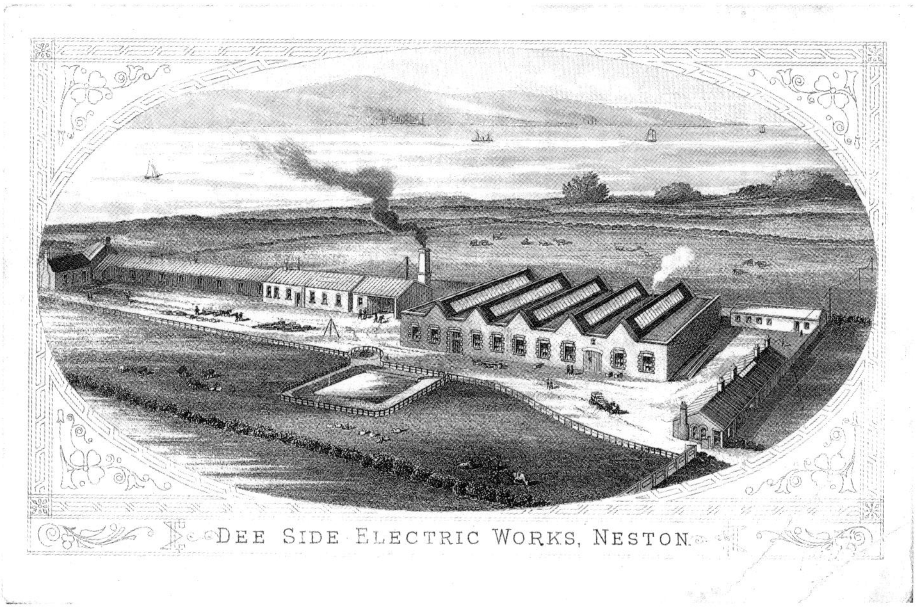

Fig. 41 Deeside Electric Works, Neston: an engraving of the cable works built in 1882.

The company had further plans for forming an iron foundry at the works, and solicited the Local Board for orders for castings and gears. The cable insulation process did not go smoothly at first, but by 1884 Crosland Taylor and Fred Whiteley evolved a process whereby the insulation was always concentric with the cable. Taylor's younger brother, James, joined the works to administer the business side, but it became evident by 1885 that the venture was not going to be successful in the Neston location.

The only railway at this time was the Hooton–Parkgate line, extended to West Kirby in 1886. Although the single line to the colliery passed near the works, goods to and from the factory would presumably have to be taken along the lane, up Moorside Lane and along Parkgate Road to Parkgate station. It has been said that not enough local labour could be found for the works and that men had to be brought in from other parts of Wirral.

The business was converted to a private company called the Telegraph Manufacturing Company, and moved to a site in Helsby in 1887. Crosland

Taylor stated in his autobiography that *"the geographical position and railway at Neston made it unsuitable"*. In addition to insulating cables, the company manufactured batteries, burglar alarms and various types of electrical equipment. Amalgamating with other companies over the years, the firm subsequently became known as British Insulated Callenders Cables (BICC).

The Taylors had installed a telephone system between the factory and their house in Thornton Hough (presumably Neston's first telephone), erecting their own telegraph poles via Liverpool Road. The equipment was transferred to Dr David Russell, Neston's physician, to use between his home, Vine House, and his Heswall surgery.

The Neston works, as far as we know, lay empty, apart from storing the Local Board's water cart in the winter, until 1896, when the Neston and Parkgate Hygienic Laundry and Cleaning Company was formed. The prime mover in this venture was Algernon Grenfell from Mostyn House, another enterprising gentleman, who resigned from the Local Board in

Fig. 42 A laundry van made in 1897 by the Gloucester Railway Carriage and Wagon Company for the Neston and Parkgate Hygienic Laundry and Cleaning Company.

exasperation at its refusing to entertain the idea of an electric light plant to light the streets. Crosland Taylor was also involved in the undertaking.

The artesian well was a welcome asset for the laundry; in later years it claimed *"We wash well with well water"*. The effluent was drained 30 feet out onto the marshes, but by the 1920s was leaving stagnant sewage and suds as the tide receded.

By 1914 the laundry was employing 80 people. The work was considered a reasonable alternative for girls to going into service. One ex-employee, now in her eighties, had the job of removing fur collars and trims from garments before dry-cleaning, and sewing them on again afterwards. She recalls mounds of serviettes and stiff collars.

By 1940 the laundry was taken over by Tranmere Laundry, in case the latter's Birkenhead works was bombed, and finally closed in the late 1950s.

Fig. 43 A good drying day for Blanche Hughes, watched by her sisters, Ruth and Amy, at the cottages by the colliery. She worked for Hollis's Laundry, nearby in Marshlands Road, Little Neston, which had been started by Mrs Ruth Hollis in 1917. About thirty people were employed here at one time. In 1960 the laundry changed to being a dry-cleaning business for ten years.

There was another laundry, too, in the years before the First World War, operating from Parkgate.

It seems that there was a certain amount of in-breeding in Neston in those days, resulting, it is said, in a higher-than-average number of retarded children. Mrs Barrett, who lived at Church House in Neston and was the widow of the Rev. William Barrett, a former curate, organized a home for the retarded girls in the basement of Ashton House (now Balcony House), in Parkgate.

With the uncompromising bluntness of the times, this was called the Home for Feeble-minded Girls and Laundry Training. Allegedly, one motive for her charity was to prevent these girls falling prey to the local feeble-minded boys. The girls were looked after by a matron, Miss Hubbard, between about 1902 and 1914. People used to hand their laundry through the windows of the basement.

MEALORS' PLOUGHS

Three generations of Mealors worked as plough-makers in Ness. Samuel Mealor and his wife, Margaret, were both born in Willaston, but had moved to Ness by 1851. They were a Methodist family, and held services in their home from 1859 until Little Neston Methodist Church was built in 1872. Their eldest surviving son, Joseph, was born in 1852 in Ness, but does not appear in the local 1871 census returns. This would suggest he was apprenticed elsewhere, since in 1881 he is shown as a blacksmith. He had probably returned by 1880, as the present company states that this date was its foundation year. The 1881 census returns also describe Samuel Mealor as retired.

Joseph Mealor built up the business and was responsible for important inventions and developments of agricultural implements. His catalogue for the 1893 Royal Agricultural Show in Chester refers to the "D-pattern Anglo Furrowing Plough", which had taken seven first prizes in four years. It cost £3 17s. 6d., and if fitted with a skimmer the extra charge was 7s. 6d. Eight other ploughs were listed, which were designed in different weights for heavy or light land.

The catalogue gives a number of testimonials from people who had bought Mealor ploughs. While this is a biased source, local anecdotal evidence supports the view given here:

Puddington Hall, Chester.
30th May 1893

I have much pleasure in bearing witness to the excellent work done by Mr Joseph Mealor of Ness, Chester, in the manufacture of ploughs. In this district he has won many prizes, not only for the high-class character of his machines, but also for the improvements he has adapted to them. He is a practical man in his knowledge of ploughs, and his ideas have met in this district with universal favour.

J. S. Harmood Banner, J.P. for the County of Chester.

This opinion was supported by evidence found by the present owners of the building. When they were making renovations they found a collection of ploughing match certificates. There were a total of ten first-class or second-class certificates won at the Raby Ploughing Society matches between 1881 and 1891.

Fig. 44 Cottages and the premises of Mealor and Sons in Ness, before the First World War.

Joseph Mealor's inventive ability is shown by two patents. The first was granted in 1898, for "Improvements in Cleaning and Weeding Implements for Agricultural Purposes". In the specification, Joseph Mealor stated that his invention would remove weeds from crops, such as potatoes, turnips or beans, which were sown on ridges. He stated that the existing machinery tended to scoop the soil away from the ridges and interfered with the manure contained therein. His new implement had adjustable, inclined feet to remove weeds without disturbing the ridges.

The second patent was accepted later, in 1899, and was an improvement of the one-way plough. Such a type of plough enabled all the furrows to be turned in the same direction, and reduced the trampling of the headlands. It was also a useful way of working narrow strips of land. Manufacturers had developed a number of versions of the one-way plough, one of the most popular being by John Huxtable in 1889. Joseph Mealor's was an improvement, as he stated:

> *The one-way plough, as at present in general use, is provided with a twin breast which turns on an under-swivel when the direction of the plough is reversed. According to my invention, I provide two separate and distinct plough breasts, one right-handed and the other left-handed, which alternately come into action, with greatly improved results.*

The company continued to produce a range of ploughs. The 1910 catalogue shows their range and refers to the company as J. Mealor and Sons. By 1935 the proprietors were Joseph Mealor, Senior, and his son, John J. Mealor. A 1930s catalogue refers to "Mealors' Famous Horse Hoe", and states that *"they sell in thousands and increase in demand each year"*.

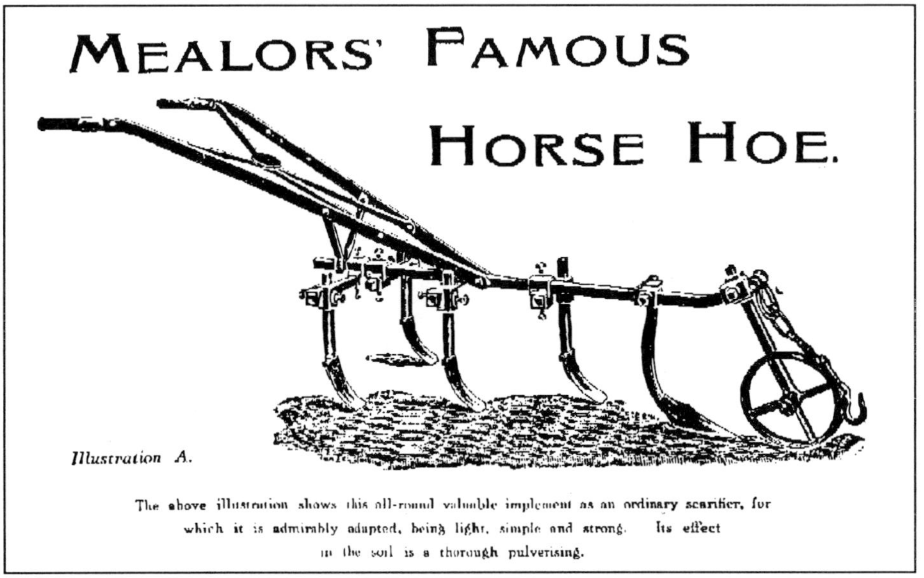

Fig. 45 "Mealors' Famous Horse Hoe": the price varied between £5 14s. 6d. for light, and £6 13s. 6d. for very heavy models.

But even though the company was in the forefront of developments in horse ploughs, it was not well placed to compete with producers of tractor-drawn ploughs. The company was small, with limited resources, and at the critical time the owners were elderly. John Mealor had left the company, and he died in 1944. His father outlived him and died three years later at the age of 94.

The business of making ploughs was continued by L. N. Shakeshaft. Then, in 1956, the present owners took over, who are specialists in the supply and maintenance of grass-cutting machinery.

Ploughs were not the only business of the company. The blacksmiths shoed horses, and the double green doors which led to the forge are still there. Other products manufactured included railings around Neston parish church (which were removed during the Second World War), and cast iron park benches.

NESS GARDENS

Ness Gardens were started by Arthur Kilpin Bulley, and were his private property. He had made money in the cotton trade, but he was a keen naturalist. Miss Bulley remembered her parents saying they had cycled all over Wirral, looking for a south-facing slope for their garden. Their search was referred to in a letter that Mr Bulley wrote to the Keeper of the Royal Botanic Garden at Edinburgh in December 1896:

> *In the last twelve months I have been hunting for a site on which to build a house and have an ideal garden. One has turned up recently with rock, sand, clay, water and south slope. I think I shall very likely buy 5 or 10 acres. I propose to develop it gradually and shall want two gardeners.*

Mr Bulley said he could recruit one gardener locally. He wanted advice on whom to choose as a trustworthy head gardener. The house was Mickwell Brow, which he built in 1898. Miss Bulley said that when she was a little girl the south slope was covered in gorse and brambles, and a lot of bramble puddings were picked from there. The site was very open, and one of Mr Bulley's first priorities was to plant shelter belts of wych-elm and pine trees. He established in their shelter seasonal herbaceous borders and a large plant-propagation area.

In 1903, in a further letter to Edinburgh, Mr Bulley said that the garden's fame was spreading, *"till it has become more like a nursery than a garden and costs a great deal to keep up"*. He went on to say that he wanted to take the plunge and start selling plants, *"if only to lessen the expenses of the garden"*. He also said that he thought *"the trade in plants the most desirable of all forms of commerce"*.

The business started under the name of A. Bee and Company, shortly before January 1905, when a co-operative company was set up, called Co-operative Bees Limited.

Catalogue No. 2, issued in spring 1903, explained the company's operating principles: it operated as a *bona fide* trading company; declared profits were divided into two parts; the first was for the shareholders, and the other was distributed to customers in proportion to their purchases. Mr Bulley was a Socialist, and his principles were reflected in his company. The catalogue was a substantial book, with 232 pages of printed lists of plants for sale, with the facing pages blank, for notes. The introduction claimed the catalogue was the most complete and up to date in existence, giving the most extensive index of English plants. The co-operative organization did not remain very long, as Bees Limited was set up in June 1906.

Mr Bulley wanted to increase the range of plants available for his garden and nursery. Miss Bulley remembered

> *My father realized that plants which grew at 2,000 feet in Switzerland would grow at sea level in Norway. That set his thoughts to the Himalayas and other such places, and it came to him that missionary societies had missionaries in the most unlikely parts of the world.*

Even though Mr Bulley was an atheist, he tried to obtain their support, and he eventually persuaded some to collect seeds. Miss Bulley said

> *Anyway, they did their best. The seeds came home with clear indications of where they came from, and they were hurriedly planted. My father soon said we had the finest international collection of dandelions. Mass dandelions had a fatal attraction to the untrained missionary mind, and so that was what led to the engaging of Forrest.*

Mr Bulley sponsored George Forrest in 1904 to collect plants and seeds in Western China. One of his discoveries was *Pieris Formosa Forrestii*, and the original plant still grows at Ness. Many of the plants took time to grow and flower, and in the 1911–12 Bees Catalogue A. K. Bulley was able to announce *"new and rare hardy plants, including our own introductions"*. Mr Bulley sponsored one other expedition himself, and was a member of a syndicate for five others.

Miss Bulley recalled that her father was very excited when the seeds arrived at Ness:

> *The seeds were spread out on the Bechstein grand piano, and Hope, of course, would be there. They used to lean on the piano side by side on their elbows, arguing furiously.*

Josiah Hope was the head gardener from 1913 to 1956. He and Mr Bulley formed a successful partnership, as the latter wanted a head gardener with definite opinions, who could test his ideas.

They also differed in their political opinions. However, Mr Hope was once working in the garden when he was approached by a man described by Miss Bulley as a *"very gentlemanly gentleman"*, who asked, *"Whose are these gardens?"* J. Hope replied, *"Mr Bulley's."* The visitor said, *"Not Mr Bulley the well-known Socialist? If I had known that, I would never have come in." "There's the gate"*, said Hope, who was a staunch Conservative.

Miss Bulley also recalled that

> *Hope would not allow anyone to pick flowers from the garden for the house. We had a concert party, and my mother slipped down and gave them one each of the famous Daily Mail roses. Next morning she told Hope, who said, "Thought so, thought so – four, wasn't it?"*

The nursery business prospered, and expanded rapidly, and an extra site was bought in 1911.

There are some clues to the numbers of people employed at the gardens from a wages book. In the spring of 1907 there were 51 employees, but most were probably doing building work. In May of that year the number fell to seventeen, and the total wages bill was £17 17s. 8d. In February 1913 eleven people were working at the gardens, at a cost of £9 19s. 2d., with a further 5s. 3d. for national insurance, which had been introduced in 1911.

Fig. 46 Staff employed at Ness Gardens, *c.*1915. Only older men, women and boys avoided conscription into the armed forces.

During the First World War many men were called up, and women were employed to replace them. They had a uniform of a brown corduroy trouser suit.

A few years later the slump in the cotton trade meant that Mr Bulley had to reduce his garden staff by nearly half. Gradually, as the economy recovered in the later 1930s, a few were re-employed. In 1939 there were seven workers in the gardens, and the wage bill was £14 13s. 6d., with 16s. 6d. for insurance. They were J. Hope, W. Cottrell, H. Vincent, F. Price, J. Evans, S. Smith and M. Coventry.

During the Second World War the gardens concentrated on producing fruit and vegetables, which were sold in Neston. Staff were also called up or transferred to war work. Only Mr Hope, who was over retirement age, and Mr Cottrell were left to look after the gardens. Mr Bulley died in 1942, and in 1948 Lois Bulley presented the gardens and house to the University of Liverpool. The gift was made on condition that the gardens should be kept as a practical and fitting tribute to her father. That principle has been followed ever since.

THE FINE ARTS STUDIO AT STAPLANDS

Between the Wars, Neston was the scene of an unlikely and unusual venture. In 1923 the house called Staplands in Hinderton Road, just below the Shrewsbury Arms, was taken by Andrea Pallis, the son of a Liverpool-based Greek merchant. Pallis had obtained a degree in biology at Cambridge, but his ambition was to create beautiful objects in metal. After studying metalwork and jewellery at the Liverpool School of Art, he opened a workshop at Staplands. His first assistant was Edward Halsall of Neston, who thought that his years there were the happiest and most fulfilling of his life. In 1926 Jack Salt was employed as a second assistant, and for a period Betty Brown of Liverpool also assisted Pallis, as an engraver.

An illustrated catalogue of the Staplands output of 1931 shows that Pallis had no truck with design such as Art Nouveau, let alone the contemporary Art Deco. Teutonic, and even Indian, influences (he had been born in Bombay) seem to predominate. A silver-gilt ciborium, two feet high, and now in Fribourg Cathedral, took three years to make. It is heavily jewelled and enamelled, with five rock crystal pillars, and surmounted by a star sapphire. On a simpler level, he designed a silver war memorial for his old school, The Leas, Hoylake, depicting St George and the Dragon. Pallis's maker's mark for the purpose of silver assay was A. P. He employed two methods of gilding — the rarely used mercury gilding, which is now illegal, and electrolysis.

Fig. 47 Two silver tankards made in the Staplands workshop.

In 1925 Pallis was joined by his friend, Aristide Messinesi, also Greek, who had studied spinning, weaving, dyeing and tapestry. He employed three assistants: they were Christine Dodd, now Mrs Hope of Neston; in 1930 Grace Mealor; and Mary Scarratt, now Mrs Sir of Neston. Messinesi disliked chemical dyes, and built a dyehouse at Staplands to use natural dyes. He advertised carpets for sale, and made some miniature ones for Queen Mary's doll's house.

The outbreak of war in 1939 brought about the closure of the workshop, but Andrea Pallis then devoted himself to painting. His brother Marco, well known as a mountaineer and author, sometimes stayed with him in Neston. The house was sold in 1947.

NESTON'S SHOPS

Unlike late-twentieth-century shoppers, we could happily have bought all our requirements from Neston tradesmen for the major part of this 100-year survey.

On a walk around the town sometime around 1850 we would have encountered several butchers, and all would have had their own slaughterhouse. Youds's was in a small thatched building where the Methodist church now stands (Fig. 48, 1). Joseph Jones had a shop at the

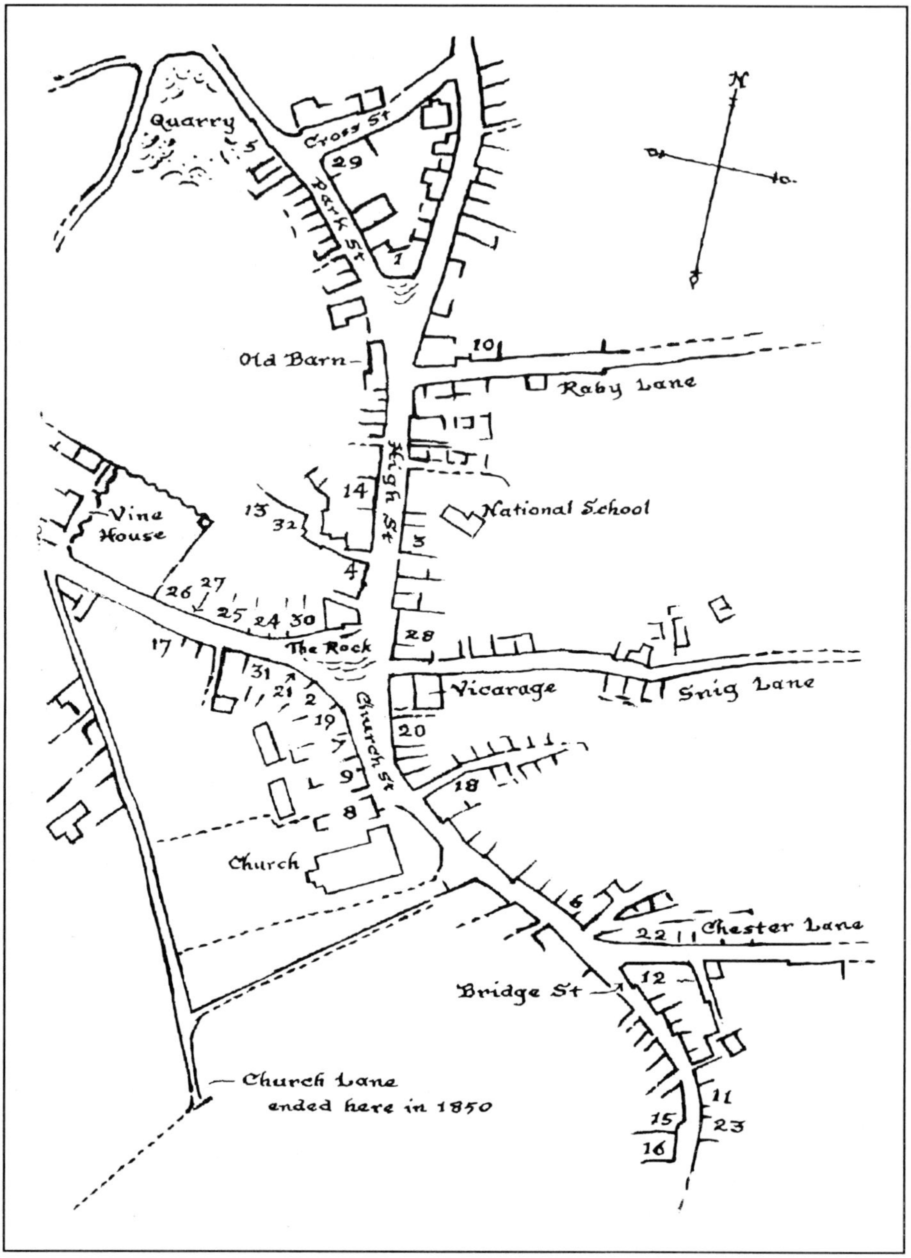

Fig. 48 Neston's shops as they were to be found in 1850 (drawn from the 1849 sale plan of the Mostyn estate).

Cross (2); it was he who in fifteen years' time would object to the idea of sinking a public well there. William Briscoe, whose family would be trading in the town for the next fifty years, had a slaughterhouse in Golden Lion Yard and a shop (3) in High Street below the present town hall site. His family also ran the post office in Neston in 1850, in the old building across the road (4) that stands gable-end to the street. Benjamin Maddox had his butcher's shop and slaughterhouse in Park Street, opposite to the end of Cross Street, in property now demolished (5).

There were several bakers in these days before lorries full of sliced white bread. Thomas Maddox, in 1850, had the shop in High Street, currently No. 33, with the bakehouse in the basement (6), which was later taken over by his nephew, Joseph Parry. In the early years of this century people recall taking their own dough to this bakery and picking it up at the end of the day when baked.

In Church Street, as the row between the Cross and the church was known in 1850, stood Thomas Mallinson's grocery and bakery business in the shop (7) that was to belong to Hancock's the butcher for many years, and is

Fig. 49 A well-stocked display at the butcher's shop belonging to William Hancock, on the west side of the Cross, in the 1880s.

now a jewellery shop. Thomas Mallinson was fined in 1880 for selling bread without weighing it. Emmanuel Mallinson (who was to die in the 1866 cholera outbreak) had a tallow chandlery nearby, in the old buildings next to the church which were soon to be demolished (8). Next to him (9) was Lemuel Welch, joiner and builder. There was another carpenter's shop and timber yard on the corner of Raby Road, next to the reservoir (10).

There were a large number of grocery and general stores. Henry Smith had a large and diversified stock in his shop in the house (11) that used to stand a few doors down from the Coach and Horses, until it burned down in the 1970s. The shop was recalled by a *Chester Chronicle* writer in the 1880s with some nostalgia – particularly for an advertisement (a rarer sight in 1850) for Warren's Blacking, showing a cat gazing intently at its own reflection in a boot. On the corner of this row and Chester Lane lived Humphrey Ellis, farmer, brewer and grocer (12).

In Golden Lion Yard (13), where an electrician now has a yard, was Thomas Garner, plumber and glazier. William Coventry was in the same trade in the High Street (14), opposite the town hall site, and sandwiched between a wine and spirit dealer and the notorious Golden Lion Hotel. The Coventrys had been in the same business in 1828 and were still in it as recently as 1932.

The townspeople could choose from four tailors in 1850. Jonathan Birch (15) and Sam Minshull (16) had shops near to each other in Bridge Street, where the present shops end. Michael O'Loughlin, another tradesman who died in the cholera outbreak, had his tailor's shop (17) in Parkgate Road.

Ann Stuart was a ladies' dressmaker in Pyke's Yard (18), off High Street opposite to the church, and Elizabeth Minshull had part of the house (19) at the Cross that bears a 1724 datestone, which did not get its shop windows for another 30 years. To complete the outfit, Jane Lovell, a maker of straw bonnets, lived across the road (20).

In the small shop (21) on the High Street side of the Greenland Fishery were Catherine and John Robinson, shoemakers. Thomas Peters had a shoemaker's shop (22) just as one turned into Chester Lane, and there was another one (23) two houses down from Henry Smith.

Thomas Henshaw was another shoemaker, whose address in 1850 was The Rock – the area on the north side of the Cross and Parkgate Road (24). Next door to him, where Lawson's the cobbler stood for many years this century, was Samuel Walley (25), bootmaker and organist in 1850. Another bootmaker, Thomas Anyon, had the small premises (26) at the end of that row, next to Vine House. Also in that row was Jane Roberts, "smallware dealer" (27), in an old building which now has large, modern, tinted windows in a Victorian frontage.

Situated in old property on the corner by the Brown Horse was chemist and druggist Maurice James (28). The only ironmonger and whitesmith was William Handley, who had a blacksmith's shop (29) on the corner of Cross Street and Park Street, in an old building on the site of the present joinery. William Handley was to become another victim of the 1866 cholera outbreak.

In the small thatched buildings on the Rock at the Cross (30) was John Johnson, saddler, employing three men. There was a smith, Thomas Powell (31), across the road adjoining the Black Bull, now part of the Greenland Fishery. He lived in the house (which now has a shop frontage) on the other side of the present access way. Another blacksmith was Samuel Pace (32) in Golden Lion Yard — yet another future cholera victim.

Many shops remained in business for decades, the shop being part of the house, rather than the separate entity which we see now. The first purpose-built shops, constructed in the 1860s with spacious living accommodation above, were those built next to the church. Built soon afterwards were the two shops on land next to the old vicarage at the Cross that now house a wine store.

One of the more noteworthy Neston stores was Oakes and Griffiths of Chester, linen drapers, milliners and clothiers, which opened a branch in Neston in the early 1870s and stayed for sixty years. The purpose-built premises were in the building in Parkgate Road that now has pillars constructed on its frontage, although it then had conventional shop windows. The firm also built the former surgery building next door and the row of cottages on the other side. The town's first "department store" included upholstery, bedsteads, bedding and carpets in its stock. Milliners and tailors worked on the premises, and the firm also arranged funerals. It had a reputation as a high-class store for the wealthier residents of Neston and district.

Pearson's, family grocer and provision merchant, was trading for over thirty years earlier this century. It opened before the First World War in an eighteenth-century building on the corner of Chester Road and Bridge Street. In 1928 a road-widening scheme meant demolition of this building, and a new shop was built across the road, now occupied by a butcher. A typical family grocer's business, the food was weighed out in the shop. An ex-employee recalls the six-pound tins of biscuits, the one-hundredweight hessian sacks of sugar direct from Tate and Lyle, sausages sent overnight from Palethorpe's in Cambridge, and cheeses from Capenhurst. Pearson's had a particularly good reputation for bacon, and people still recall the smell of roasting coffee in the vicinity.

The Chester Co-operative Society Ltd opened a branch in 1908 on the site of the old Golden Lion Hotel, selling groceries, clothes and shoes, although a site reserved for a Co-op butcher remained empty for years. Housewives could take an order into the shop early in the week to be delivered on Friday, wrapped in brown paper. People recall the small cash containers sent along wires to the cash desk. Customers gave their "divvy" number and received a quarterly payout which many used to pay off goods they had bought on credit. The Co-op built new premises on the site in 1937.

Fig. 50 Pearson's "new" grocery shop, in Bridge Street, Neston, with George and Dick Pearson and Andrew Cavanagh standing in the doorway.

TWO NESTON BUSINESSES

Two very different accounts of businesses — the plumbing and decorating firm of Joseph Johnson in the late nineteenth century, and the Camerons' cycle and electrical firm in the twentieth century — now complete our survey of the shops and craftsmen of Neston.

JOSEPH JOHNSON, PLUMBER AND DECORATOR

Having been apprenticed as plumber and painter to Thomas Bainbridge, of Charing Cross, Birkenhead, Joseph Johnson started his own business in

Parkgate Road in 1882 as a plumber and painter, later moving to High Street, Neston.

From two ledgers, partly covering the years 1882–87, it can be seen that he was running a small concern with a flexible work-force, engaged in plastering, plumbing, painting, roofing, glazing, gas installations and general repairs, his customers ranging from ordinary householders having their ceilings whitened and their rooms papered and painted in the fashionable colours of the period — chocolate, stone, green and Venetian red —, to more prosperous clients, the Comber family at Richville (now familiar to us as the Parkgate Hotel) and Backwood and Ashfield Halls, which might require bell-hanging, with copper wire throughout, for servant bells. There was much repairing of pumps, kettles and teapots, "graining" of water tins, and, intriguingly, "repair to parrot cage" at Miss Young's Ladies' School! Apart from this type of work, he procured subcontract work from larger local companies, such as Pritchard's at Little Neston, and he and his men worked as far afield as Birkenhead, Eastham, Heswall, Thornton Hough and Liverpool. It is interesting to note from his records that reglazing of lamps was frequently requested by the Neston Local Board — an indication of stone throwing and vandalism, perhaps?

By 1892 a shop in High Street complemented his existing business, selling such items as gas mantles, paint, varnish, turpentine, paint brushes, red lead, whitening and linseed oil. Wallpaper was delivered in round bales, but customers were able to order their preferred choice from pattern books. Paint was mixed on the premises. An eye witness describes the shop as having no counter, just a large roll-top desk, the slide being pulled out to support pattern books, while the customers sat in a chair provided. There were pigeon holes for rolls of wallpaper.

The original shop window was a plain kitchen window, and in time Mr Johnson changed this to a proper shop window, within which he displayed WCs, sinks, taps and suchlike items. Out-of-date pattern books were given to local children, who loved to cut out the flowers and decorative patterns for their scrapbooks.

As might be expected, seasonal factors affected the amount of work available. From January to April in 1884 there appears to have been sufficient trade to employ himself and one man, averaging together some 58 hours a week. From May to August in the same year, Mr Johnson and two, sometimes three, men, averaged 181 hours a week. The final period of the year shows him and generally two men averaging 120 hours a week. This work-force was supplemented throughout the year by the hiring of plasterers on a daywork basis.

An account with Neston gasworks in October 1882 details that a meter was fitted for a Mr Mathews of Parkgate, at a cost of 1s. 6d., and in January

1883 Oakes and Griffiths, Neston's department store in Parkgate Road, had gas lights installed in the tailors' room and over the tailors' table, at a total cost of 15s. 9½d.

Accounts for the Neston Local Board would often show a credit for reclaimed lead at 1d. a pound, whereas new lead was charged out at 2½d. a pound.

Fig. 51 Joseph Johnson outside his premises (now Barnes's shop) in High Street, Neston. The double gates are still there, but are now surmounted by an arch.

In 1898 Joseph Johnson employed thirteen men, at varying rates of pay. Joiners and plumbers received 9½d. an hour, and painters, paper hangers and glaziers were paid 8½d. or 9½d. an hour. Weekly-paid employees included the long-serving Henry Smith, who was paid 16s. (3¼d. an hour) for services which entailed carting, labouring in the workshop, and caring for the horse and cart. Overtime was paid at the hourly rate, and a week was 49½ hours. A group of four apprentices were paid on a sliding scale of 3s. 6d., 4s., 7s., or 8s. weekly, probably dependent on age, and overtime was an approximation of an hourly rate – either 1d. or 2d. an hour.

THE CAMERON FAMILY

Roy Cameron was born in 1912. His father, John Cameron, had been apprenticed to motor engineers at Falkirk in the early 1890s, while his mother, Carry (Constance Brison), had been in service and had travelled with the family to Egypt, Germany, Norway and Sweden. After their marriage, John Cameron was employed as chauffeur by Lord Massereene at Antrim Castle in Ireland. Their elder son, Ian, was born eighteen months before Roy. When Lord Massereene left Ireland for London, John was left without a job, and he contacted his mother's brother-in-law, R. W. Jones, who was the first head of Neston's council school in Burton Road. With Jones's help, John obtained a shop with a workshop at the back, on the north side of Neston Cross. In 1912 John Cameron established a motor and cycle dealing and repair business there. He also maintained the electric light plants in large local houses, and had the Raleigh agency.

During the First World War, John had to work in a munitions factory at the John Summers steelworks, but in 1916 he was called up and served as an engineer in the Royal Flying Corps. His wife was a very good business woman, and she carried on the business with the help of mechanics.

Roy went to his uncle's school in Burton Road, and thence to the City and County School for Boys at Queen's Park, Chester. He was subsequently apprenticed to the Vulcan Motor Engineering Company at Southport, which made cars, buses and lorries. But the depression put the company into financial trouble, and in 1930 Roy got a month's notice. He found work in Chester with the Grosvenor Motor Company and the Dee Motor Company. After two years he joined the family firm in Neston, and at about the same time his brother Ian left Metropolitan Vickers to specialize in the radio and electrical side, part-time at first, while working in Chester.

The Camerons acquired the BSA agency, previously held in Neston by W. E. Chrimes where Manning's the cobbler is now. They sold BSA, Royal Enfield and other motorcycles, which they obtained through Davies Brothers of Chester.

Roy played the organ for Neston parish church from about 1930, but he also played at Caldy, Burton, Thornton Hough, Woodchurch and Eastham. He also played the piano for dance bands.

When the Second World War came, Ian served as an electrician in the RAF, and Roy became a motor engineer for Birkenhead Corporation Transport. Their wives managed the business with the help of an apprentice, and of Roy in the evenings.

The shop was sold in 1973, although the workshop behind remained in use for some years under different management.

SOURCES

This chapter, like Chapter Two, has been the joint effort of many hands and memories.

George Tilley was interviewed by Edward Hilditch.

Edward Hilditch wrote the section on Coal Mining. His sources were the Mostyn papers at Bangor (6959); the Arundel Castle archives (MD 1244); W. Fairlie, *Practical notes on the geology of Wirral*, in *Transactions of the Federated Institute of Mining Engineers* (Vol. 4, 1892); Peter Barton's MA thesis, *The coal industry of Neston, 1759–1927* (Liverpool, 1991); an article in the *Heswall and Neston News* (21 November 1968), quoting Mr Millington; and interviews with Cyril Oxton, Jack Jones, Harry Sowden and George Shaw. Lyn Miles and Geoffrey Place helped with the early years, and the numbers employed at the mine came from the Home Office List of Mines in the UK [from 1920, the Mines Department of the Board of Trade].

The section on Quarries and Building was written by Susan Chambers, assisted by the minutes of the Local Board of Health and the Urban District Council; trade directories; census returns; and the memories of Tom Bostock, Arnold Whiteway and others.

The Cable Works and the Laundry section was also written by Susan Chambers.

The sections on Mealors' Ploughs and Ness Gardens were written by Edward Hilditch, with help from Lois Bulley, Miss Hope, Ken Hulme and Mrs Maclean who researched Arthur Bulley's letters.

The Fine Arts Studio at Staplands was researched by Clare Johnson, with the help of Mrs Hope, Mrs Sir and Mr Halsall.

The section on Shops was written by Susan Chambers, helped by the memories of Mrs Mary Chrimes, Mrs Mannion, Mrs Elsie Rigby and others; the details of the 1849 Mostyn estate sale; directories; and census returns.

Clare Johnson wrote about Joseph Johnson, and Roy Cameron was interviewed by Clive Edwards.

CHAPTER FOUR

THE THREE Rs

Neston had had a parish school since 1610, when six Neston yeomen were granted as trustees some land on Windle Hill on which to build a school. The schoolhouse probably stood on the Chester side of the road now called Quarry Road, Hinderton, opposite the end of School Lane. This school was no longer in use by 1779, and a new initiative to found a parish school was launched in 1814. The next year the vicar, Thomas Ward, wrote

> *Within the last year we have established a school on the National Society's plan of instruction, which consists of 80 boys and 50 girls ... our room will not contain a greater number, nor does it seem necessary at present ... to enlarge it.*

The new school was housed on the site of the present town hall, but was set back from the road behind another small building. The school was therefore intended, first and foremost, to serve the town of Neston, whereas the Windle Hill school was sited centrally for the whole parish.

The "National Society" referred to by Thomas Ward had been founded in 1811, with the resounding title of The National Society for Promoting the Education of the Poor in the Principles of the Established Church. The Society still exists, although it is now more modestly known as The National Society (Church of England) for Promoting Religious Education. An offshoot of the SPCK (Society for Promoting Christian Knowledge), the National Society offered financial help and advice on forming schools, printed matter such as tracts, and originally a teaching method, the "monitorial system" of Andrew Bell. The school at Neston did not seek or receive either help or advice from the National Society at its foundation, although it was usually known as the National school. The apparently loose link was formally recognized in 1829 when the school at Neston was granted union with the National Society. In 1841 the parish established an infants' school at Little Neston, which was at once placed in union with the National Society. Although the rules of the new school hopefully referred to *"pecuniary aid"* from the Society, no money ever seems to have come from that source before 1858. Both schools were supported by voluntary contributions and collections in the parish church.

The rather scrappy accounts that survive make no mention of any school fees before 1858, so it is probable that the schools were free until that year — hence the alternative name, Neston Charity School.

This, then, was the situation in 1840. James Woodward and his wife Jane ran the Neston school. Their joint salary was £70 a year, which Mr Woodward supplemented from three sources. He was secretary of the Neston Ladies' Club; he was actuary of the Neston Savings Bank (a branch of the Liverpool Savings Bank); and he steadily embezzled the funds of that bank for over thirty years by forging the directors' initials in the passbooks. Woodward left the school in 1850, became a land surveyor and took private pupils, but continued his other activities. In 1862 it must have seemed that a useful public life was crowned with recognition when he received a testimonial gift to mark 30 years as secretary of the Ladies' Club. He had also put his son through university and seen him ordained. Two years later, however, in 1864, fate overtook him: Woodward was found guilty of false pretences, forgery and embezzlement, and was sentenced to five years' penal servitude.

A parish infants' school at Little Neston, established in 1841, seems to have been a response to the following circular letter:

> *The township of Little Neston* [and also Ness] *belongs almost exclusively to Roman Catholic proprietors ... whilst the resident population is almost entirely Protestant. The barren neglected condition of this district, as regards the means of moral and religious instruction, has long been a subject of loud complaint, and its natural consequences have been but too visibly developed in the general character and habits of the people. The united population of these townships is about 650, composed with few exceptions of the very lowest order of society, and the only school in either is kept by a Roman Catholic, the majority of whose pupils (about 20) are the children of Protestant parents.*
>
> *It is now proposed to erect a suitable building for a daily school.*

In the event, no school was built at this stage, but a house in Little Neston was leased, to be replaced by a different building in 1849. We do not know where either of them was.

There survives from 1841 a set of the rules of Neston Charity School, with amendments to suit the new infants' school. We do not know when they were printed, but they appear to date from before the union with the National "Society" in 1829. Boys were admitted between the ages of 8 and 12, girls between 7 and 12. Only one holiday a year is mentioned — a fortnight in the summer for the "gleaning season". While Saturday was a holiday, Sunday certainly was not: the pupils had to be at school at 9 a.m. and at 2 p.m., to go to church with their master or to learn the catechism.

By the late 1850s, three elements conspired to encourage some great improvements in the parish school system. First, the old building in use from 1814 was described as *"forlorn"*, and could no longer contain a growing child population. Secondly, the finances relied too heavily on subscriptions from a very few people, and quite often there was an annual loss. From 1833, Government subsidies could be channelled to schools through the National Society, and the first such grant, of only £5 5s., reached Neston in 1858. Thirdly, a vigorous new vicar who was formerly a headmaster, and a rich new landowner with a strong interest in education, together seem to have turned the tide of local opinion. Richard Gleadowe became vicar in 1853, while Christopher Bushell started to build Hinderton Hall in 1856. It was in that same year that the Bishop of Chester preached the annual schools sermon in Neston parish church, in which he called for new schools to be built. There may have been a fourth reason — competition from elsewhere —, which will be revealed presently .

Fig. 52 The architect's drawing for the Church of England school, known locally as "the Top School", in Liverpool Road, Neston. The windows were later altered to let in more light.

The Chester architect Thomas Penson was engaged to design two schools: an elementary school for 166 juniors and 100 infants (or twice the number the old school would hold) in Liverpool Road, Neston; and an infants' school for 60 at Parkgate. The Neston school, which had a house adjoining for the schoolmaster, was opened on 11 January 1859 with considerable festivities, including peals on the church bells. The school at Parkgate opened with less acclaim, so that we do not know the exact date, but it was apparently in 1860. Penson's designs looked attractive on the outside, particularly their patterned slate roofs, but the more practical details were poor. In 1886 the heating, ventilation and sanitation of the Liverpool Road

Fig. 53 A typical school photograph: children at the Liverpool Road school *c.*1883.

school had to be redesigned. At Parkgate the heat, light and ventilation were constantly criticized: in 1886, for example,

> *Four large holes in the roof, made for ventilation, produce an intolerable draught.*

The conditions were still being criticized by the inspector in 1904.

In 1870 the church infants' school in Little Neston was replaced by a newly built elementary school. The building was similar in style to the Neston and Parkgate schools, so it is probable that Thomas Penson's designs were again used or adapted. The disadvantages also seem to have been copied, for in 1910 an inspector was very critical of the ventilation and sanitation.

Children of Roman Catholic parents had been provided for since 1841, when a school was built in Burton Road. Two years later, the school building was turned into a church, the present St Winefride's, and the school classes seem to have been continued in the church until a new school was built a little further along the road, opening in January 1857. It may well have been the knowledge that the Catholic community was building a new school which spurred the Church of England into action at roughly the same time. There was also a Roman Catholic school in Ness, which continued until about 1865.

Fig. 54 The infants' school at Parkgate was built in 1860, immediately after the Liverpool Road school. The school was transferred to new premises in 1968, and the building became a private house in 1977.

There was as yet no national system of education, but the Electoral Reform Act of 1867 gave parliament a fresh incentive to provide one, because *"our new masters"* in the increased electorate needed to be educated into civic responsibility. In 1870 the Elementary Education Act required that any district not already provided with adequate school places by the religious societies should have new schools built, to be run by locally elected school boards. But Neston did not qualify, because its church schools contained ample space. The inspector who made the assessment in 1873 was very generous in his numbers, listing 357 places at Liverpool Road, about a hundred more than it was built for.

Between 1876 and 1880, school attendance became compulsory, at first to the age of 10, being raised to 11 in 1893, and to 12 in 1899, while children

Fig. 55 Little Neston elementary school was later renamed Ness Holt school. It was demolished in the 1970s, and the stone was reused for walling at Ness Gardens.

under 13 could leave school only if they had achieved a certificate of attainment. In the Neston area it had been rare for children to be employed below the age of 14, but that did not necessarily mean that they all went to school. Genuinely compulsory education required some painful adjustment. In 1892, on the occasion of an inspector's visit, it was written of the Neston schools:

On the passing of the Act, when every child was hunted up in the district, and compelled to attend school, the first few years after it was opened under the new regime it was in a most disorganised and unsatisfactory state in consequence of the turbulent character, the wild Arab like condition and dreadful ignorance of the children thus driven out of the streets, lanes and alleys, nearly all of whom had been compelled to learn what it was to be obedient, truthful and cleanly and to give way to systematic control.

For some children there was a cultural shock in store:

Boys [infants] *had their first lesson in sewing this afternoon. Several commenced crying when needles and cotton given to them. Miss Seager spoke to them about tailors, shoemakers etc. using needles and cotton and stitching which seemed to pacify them.*

And some parents also suffered from the strain!

> *Mrs Broster requests that her child may not be taught Arithmetic. Says she is adding figures aloud in her sleep all through the night.*

There were, as well, difficulties with getting children to school: lack of school fees and lack of boots. We have records of the fees paid for infants only. For them the charge was probably 1d. a week from 1858, raised to 2d. a week in 1875. The First Standard of the infants had to pay 3d. a week from 1883. *"Lack of school pence"* was occasionally recorded as a reason for absence. Elementary education was made free in 1891, and parents expected that there would be no fees when their children returned in September for the new term; but the managers would not implement the Act until November, which was then the official start of the school year. It was customary to move children out of the infants to the senior department (from Parkgate to Neston, for example) in November each year, which was actually the middle of term. The school year was not made to begin in August until 1905.

The surviving school log books before 1900 are all for infants, and they show that a lack of boots, and occasionally clothing, could keep children from school. Children were not allowed to come to school barefoot: in 1884 a boy was cautioned for doing so. Christopher Bushell gave boots or shoes to Neston children on several occasions. In 1871,

> [four girls] *presented with a frock by Mr Bushell. The mother of another girl called to know why her daughter had not got one.*

In February 1929, in bitterly cold weather, the teacher at Parkgate, Elsie Young, arranged for stockings and underclothing to be given to children who needed them.

The performance of these schools, judging by those inspectors' reports which survive, naturally varied with the abilities of changing teachers, but was often very good. In 1867, for example, the infants' school at Neston received this praise:

> *The infants are taught with great spirit and success. I do not know that I have ever seen little ones brighter or more cheerful.*

But the social conditions associated with the colliery were the cause of problems at Little Neston, where in 1914 *"very low standards of attainment"* were blamed on ill-health, *"very low mental capacity of children"* and unhelpful home backgrounds.

Before the First World War, elementary schools often produced their own teachers through the pupil teacher system. For example, Annie Bushell was a monitress, or senior pupil who assisted the teacher, at the Parkgate infants' school in 1891. When she left (Neston) school the next year she became a pupil teacher at Parkgate. She signed her indentures in 1894 and taught at Parkgate until 1896. She returned as the mistress in 1906 and ran the school until 1919. Then she became head of the Liverpool Road infants' school for the next ten years.

We have more details about the career of Catherine Norman, who came to Parkgate as a pupil teacher in 1903 at the age of 13. A year later she passed the Admission Certificate for pupil teachers, and in 1907, on passing the Preliminary Certificate Examination, she was appointed assistant mistress. Her salary had started at £5 a year, going up each year to £8, £10, £18, and £20. When she finally qualified as a teacher in 1910, at the age of 21, she was entitled to £45 a year. This was too much for Parkgate, so she went briefly to the Liverpool Road school before being appointed in 1911 as assistant teacher at Little Neston for £55 a year. She left to become Mrs Scott in 1921, and died in 1979 at the age of 90.

There were schools of other types in the Neston area. In 1815 it was stated that

> *there are many small day schools in the parish, but it is impossible to collect with any degree of accuracy the number of children that attend them, as in general they go only for a few weeks at a time, when their parents can spare money to pay for them.*

These were the so-called "dame schools", essentially one-teacher schools providing the simplest kind of schooling. If they were too small and simple to advertise, they have left little trace behind them. Although the need for them was greatly diminished by the advent of effective parish schools from 1859, some of them continued to find a niche, educational or social, just above the elementary level. An example was the school run by Elizabeth Molyneux from 1891 to 1915. Her brother ran a bakery in Park Street, and he erected a corrugated iron building, stated then to be temporary, for his sister Lizzie. The building is still with us as the "Labour Hut". At roughly the same time two sisters, the Misses McCall, ran a small school of about twenty pupils in the basement of the Presbyterian church in Parkgate Road: it was called Moorside Private School.

A school with slightly higher aspirations was the one kept in the old vicarage at the Cross (where Tesco now stands) from 1861 to *c*.1923. For its last forty years it was run by Mrs Ann Pakenham-Walsh. She taught in the kitchen; her pupils had no desks and used slates. If Mrs Pakenham-Walsh gave a piano lesson in the parlour, the other pupils would go with her and work at a long table, accompanied by the music lesson. Another teacher gave French lessons in an upstairs room.

A school which bridged the narrow gap between a church-run elementary school and a private school was Dr Riddock's school at Little Neston. Its

Fig. 56 The old vicarage in Neston ceased to be a vicarage in 1857, and was used as a school from 1861 until *c.*1923. The building was demolished in 1930, and Irwin's grocery shop (later to become Tesco) was built on the site.

building, on the Neston side of Little Neston Green, was erected in 1839, by whom is not known, but possibly as a response from the nonconformist churches to the Anglican initiative already mentioned. In 1851 it housed a day school *"of independent denomination"* (which nearly always means nonconformist), with room for 150 pupils. One of the school managers in 1851 was James Woodward, who had just retired as master from the Neston school. Whatever the status of the school had been, it was bought by Robert Macfie, the rich sugar refiner who launched Presbyterian worship on Neston and Parkgate, about 1859. He installed a Presbyterian schoolmaster, who from 1864 was Dr John Riddock. We shall hear more of Dr Riddock presently. The school was supported by Macfie personally, with £100 a year in 1873, and when he decided to retire to Scotland, the Presbyterian church session would not pay more than £20 a year. Riddock therefore broke the church connection in 1874, and ran the school privately for the next thirty years. Because he was then reliant solely on fees, he described it as a *"middle class school"* — with a higher class, that is, beyond the elementary level. But numbers were small: in 1892 he had on average 35 boys, and 25 in 1902. When Riddock retired in 1904, his school came to an end, but the building was used as a temporary council school, between 1905 and 1909, while the Burton Road school was being built. It then became a working men's club, as the Little Neston Institute, until it was demolished in 1928.

Fig. 57 Dr Riddock's school is the building next to the Green in Little Neston, at the left of the picture. Lees Lane, Rodney Row ("Sebastopol") and the Durham Ox are on the right.

It may be worth pausing here, to wonder why parents would send their children to, say, Lizzie Molyneux, when substantially the same education could be had for nothing, just round the corner in Liverpool Road. Sometimes, as here, in 1881, the reason had to do with social aspirations:

Mother thinks [the private school] *more refined than the National school.*

Often the reason had to do with size of class, for the National schools were often overcrowded. But there was a more pressing reason why parents who could afford private schools might choose them — health and cleanliness. It was not until the First World War that most Neston houses had running water and adequate sanitation. The new infant teacher at Neston in 1875 was *"surprised to find many of the children very dirty and untidy*". The schools were often closed for weeks for epidemics of diseases like diphtheria, from which some children died. In 1894 the summer holidays lasted nine weeks instead of four because of scarlet fever, while in 1906 the reason was measles. It is certain that one reason for avoiding the public elementary schools, right up to the Second World War, was the fear of infection.

A similar concern for health could make or break the private boarding schools. Parents were quick to remove their children from a school which lost its reputation for good health, and indeed, one of the stated motives for building a school chapel at Mostyn House in 1895 was to put an end to the risk of exposing its pupils to infection in Neston parish church. Boarding schools therefore isolated themselves if they could, in salubrious places like Parkgate.

There are records of boarding schools at Parkgate, often advertising the health-giving effects of sea bathing, from at least 1804. From 1810 until about 1865 there was a girls' school at Mostyn Place, in the house now called Brockleigh. For over thirty years John Salkeld ran a boys' school at the Warren, from 1831 to 1865, offering "*a classical and commercial education*", and there survives a set of letters home by one of his pupils between 1837 and 1842. Dee House, at the foot of Moorside Lane, housed a boys' school from 1822 until the 1850s. In Neston, Ashfield House in Park Street (where the telephone exchange now stands) was a school for a hundred years. It had its own water supply and eight acres of grounds. There was a succession of girls' schools there from 1813 until the 1890s, followed by a short-lived boys' school, called the Priory, until about 1910.

A later example was the girls' school opened by May Richardson in 1913 at Moorside Cottage, which stood in Moorside Lane opposite the entrance to Old Quay Lane. In 1918 she moved it to more sumptuous premises in Parkgate — a house called Leighton, which is now the Parkgate Hotel. The school lasted until 1940, when the army requisitioned the building.

These, with Mostyn House, were the long-running schools, but there were many of shorter duration, such as "Neston High School for Girls" at Church House in High Street in 1894, which failed to attract a clientele.

The boarding schools played a considerable part, equivalent to hotels, in the local economy, providing employment and bringing in money. How much they served the local population as schools is unknown, except in the case of Mostyn House, which educated the sons of such local gentry as the Rev. Richard Gleadowe and Dr Russell.

Mostyn House School opened in the old Mostyn Arms Hotel in the summer of 1855, having been established in Tarvin eighteen months earlier. The hotel's owner and landlady, Mrs Briscoe, had died, and there was no longer enough sea bathing business to keep the hotel open. The school

Fig. 58 Ashfield House was first a girls', and then a boys' school (the Priory), before the telephone exchange was built on the site.

Fig. 59 Joseph Rich built his residence, Richville, in Parkgate in 1862. Between 1918 and 1940 it housed Leighton Girls' School, and has since become the Parkgate Hotel.

Fig. 60 Mostyn House School was founded in Tarvin, but moved to the buildings of the Mostyn Arms Hotel, Parkgate, in 1855. The domed structure on the right is a covered playground which was built in 1891, and the large building between that and the original hotel was built in 1898.

contained about sixty boys, but the first headmaster, E. H. Price, was eventually to sire thirteen children of his own; and when space became cramped, he moved his family to a new school in Surrey, and left his nephew, A. S. Grenfell, in charge at Parkgate.

A. S. Grenfell's eldest son, A. G. Grenfell, was to become headmaster in 1890, while his second son, later Sir Wilfred, became internationally famous as a medical missionary in Labrador. A. G. Grenfell was a dynamic character. He found his inheritance in a bad state in 1890, with only twenty pupils in an ancient and decaying building. In five years he had brought the numbers up to a hundred, which was very large for a boarding school in those days, and he then embarked on a building programme which by 1906 had transformed the school into the most up to date of its kind. He made it a wholly preparatory school, preparing boys to go to public schools at the age of thirteen.

After A. G. Grenfell died in 1934, the school continued under his son and grandson. In 1986, responding to changing parental expectations, it became entirely a day school, and extended its age range.

Fig. 61 A. G. Grenfell was the headmaster of Mostyn House School from 1890 to 1933. Under his long tenure of office, it became one of the most up-to-date and respected preparatory schools in the region.

The new century which dawned in 1900 brought with it something of a new spirit to schools, as the growing pains of compulsory education began to subside, although the leaving age was raised again, to 14, in 1918. In 1909, medical inspections, often by the medical officer of health, were first reported; and in 1911, for instance, the county nurse excluded five children from the Little Neston school for ringworm and facial sores. An oculist visited the Liverpool Road school in 1909, and from 1929 a dentist attended the Burton Road school to which patients from other schools were sent.

In 1900, as we have seen, all free schooling was tightly under the control of the churches. When a growing population made a new school necessary, it was decided to build a council school in Burton Road. Council schools did not provide a wholly secular education, but their religious teaching had to be non-denominational. Whether for reasons of bigotry or not, there were some murmurs locally when the council sent leaflets advertising the new school to all parents of school-age children in Neston and Parkgate:

> *There have been reports that parents have been warned against sending their children to the new Council school in Burton Road: stories that the children will be moved down a grade, or that attendance there will not count towards exemption certificates.*

These misgivings were quite unfounded, and the new school quickly settled down among the others, particularly when cookery, laundry and handicraft rooms were built and made available to children from other schools in the area.

The council school was actually established in 1905, when it occupied the buildings formerly used by Dr Riddock's school. Its first headmaster, for 22 years, was R. W. Jones, who caused some embarrassment by quarrelling with his staff in the early years, and with the governors in his later years, and for being too heavy-handed with the cane. The new premises in Burton Road were first used in 1909.

Before leaving the elementary schools, we shall look briefly at the other parts of the old Neston parish.

In Willaston, the first village school was built on the village green in 1859, largely at the expense of Duncan Graham, who lived at the Lydiate. In 1882 Graham transferred the school to the vicar and churchwardens. The deed stated that the school should be used for the education of "*children of the labouring, manufacturing and other poorer classes in the parish of Willaston*". It was run according to the rules of the National Society. Plans for improvements were delayed by the First World War, and in the 1920s an inspector was horrified to see some cows wandering across the unfenced playground, which was the remainder of the village green. The trustees, in rejecting his fears that the children were in danger, considered that in an agricultural village they were well used to cattle.

In 1928, when there was a suggestion that a council school would be built in Willaston, the parishioners decided to build a new church school by public subscription. It opened in 1930.

Fig. 62 The first village school at Willaston. The half-timbered Red Lion public house may be seen in the background.

Joseph Hirst, who paid for a church in Thornton Hough, built two schools. One opened in Thornton Hough in 1868, and the other, for infants, in Raby in 1877. The infants from Raby moved up to the Thornton Hough school when they were old enough. That school's log book for 1888 suggested that the school at Raby should be closed, and probably in the 1890s it was. Hirst's school was attached to All Saints Anglican church, and in 1905 William Lever, the new landowner and a friend to nonconformism, helped to establish a non-denominational school in Thornton Hough, the Lever council school. Lever's school closed in 1939, and Hirst's school was superseded in 1953.

A former pupil of the Roman Catholic elementary school at St Winefride's recalled the grimmer side of school life in the late 1920s under the formidable Miss McNeil:

> *9 to 9.30 a.m: Religion. We knelt on the wooden seat of our desks for the half hour and if we moved, then we were punished. Two or three strokes of the cane, or we were sent into the porch and made to kneel on the concrete floor; or if it was winter, we stood about a foot from the fire until the sweat was running down our backs and then sent into the porch.*

St Winefride's became a very decrepit and worn-out school building long before it was replaced by a new Catholic primary school in Mellock Lane by stages, in 1967 and 1974.

There was no provision in the Neston area for secondary education before the Second World War, and it was only the occasional pupil from the elementary schools who was recorded as winning a place at a grammar school. The first named in the log books for Little Neston were a boy for Calday Grange in 1924, and a girl for West Kirby in 1928. Other pupils might have to go as far as Birkenhead or the Liverpool Institute. The county bought a field in Mellock Lane in 1931, with the intention of building a secondary school on it, but it was later reserved for allotments. The managers of the Burton Road school offered to discuss the provision of secondary education with the managers of Liverpool Road, but the latter refused. It was not until 1959, when a county secondary modern school opened in Raby Park Road, that the Neston schools ceased to be elementary. Liverpool Road became an infants' school until it was closed in 1992; a new Parkgate primary school opened in 1968, and the old school was sold, later to be converted to a dwelling; Burton Road became a primary school; Little Neston became an infants' school in 1959 (then being called Ness Holt school), and closed in 1969 when its pupils moved to the school in Woodfall Lane which had opened two years earlier.

If secondary education was not catered for locally, adult education certainly was. The Liverpool Road school was built with adults in mind:

> *The schools are so arranged as to form one large room, which is found most convenient for public meetings and lectures, the latter being given every alternate week during the winter season.*

The first lecture, in March 1859, was on "Nineveh".

Even before this, in 1856, a series of lectures on chemistry had been given in Parkgate's Assembly Room. From then on, a variety of societies were founded with more or less educational aims: the Floral and Horticultural Society in 1867, the Musical Society in 1877, the Neston Vocal Society in 1878. But a cultural diet did not suit the temperament of all Neston's inhabitants. In 1881 a lantern-slide lecture was broken up by a mob of "*dirty urchins*" who forced their way in. Sometimes we read of determined efforts at paternalism: from 1882, a wealthy resident of Parkgate called Reginald Haigh arranged concerts for the local fishermen, while in 1895 a series of three instructive lectures for the same audience was arranged.

Perhaps the most important of these movements was the Literary and Debating Society, which Dr Riddock founded in 1881, because from this society there grew the Neston Library. There had been a small circulating library in Parkgate, established for the sea-bathing visitors, throughout the nineteenth century. When the Liverpool Road school was built, Christopher Bushell's two sons set up a small library in it and taught people to read, although this initiative soon seems to have lapsed. The suggestion was made, when the town hall was being discussed in 1887, that it should contain a public reading room. But the vicar, Gleadowe, said that the level of literacy in Neston did not justify a reading room, judging by his experience in the National school. When the Literary Society started its own library, first at Riddock's school, and from 1890 in the town hall, Gleadowe encouraged it by passing to it £30 he had been given for "*the local benefit*".

After Queen Victoria died in 1901, it was proposed that Neston's memorial to her should be a public library. To this end Neston Council invoked the Public Libraries Act and took over the library in the town hall. Riddock, as its librarian, wrote to Andrew Carnegie for funds: Carnegie, a Scottish-American steelmaker, had promised to provide a library to any town which would support one. He offered £1,200 if a site were donated, and if the council would levy a penny rate in support. A field was given by the Russell family who lived opposite, in Vine House; and their son, Frank, whose firm acted as consulting architects for Neston Council, designed the building. It was opened in January 1908, six months before Riddock

Fig. 63 The field on which Neston library was to be built. The footpath on the left was known as "the Doctor's Stiles".

died. Until 1934 the library was open for very short hours: one hour on two days a week, and half an hour on a third. It was not until Daisy Taylor became the first paid librarian that the library was open full time and the books were placed on open access.

In 1892 the council had invoked the Technical Instruction Acts, though what this led to in practice is uncertain. When the Burton Road school opened in 1909, it included the workshops already mentioned, which were used for adult evening classes. The handicraft teacher from 1910, James Hacking, was the chairman of Neston Urban District Council in the 1930s.

As a tailpiece to this educational chapter, here is a schoolboy's letter of 1840, written in impeccable copperplate by Robert Topham, aged thirteen. He was a pupil at John Salkeld's school at the Warren in Parkgate.

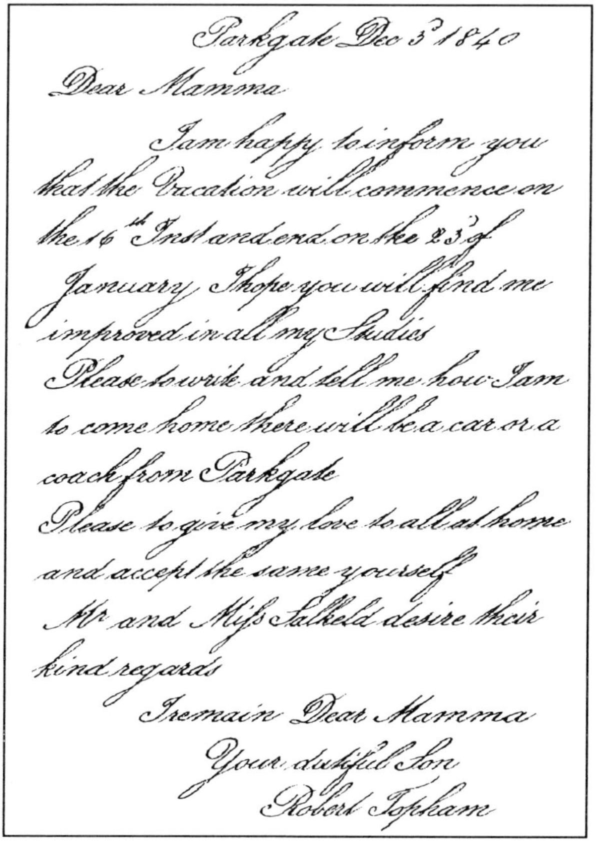

Parkgate Dec 3d 1840

Dear Mamma

I am happy to inform you that the Vacation will commence on the 16th Inst and end on the 23d of January. I hope you will find me improved in all my Studies

Please to write and tell me how I am to come home there will be a car or a coach from Parkgate

Please to give my love to all at home and accept the same yourself

Mr and Miss Salkeld desire their kind regards

I remain Dear Mamma

Your dutiful Son

Robert Topham

Fig. 64 Robert Topham's neatly penned letter.

SOURCES

This chapter was written by Geoffrey Place.

Documents in the Cheshire Record Office have supplied information on the 1610 foundation of the Windle Hill school (DDX 178/27); the 1814 foundation (EDA 6/9/36); the accounts of the Liverpool Road school (P149/3035); and the letter concerning education in Little Neston *c.*1840 (P149/12/1).

Documents from its archives were kindly provided by the National Society.

The trial of James Woodward was reported in the *Birkenhead Advertiser*, 16 January and 9 March 1864.

Details of Dr Riddock's school were supplied from the Congregations Committee Minute Book kept at the United Reformed Church, Neston.

We are grateful to Fr G. Courell and Tony Morton for permission to quote from Mr Morton's diary in *St Winefride's, Neston, 150 Years* (1993).

Teaching contracts belonging to Catherine Norman were supplied by David Scott.

Information about some of the private schools is derived from the memories of Alfred, Tom and Ann Johnson.

We have studied the following school log books: Liverpool Road infants', 1864–1902, and mixed school, 1910–31; Burton Road managers' minute book (Cheshire Record Office SL288/1/1); Little Neston infants', 1900–34, and main school, 1907–41; Parkgate, 1885–1933.

CHAPTER FIVE

CHURCH AND CHAPEL

The only truly thorough enquiry into the religious habits of the British people was made at the time of the ten-year census in 1851. Unlike the compulsory census of households, the ecclesiastical census was voluntary. Those in charge of religious buildings were requested, but not obliged, to state the date of the building, the number of seats which were free or rented, the attendance at each service on 30 March 1851, or if preferred, the average attendance over the past year.

The census was taken against a background of concern that religious belief and worship were breaking down in the large towns, and that the position of the Established Church was under threat. The results were difficult to interpret nationally, because attendances were recorded, not the number of individual members. It is clear, though, that regional differences were considerable, and that religious attendance was higher in the south of England than the north. As one might suppose, the Church of England had a greater hold where the social pressures from a strong middle class were to be found.

Horace Mann, the official census statistician, devised a formula to deduce the number of worshippers from the attendances given. He counted all the morning congregation, plus half the afternoon and a third of the evening congregations. By this formula, the returns from Wirral Registration District (Birkenhead, Neston and the Wirral villages) yielded 41% of worshipping Anglicans, 16% Protestant dissenters, 11% Roman Catholics and 32% non-worshippers. These figures for worshippers are relatively high for the country as a whole and indicate, if nothing else, that the people of Wirral as a whole took religious matters seriously.

For Neston itself it is not possible to give the figures for religious attendance, because the vicar of Neston parish church, the Rev. Robert Yarker, declined to give any attendance figures, either for the Census Sunday or for the annual average. We are therefore spared, as he no doubt intended, the somewhat risky numbers game of comparing the strengths of denominations. He was not alone in doubting the efficacy of giving numbers, for William Daniell, Congregational minister at Parkgate, wrote *"the state of the weather affects this place"*.

Yet Neston, like most of Victorian England, offered the Christian worshipper a choice. This had not been so in the previous century, when the parish church had little competition from a handful of Roman Catholics, who were carefully listed from time to time by the watchdogs of the Establishment, and from a few Methodists in the later years. The old Dissenting sects, like Baptists and Congregationalists, seem to have taken no root in Neston before the nineteenth century.

There was a much greater variety available in 1851. The choice lay between the parish church of St Mary and St Helen which had 875 seats; the Wesleyan Methodist chapel in Parkgate Road with 150 seats; the Congregationalist chapel in Parkgate with 300 seats; the Roman Catholic church of St Winefride with 160 seats; an Independent chapel in Little Neston with 150 seats; and a Primitive Methodist congregation which met in a dwelling house in Little Neston with room for 50. In addition Willaston had a Primitive Methodist chapel with 120 seats and Ledsham had a Methodist Great Connexion chapel of unrecorded capacity.

Before we look at the diversity of religious observance available to the worshipper, it is worth noting that Neston may not always have proved very fertile ground for any denomination. A Yorkshire evangelist called Squire Brook

> *was so discouraged at Neston that he said on the last night of his visit there that some day the devil would run away with it!*

Several congregations were supported by wealthy patrons, only to fail financially when their benefactors left them. Thus the Congregationalists of Parkgate could not maintain a chapel which was built by a visiting Yorkshireman and relied too heavily on the seabathing visitors in the summer. Their successors the Presbyterians, who were installed by the munificence of the temporarily resident Scot, Robert Macfie, were severely troubled when Macfie returned to Scotland. The non-denominational mission hall built by Captain Ward was bought by its congregation when Ward died, but they could not find the money and were taken over by Methodists from Rock Ferry.

Occasionally those who were not in church at all found the means to express their indifference to religion. In 1864 the members of the Neston Rifle Volunteers' band, piqued that they had not been considered good enough to play for the annual Ladies' Day parade, interrupted the service by playing loudly outside the east window of the parish church.

The most striking occasion when Neston cocked a snook, certainly at the vicar if not at religion in general, was in the same year, 1864, when John Ashbrook was acquitted of a charge of manslaughter. Ashbrook was a Neston farmer whose horse ran away with him in Liverpool Road. Ashbrook was thrown out of the trap and the horse knocked down an old woman, Margaret Brien, who died. An inquest returned a verdict of accidental death. The case was reopened, however, at the petition of Ebenezer Baker, a scripture reader attached to the parish church, who claimed that Ashbrook had been drunk. It is clear from the newspaper accounts that Ashbrook did not attend church; indeed he may have been a thorn in the clerical flesh for many years, for the churchwardens' accounts for 1837 contain the laconic entry, *"John Ashbrook broke the church rails"*. Be that as it may, Ashbrook was tried at Chester Assizes for manslaughter and acquitted. When he returned to Neston he was welcomed with noisy enthusiasm, and the Volunteers' band played "See the Conquering Hero Comes". Ashbrook's friends the bellringers persuaded the sexton to unlock the church door and they rang a merry peal on the bells. That brought out the vicar who, furious, dismissed all the bellringers, as well as the sexton.

There was fierce competition between the religious denominations, and the rivalry led at times to intolerance and rudeness. William Daniell, whose chapel at Parkgate was falling on hard times, reported in 1850 that

> *Church* [i.e. Anglican] *wealth and church zeal are very influential in many a rural district, and their influence is not unfelt at Parkgate. The children are bribed from their school and their parents urged to discontinue their attendance at the chapel. Popery, moreover, is of considerable strength and has great influence in the neighbourhood.*

A rather nasty little row was reported in the newspapers in 1860 under the headline, *"Shameful Proceedings at Parkgate"*. It seems that the Presbyterian minister, Macdonald Halket, was visiting a sick woman when one of the Church of England curates, Thomas Dean, called at the house and ordered Mr Halket out of the room. *"This is only one of many disgraceful proceedings which occur in this neglected place."* A war of words was waged in the newspaper for a full month. The original correspondent denied any knowledge of the incident; Dean's fellow curate, Arthur Watson, had told another woman not to pray with Mr Halket; Halket had written to the vicar to complain but did not think that he, Mr Gleadowe, sympathized with Dean's attitude.

In 1882 there was religious ferment among the coalminers, many of whom were Primitive Methodists, when a Society of Free Gospellers was formed. There were complaints that miners were being pressurized at work to attend the Free Gospellers' meetings. It has to be said, though, that it was usually the Church of England which was indicted for intolerance. Colonel J. C. Lloyd, *"a man of evangelical zeal"*, and originally a member of the Church of England, was forbidden to teach in the Anglican Sunday School because he also joined Methodists at prayer. He led a New Year service, mainly for nonconformists, at Neston Cross every year for fifty years before he died in 1912.

The most notorious case of intolerance was in 1882, and was publicized by Sir Wilfred Grenfell in his autobiography, *A Labrador Doctor*:

> *An incident which happened on the death of one of the boys at my father's school interested me temporarily in religion. The boy's father happened to be a dissenter, and the vicar refused to allow the gates of the parish churchyard to be opened to enable the funeral cortège to enter. My chum had only a legal right to be buried in the yard. The coffin had therefore to be lifted over the wall and as the church was locked, father conducted the service in the open air. His words at the graveside gave a touch of reality to religion, and still more so did his walking down the aisle of the church the following Sunday when the vicar referred to the destructive influence of anything that lent colour to dissent.*

The boy who died was William Henry Ward, the twelve-year-old son of H. J. Ward, a prominent Neston citizen, keen evangelist and the provider of the mission hall at the junction of Liverpool Road and Park Street that later became a Methodist chapel. The boy attended Mostyn House School, and his headmaster, Wilfred's father, was A. S. Grenfell, an Anglican clergyman and a man who for twenty years had served the local community – as a member of the Local Board, to give one example. The boy had died of *"rheumatism of the brain"*, and was buried on Saturday 27 May. The sermon the following day was preached, not by the vicar (who was away) but by his curate, the Rev. A. Ogle. Ogle was about to leave the parish and his parting shot was the sermon in which he roundly condemned the amount of dissent in Neston, and anyone who lent them support. An angry correspondent to the *Chester Chronicle* wrote:

> *Only on the previous day a Nonconformist burial had taken place in the churchyard. One member* [of the congregation] *at least had the manliness to testify his disapproval of such ignorant bigotry by marching out of the church.*

For an ordained priest of the Church of England to walk out of a service in his parish church must have caused a tremendous upheaval. It seems likely that A. S. Grenfell never recovered from the stress of the incident. Within a few months he had given up his post as headmaster, left the district and become chaplain at the London Hospital. There he suffered a severe nervous illness from which he never emerged. Mr Ogle had a lot to answer for.

The remark by William Daniell that *"the children are bribed from their school"* foretold the battle of the Sunday School treats which was evident from the 1870s. In 1878, for example, the attendance at the Liverpool Road infants' school was depleted in June for the mission hall treat, and twice in September for an outing at Ashfield Hall, Robert Macfie's house, followed by the vicar's fête. In most years the adept infant could attend both the Presbyterian and the Anglican treats. The Salvation Army sometimes offered a treat, and during and after the First World War, Sir William Lever's Sunday School treat was likely to be followed by the church fête.

Fig. 65 A typical start to a Sunday School treat — children setting off from the Presbyterian church in Parkgate Road, June 1909.

The vicar, however, Richard Gleadowe, did not rely solely on treats to encourage his flock, for he had his own, more direct, methods. For Mrs Oxton recalled,

> *If we didn't go to Sunday School, he used to run after us with his knob stick. We were frightened to stop away.*

But Mrs Oxton was only five years old when Gleadowe died, and so this story was probably hearsay, or even a legendary tale.

One shining example in the nineteenth century of tolerance in religious matters was Robert Macfie. Although an ardent Presbyterian he

> *was most munificent and catholic-minded. He repeatedly entertained the people of the district to tea on the lawn of the* [Ashfield] *Hall without respect to religious conviction or political creed, there being present Roman Catholics and members of the Church of England, as well as members of his own community.*

When Macfie thought that the elders of the Neston Presbyterian church were in danger of bigotry in trying to prevent Methodists from establishing themselves once more in Neston, he said that he would not be a party to such a thing.

The Reverend Richard Gleadowe, vicar of Neston for forty years, was the outstanding figure on the ecclesiastical scene. His long tenure was overtaken by the Rev. John Towert, Presbyterian minister for 48 years, but Gleadowe held office during striking changes in both church and community. He was born in 1811, the son of a Shropshire vicar, and after ordination became a curate at Pickford, where he eked out his stipend by teaching at Stainford Grammar School. In due course he became headmaster of the Cathedral Grammar School, Chester (King's School), which in those days could scarcely claim to be a grammar school and was not held in high esteem in Chester. Gleadowe perceived that the school would not flourish unless it was separated from the cathedral choir, and this separation he achieved before he was appointed vicar of the parish of Neston in 1853.

During his tenure at Neston, Gleadowe presided over the great changes from administration through the parish vestry to elected government; the break-up of the ancient parish and the provision of churches for the outlying villages; the provision of schools and the development of education; and the rebuilding of the parish church. He pursued these goals with the paternal authority of the headmaster he had recently been, and no doubt some of the resistance he encountered was provoked by his masterful manner. Yet he seems to have been greatly respected and to have held aloof from some of the local controversies which might otherwise have engulfed him. But he was ready to speak his mind, whatever people might think. He was not at all popular for opposing the annual Neston Races, which he regarded as a festival of wickedness; and he was very critical of some aspects of Ladies' Day, which he feared might also become one.

Before Gleadowe's arrival, it must be said, the church scene was a lot more peaceful. Unwin Clarke, who was vicar from 1828 to 1847, was also vicar of Eastham, where he lived, and Neston was looked after by a curate. Wright Willett was the curate from 1838 to 1846, and he may have been something of a new broom, for in October 1838 it was recorded that 330 boys and girls were confirmed in Neston church. Perhaps he had rounded up ten years' worth of strays.

The chief event for the Church of England in this period was the complete renewal of the inside of the church, which was *"thoroughly repaired"*. The old pews were taken out and far more seating was provided. The commissioners were to provide *"from eighty to ninety sittings for the free use of the poor"*. The only clue to this considerable change is a payment in the churchwardens' accounts *"for beef mutton & cetra at the finishing of the alterations in Church"*.

For six years from 1847, Neston regained a resident vicar in Robert Yarker. He was a generous man who bought a cloth for the communion table and two chairs to flank it, lent £50 when a new heating apparatus was ordered, and gave £700 for a new church and school at Willaston.

The degree to which the vicar and his parish officers were both required and expected to take the lead in civil affairs was to alter greatly during Gleadowe's tenure. Part of the resentment felt towards the Church of England, whether by nonconformists or by those with no willing religious affiliation, must certainly have represented opposition to civil rather than purely religious authority. Equally, the paternalism, even arrogance, shown by the Anglican clergy at times must have reflected a feeling that the status of the Established Church represented duties which demanded respect from people.

As Chapter Six, which deals with local government, tells in greater detail, the parish vestry had civil duties which increased greatly after 1849. The church ley, originally a rate used mainly for the upkeep of the church itself, became a general rate used for both ecclesiastical and civil purpose until 1861, when a separate church rate became voluntary. The vestry meeting proposed in 1866 that a Local Board of Health should be formed with the power to raise considerably more money. But when the ratepayers of Neston realized just how much money they would have to find to finance the new waterworks, the reaction was bitter. In February 1869 placards were posted throughout Neston which read

> *When the Rev. Dick Gleadowe is missing he will be found at the bottom of the quarry with the Local Board and Government inspector at his neck and the short-sighted draper close up.*

A short time afterwards, Gleadowe resigned from the Board.

Another bone of contention was the payment of tithes. Until the 1840s this ancient form of rent was still payable in kind, in theory one-tenth of all produce. Before the Reformation this rent had been paid to the Abbey of St Werburgh in Chester as rectors of the parish of Neston, and the Abbey used part of this income to support a vicar. By the nineteenth century the kinds of payment were so confused that the Tithe Commutation Act of 1836 appointed commissioners to turn all these payments into a money rent payable on land.

The tithe commissioners for the parish of Neston called a meeting at the Mostyn Arms Hotel in Parkgate in May 1843 to decide what the rent-charges would be. They learned that for the township of Great Neston, the major landlord (Edward Lloyd Mostyn) was entitled to the tithe of corn and grain, while the vicar received all the other tithes, including certain customary payments: 1½d. for each cow in lieu of the tithe of milk, 4d. for each colt, 3d. for each homestead in lieu of the tithes of eggs and garden produce. In Willaston the vicar of Neston could claim the tithes of hay, hemp, flax, pigs and geese, with customary payments for milking cows, barren cows, cocks and hens, and hives of bees; Sir William Stanley claimed everything else.

It took the commission five years to report, which they did at several local meetings in 1848. Every piece of land was given a permanent annual rent, and 44% was paid to the vicar of Neston, amounting to £728 a year. The rest went to various landowners who had at some time bought the rights to it. The absurdity of a rent which supported the Church of England but was payable by all, whether they belonged to that Church or not, continued until 1936, when the Tithe Act finally abolished rent-charges.

As the need for the vicar to be involved in civil affairs dwindled, so did his proper concern for moral matters become more prominent. Alas, in Neston a firm stand on moral issues was only too likely to be seen as an infringement of civil rights. Good examples were the vicar's attitude to Ladies' Day and to Neston Races. The problem with Ladies' Day was that it ended with dancing on the Green behind the Golden Lion. In 1879 a correspondent to the *Chester Chronicle* complained that servant girls were encouraged to stay out all night; but in 1887 another correspondent, noting that Neston's *"annual wave of dissipation"* ended with dancing on the Green, said disapprovingly that *"there are those who would fain deprive the young people of this"*. Richard Gleadowe was remembered as one of these killjoys.

If Ladies' Day could end indecorously, Neston Races were dissipated throughout. Every year pickpockets and gamblers were arrested. The gamblers were not bookmakers, but men with the three-card trick or with games at which the customer could not win. In 1885 Gleadowe preached a sermon which criticized the morality of a race meeting where 50 or 60 policemen had to be brought in. But in 1879 his contempt for the races had caused him considerable embarrassment. He had announced that the annual vestry meeting would be held at 2.30 p.m. on Easter Monday, the day of the Races; and he was asked to change the time to 11 a.m., *"to meet the wishes of some of the parishioners who desired to attend the steeple-chase-races at Neston on that day"*. But Gleadowe would not agree, whereupon a letter of protest was delivered which claimed that his meeting was illegal. Although he had given a week's notice, he had not given three days' notice from a Sunday as the law required, so that he was forced to climb down and appoint a later date. One of the signatories to the letter of protest was Thomas Parry, the people's churchwarden.

Although Gleadowe was a stern and headmasterly figure, some of his young curates entered into local affairs with the enthusiasm of "muscular Christianity". As a means of encouraging manly sport and keeping young men out of the pubs, the Rev. K. Kempston formed a cricket club in 1884. The Rev. William Barrett founded a quoits club and was active in the local bowling and football clubs.

While Gleadowe's stern manner was remembered with awe, he was also remembered with great respect. During the cholera epidemic of 1866 he was said to have gone boldly into infected houses showing no fear for his own safety.

After the parish church was rebuilt in 1875, and new bells were provided in 1884, there was less for Gleadowe to sink his formidable teeth into. And he was growing old. For the last years of his tenure he was inactive, sometimes ill, and increasingly reliant on his curates. Yet even at the end he caused some controversy by failing to hand over his living when it was thought he should have done. In 1890 when he was 78 years old, he handed control of the parish to his senior curate, William Barrett. Barrett had been ordained in 1885, while headmaster of Mostyn House School, with the intention of ministering to the needs of Parkgate. He left the school at the end of 1889 to look after the whole parish, where he was already greatly respected as a man who *"keenly interested himself in every movement which was calculated to benefit the neighbourhood"*. In November 1892 he died of pneumonia, but was generally thought to have exhausted himself by overwork. While Barrett was ill, Gleadowe sent Mrs Barrett a letter to say that he intended to resign as vicar at Christmas, and that he would put her husband's name forward as a worthy successor.

The chief problems for the Church of England during Gleadowe's tenure concerned finance. It was a striking feature of the eighteenth-century parish that, because most people were required to pay for the maintenance of the church, whether through tithes, pew-rents or the church ley, nothing seems to have been done voluntarily. Bellringers, and later on the organist and singers, were paid for their services. The idea of voluntary work for the church came in the nineteenth century, with increased prosperity, increased leisure and less certain church income.

The church ley was an annual rate levied on the whole parish, whether Anglicans or not, which was used to maintain the fabric of the church and any running costs other than the vicar's stipend. A few purely civil expenses were paid from the church ley: a payment for the destruction of sparrows was paid until 1848. As we shall see, the parish vestry (in effect the church council) became heavily involved in civil affairs between 1847 and 1866, with the result that some people began refusing to pay the church rate, apparently from 1859. Why it was meekly paid until this date remains a mystery. In 1861 it was decided to levy a voluntary church rate, separate from the general rate, but this did not bring in enough money.

After a reorganization of pews in 1842, rents were charged for the pews which were permanently reserved, but this was ended in 1855 after the induction of Richard Gleadowe. It was resolved that

> *no pew or sitting be let either in the body or any other part of the church ... the said practice being illegal will not in future be permitted.*

However, pew-rents were resumed on a supposedly voluntary basis until 1871, when a collection began to be made at services.

One part of the parish church continued to serve the entire community, regardless of denomination, and that was the graveyard. Although burial fees were charged, a sexton had to be paid and a hearse maintained. A new hearse complete with plumes was bought in 1835. A few burials took place in the Congregational chapel graveyard at Parkgate between 1847 and 1882, and a Catholic cemetery was in use at St Winefride's from 1851, but everyone else used the parish graveyard. In 1868 the parish spent £642 on an extension of the burial ground to the north, including a railed footpath to discourage people from walking straight across the graves. In 1899 it was thought that there was almost no further room for graves, and Neston Council provided a cemetery in Raby Road, which was opened in 1906, with the burial plots for different denominations rigidly segregated, even in death.

Neston's church tower contained a ring of six bells, cast in 1731, one of them being recast in 1804. The team of bellringers were paid to ring before Sunday services and on other special occasions, such as the Queen's birthday, or the opening of Neston school in 1859. In 1860, when money was tight, it was decided to stop paying the bellringers, but they were being paid again in 1863. The sacking of the bellringers in 1864 for celebrating John Ashbrook's acquittal has been mentioned; in 1855 also, the entire team of ringers was dismissed for a reason not recorded. A set of four new bells was cast in 1884, replacing two of the earlier set, to make a ring of eight bells altogether.

One function of the belfry was to give notice of a death, as far as possible at the moment of death. Three tones of the passing bell, followed by a pause before the next three tones, and rung for a few minutes, would tell the listeners that a child had died. Two tones were rung for a woman and one for a man. At some stage, probably just before the First World War, it was decided that to ring the passing bell while someone was dying, so that they might well hear their own obsequies, was too morbid, and after that the bell was only rung when death had finally occurred. Until the Second World War there was also a curfew bell, rung at 8 p.m. In 1939 all church bells were silenced, for they were to be rung only if the Germans invaded.

Fig. 66 The old parish church of St Mary and St Helen, before it was replaced in 1875.

Fig. 67 J. F. Doyle's design for the new parish church. The tower was the only part of the old structure to survive, though with alterations: the height was increased, for example, and the top was given battlements.

It was feared that paratroops might be dropped on the Dee estuary, and the church tower was provided with a wooden hut from which the Home Guard kept watch.

An organ was first installed in the church in 1809, and this instrument was replaced in 1842, to be replaced in its turn in 1909. When the decision was taken in 1882 to provide robes for the choir, at least one reason was the hope that wearing surplices might make the choirboys behave better. The effect, if successful, may have worn off in time, for in 1914 Mrs Ariel Gray gave £50 to be invested for a prize to the two best-behaved choirboys, chosen annually by the boys themselves.

The church building itself had been greatly altered over the centuries, and could not be called an attractive piece of architecture. Inside, four galleries had been built between 1725 and 1816 to provide extra seating. To ensure a good view of the pulpit at least two pillars had been removed. As a result the church needed massive repairs by 1874. The architect, Francis Doyle of Liverpool, hoped to preserve a large part of the old building, but he found that burial vaults had undermined part of it, and that the south wall had never been given a proper foundation. Therefore the whole church had to be rebuilt, apart from the tower, and even that was raised by three feet and given battlements. The new church was opened on 5 November 1875.

When Gleadowe became vicar he wanted a more modern house than the ancient vicarage which stood at the Cross. With its cowhouse, piggery, poultry-house and two walled gardens, it was an echo from the age when the vicar supplemented his income from the land. It was sold in 1857, and Gleadowe had a new vicarage built in 1859, just off the town end of Wood Lane, a house now known as Woodlands. But this house was too big for Gleadowe's successor, E. C. Turner, and for him a newly-built house in Parkgate Road was bought in 1903. This house remained Neston's vicarage until 1985.

The affairs of the parish became considerably simpler as new provision was made for the outlying villages. The first was Willaston. Robert Yarker had given £700 for a new church, and Gleadowe, his successor, proceeded to get it built. It was opened in 1855 but remained a chapel-of-ease for ten years until a new parish was created for it. The next new church, built at Capenhurst by the local squire, the Rev. Richard Richardson, served Ledsham, the furthest outpost of the ancient parish, so far away that its people had often preferred to go to Burton or Shotwick churches. Capenhurst church was assigned a district, making it into a parish, as soon as it opened in 1859. The third new church was built at Thornton Hough by the local landowner, Joseph Hirst. He was a Yorkshireman, and he imported Yorkshire craftsmen to build it. His church opened in 1867, and a new parish was created for it, including Raby, two years later.

Of the original eight townships in the parish, the inland four (Raby, Thornton Hough, Willaston, Ledsham) had been hived off by 1870. To help serve the remaining four (Leighton, Great Neston, Little Neston, Ness), two chapels-of-ease, or daughter churches, were provided under the vicarship of C. Brooke Gwynne, who succeeded Edmund Turner in 1909. In Little Neston, St Michael's mission church was built in 1913; and in Parkgate the disused nonconformist chapel, which had been rented by the Church of England since 1910, was finally bought in 1917 and dedicated to St Thomas.

The upheavals in the Victorian Church of England when the High Church followers of the Oxford Movement tried to impose strange and apparently "Romish" ways on their conservative Low Church congregations, scarcely touched Neston. When the choirboys were first put into surplices in 1882 for reasons that may have been more practical than liturgical, the vicar was at pains to assure everyone that surplices were not a sign of ritualism. In 1893 his successor, Turner, made the choir turn to the east during the creed; some refused and were replaced.

Another change made by Turner may offer one explanation why some people had preferred the nonconformist chapels to the parish church. Until 1893, only the coffins of gentlefolk were carried to the chancel steps for the funeral service; the coffins of lesser folk had to stand at the door. Turner decreed that every coffin must travel the full distance of the nave.

The parish vestry, a committee which controlled the church's expenditure, and had once had a considerable say in the running of the community, lost most of its powers in 1910, when Brooke Gwynne formed a finance committee; and just as he retired in 1920 the new system of a Parochial Church Council was begun.

Roman Catholic observance in Wirral was, until the early nineteenth century, centred on the seats of the Stanley family at Hooton and Puddington. One of the wings of Puddington Hall contained a chapel, with its own resident priest, who served the whole of west Wirral until the 1840s. It was in 1841 that the chaplain at Puddington, Richard Gillow, built a school at Little Neston. The building was paid for by a bequest from a former chaplain, Father Ralph Platt, who died in 1837, and a contribution from the Catholic Earl of Shrewsbury, who gave the land. Augustus Pugin, an architect who believed strongly that Gothic architecture and Christianity were closely intertwined, designed the building, but the money available made it a *"very humble"* one.

The original school failed, and Father Gillow sent the Rev. James Kershaw, whom he had prepared for ordination at Puddington, to convert the school building into a chapel. A formal lease was taken on the land, which was eventually bought by the diocese of Shrewsbury in 1897.

The new chapel was opened for worship in November 1843, on the feast of its patron saint, St Winefride. The shrine of this saint at Holywell, just across the estuary, had long been a place of pilgrimage, the only one in Britain to receive pilgrims continually throughout the long years of religious upheaval.

Fig. 68 St Winefride's church, Little Neston, as drawn in 1979.

Father Kershaw was in poor health when he was inducted, and he died in 1845. His successor, James Pemberton, was to remain as parish priest for over thirty years. He laid out a burial ground in 1851 so that for the first time the local Catholics could be buried in their own ground, rather than in the public graveyards at Neston or Burton. A year later he enlarged the chapel, lengthening it by twenty feet and adding a gallery. The Neston Catholic parish was extensive, including Burton and Puddington and, until 1928, Heswall as well. In 1856 Pemberton was able to revive the project for a school: a gift of £500 enabled him to build a new one next to the church.

Pope Pius IX announced in 1850 that his eight apostolic vicars in England, who performed the duties of bishops, were to be replaced by an archbishop and twelve bishops, with a regular diocesan hierarchy. So in 1851 the diocese of Shrewsbury, which included Neston, was formed. The change, described by the cautious English Catholics as administrative only, was hailed less diplomatically on the Continent as part of a crusade to convert England to the Catholic faith. There was a brief public outcry at this so-called Papal Aggression, represented locally by lectures in protest at Chester, but such intellectual controversies do not seem to have disturbed Neston at all.

An unusual visitor to the church during the last twenty years of the nineteenth century, and who is buried in St Winefride's churchyard, was Teresa Higginson. She was a mystic whose profound contemplation of the sufferings of Jesus on the Cross, allegedly since she was four years old, caused her to show the signs in her own body of the stigmata, the five wounds of Christ, in 1874 while she was teaching in Wigan. It was during the 1870s that her two sisters came to live in Neston: Louisa as mistress of the Catholic school, and Frances as her housekeeper. Their mother lived with them. In 1879 Teresa came to stay with them for a while, and she visited from time to time. She always dressed in black with white at the throat, and her vow of poverty gave her clothes an eccentric appearance. During the 1890s she was at a convent in Edinburgh, where she was noted for her devotion to the Sacred Head of Christ as the seat of divine wisdom. She died in Devon in 1905, and Louisa brought her body to Neston for burial. At one time, pilgrims used to visit her grave by the coachload.

As the population increased, St Winefride's became inadequate, and in 1920 the parish priest, Father John Ryan, began a mission in Heswall which gave rise to a parish of its own in 1928.

When St Winefride's was built, or rather converted from the original school building, it was opened with a simple service of blessing. There was no formal act of consecration, possibly because the building was not owned by the church until 1897. When the Rev. Dr George Worsley became parish priest in 1936 he set about improving the church; he refurnished the sanctuary with a new altar, while new lights, panelling and pulpit were provided in the chancel. It was to reopen the sanctuary that, for the first time, a service of consecration was held by the Bishop of Shrewsbury in August 1939.

The first of the Protestant denominations outside the Established Church to reach Neston were the Methodists, in the late 1750s. A Methodist chapel, where John Wesley preached, was built just off the road from Neston to Parkgate in 1762. When divisions arose within the Methodist movement, particularly after 1812, this chapel's congregation became Wesleyan Methodists, whereas Primitive Methodists were to be found in Little

OPENING

OF THE

Primitive Methodist New Chapel,

LITTLE NESTON, CHESTER CIRCUIT.

On Sunday, October 6th, 1872, SERMONS will be preached Morning and Evening by the REV. W. HALL, (Superintendent of the Circuit); also in the Afternoon by CAPT. H. J. WARD, and on the Monday following, at 2.45 p.m., by the REV. VERNER M. WHITE, LL.D., of Liverpool. At 4 o'clock a TEA will be provided, Tickets 1s. each, after which, A TEMPERANCE MEETING will be held, Chair to be taken at Six o'clock by T. MATHESON, ESQ., of Poulton Hall, and Addresses delivered by Dr. White, W. Hall, J. Hall, H. J Ward, F. Caldwell, and J. Postlethwaite.

SERMONS will be preached on Sunday, October 13th, in the Morning by CHARLES LEE, ESQ., of Chester, and in the Afternoon and Evening by J. CALDWELL, M.A., of Ledsham. And on Sunday, October 20th, in the Morning and Evening, by the REV. WILLIAM INMAN, Birkenhead, and in the Afternoon, by J. POSTLETHWAITE, ESQ.

A Collection will be made at the close of each Service in aid of the Building Fund.

Service to commence on each Sabbath at 10.30 a.m., 2.30, and 6 p.m.

N.B.—Refreshments will be provided on Sundays in the School Room for Friends.

On Monday, Trains will leave Chester at 1.55; Liverpool Landing Stage, 1.10; Birkenhead, 1.30. Tickets, including Tea, 2s. each.

Your presence and support are respectfully solicited.

CHESTER: JOHN THOMAS, BROOK STREET STEAM PRINTING WORKS.

Fig. 69 The opening of the new Primitive Methodist chapel in Little Neston was expected to attract people from some distance.

Neston and Willaston. In Willaston they built a chapel in 1838, followed by a larger replacement in 1889. Three local dignitaries laid the foundation stone of the later building, including the MP for Wirral and the landowner Duncan Graham. As Graham remarked, it was *"a better building on a better site"*. He added that some might wonder that he, a churchman, should be involved in such a proceeding: but as an elected representative of the county council he should not be narrow minded.

In Little Neston the Primitive Methodist Society was founded in 1819, and services were held in a number of different places. In 1859, for example, the services were moved to the cottage of Samuel Mealor, next to the plough works in Ness. In 1872 the chapel in Little Neston was built, partly with the help of some stonemasons who were members of the local Methodist congregation.

Methodist churches are grouped into circuits. Little Neston was part of a Chester circuit. Ministers and lay preachers would travel from Chester, and would usually take both Sunday services at Little Neston. Some cycled all the way; others came by train to Hooton, and if there was no suitable train from Hooton to Neston, the visitor would be met with a donkey cart. But if the donkey could not be persuaded to go, the preacher had to walk!

Another group of Wesleyan Methodists met at Raby, in a *"preaching room"* erected in 1846; and at Ledsham there was a congregation of the Methodist Great Connexion, which built a chapel in 1855. These various strands of Methodism were eventually reunited in 1932.

Next on the Neston scene were the Congregationalists, whose cause never took permanent root, possibly because it owed too much to outsiders. They were first reported at Parkgate in 1808, where a year later there was *"a neat chapel erected by our Chester friends"*; this was a building near the Watch House. But Congregationalism in Parkgate lapsed until 1833, when Mr S. Rawson of Leeds initiated services in the Assembly Room, behind what is now called Balcony House. These services continued until George Rawson of Pickhill Hall near Thirsk, Yorkshire, built a chapel largely at his own expense. The chapel was opened in May 1843.

The causes of both Methodists and Congregationalists seem to have been faltering when the wealthy adherent of another denomination, Presbyterianism, came to live in Neston. This was Robert Macfie, a Scot who owned a sugar refinery in Liverpool, and who settled at Ashfield Hall, just inland from Parkgate, in 1857. Finding that the Congregationalist chapel at Parkgate was deeply in debt, he bought it; he also bought the school *"of independent denomination"* on Little Neston Green, and in 1860 the Wesleyan Methodist chapel in Neston. All three buildings were then used for Presbyterian worship, under the ministry of the Rev. A. M. Halket, who used to refer to himself jocularly as the Bishop of Parkgate.

Fig. 70 The Congregational chapel in Parkgate was later used by the Presbyterians, before being dedicated to St Thomas by the Church of England.

Fig. 71 Neston's Presbyterian church was built in 1884 by the architect of the new parish church.

The Presbyterian cause was therefore flourishing, at least while Robert Macfie subsidized it. But he returned to Scotland in 1871, before which the prospect of losing his financial support horrified the officers of the church, and negotiations continued for several years. The three chapels were gradually reduced to one. The school at Little Neston was cast adrift almost at once, and Sunday services there ceased. After some awkward years, John Towert became the minister in 1875, and the first steps were taken to build a new church. Its architect, Francis Doyle, had already designed the rebuilt parish church; he designed several other churches locally, including Heswall. The new Presbyterian church at the head of Moorside Lane was opened in July 1884.

The Swedenborgians were the only other denomination recorded during the nineteenth century. They had 50 adherents in 1829, but in 1850 it was recorded that their Neston chapel had been taken down some years before.

The new century brought with it some fresh enthusiasm. Just as the Rawsons and Hirst from Yorkshire, and Macfie from Scotland, had strongly buttressed local religious observance, so did the Lancashire presence of William Lever, later Lord Leverhulme, strengthen the cause

Fig. 72 The Wesleyan Methodist chapel in High Street, Neston was built in 1908.

of nonconformists. Although it was a Congregational chapel that he built, elaborately, near his home in Thornton Hough in 1907, he was ready to help any of the Free Churches. His wife laid the foundation stone in 1908 of the new Methodist chapel at the head of Neston High Street.

Wesleyan Methodists had returned to Neston in 1899, when they had taken over the bankrupt mission hall which had stood on the same site. The non-denominational mission hall had been built in 1874 by a mariner and tug-owner, Captain H. J. Ward, and was served throughout its existence by its pastor, Joseph Grylls. When Ward died in 1890, the congregation tried to find the purchase money for the hall, but failed.

William Lever himself opened a Baptist chapel in 1909, at the colliery in Little Neston. The colliers were already served by a mission, jointly supported by the Presbyterians, the Primitive Methodists and the mission hall which later became Wesleyan. The Baptist chapel continued until 1925, when it was removed, as we shall see, to Neston.

In the same year, 1909, Lever leased part of the old Liberal Club, by then known as the Institute, to the Congregationalists, who thus made a brief return to Neston. He had earlier offered space to the Methodists, but they preferred to build their own chapel. The Congregationalists also built a wooden chapel, which closed through lack of support in 1927, reopened in 1929, and finally closed in 1938.

Another nonconformist body in Neston was the Salvation Army, which met in Park Street and held meetings at the Cross every Saturday. The Salvation Army was well supported until its leader, Captain Peate, went off with a married woman, it is said, and the citadel crumbled.

During the First World War an evangelist named Dempsey preached that his hearers should love everyone, including the Germans. There was a riot, and Dempsey had to be rescued by the police.

We have seen that this renewed activity after 1900 under the wing of William Lever, accompanied, as it was, by an increase in population, was echoed in the Church of England by the provision of two extra churches — St Thomas's at Parkgate and St Michael's at Little Neston. When the war was over, much of the steam seemed to have gone out of religious rivalry, and although ecumenicism was still a long way off, the different denominations seem to have coexisted more peacefully, and their development was mainly of internal interest. The Church of England built a church hall in 1927, next to the church, designed by Frank Russell, who had also designed the library and St Michael's.

An assembly of evangelical Christians, originally calling themselves the Open Brethren, was founded in 1921, perhaps carrying on the spirit of the old mission hall. At first this group met in Riddock's old school by Little Neston Green, and later in the Salvation Army hut in Park Street. The group then bought land in Burton Road and built a chapel there, called Salem Hall. The building was designed by the leading member of the group, Oulton Lee, a solicitor, and was built entirely by the hands of its members between 1936 and 1938. The congregation later decided that the term "Brethren" carried overtones of strictness and exclusiveness, and they now call themselves the Salem Christian Fellowship, an independent evangelical church.

Occasionally, one might even have glimpsed, in the 1930s, the saffron robes of a Buddhist monk, a guest of the Pallis family of Hinderton Road, where Marco Pallis was a convert to Buddhism.

One denomination which did not flourish was the Baptists. Their charismatic minister, the Rev. Arthur Price, known by his detractors as Black Mick (he had a full dark beard), or as "von Price" for his authoritarian manner, decided in 1924 that the days of the colliery were numbered, and he got his congregation to build a new chapel in Bushell Road. It was built in 1926 – very badly, as later buttresses to the walls bear witness, and without planning permission, for which Price was prosecuted. One of Price's successors as minister went to prison for sexual offences, and the last minister joined the Church of England. The chapel was sold, after the Second World War, to the Neston Lodge of Freemasons.

In 1851, we have remarked, the Church of England held greatest sway where middle-class social pressures existed. In Neston between the wars, those social pressures were still felt. Local families of good social standing did not welcome the Bulleys of Ness, who, though clearly and fully equipped with those humane qualities which Christians like to claim as "Christian virtues", were declared atheists. It was not until after the Second World War that these social pressures eased, and religious observance truly became a matter of personal choice and individual conscience.

SOURCES

This chapter was written by Geoffrey Place.

Many references, particularly anecdotal ones, are taken from the *Chester Chronicle.*

For the Church of England, the Churchwardens' Accounts 1803–1921 (Cheshire Record Office, P149/9/2,3) were useful, as was W. Bidlake, *Neston Church and Parish,* (1936). The scandal in 1862 was described in W. T. Grenfell, *A Labrador Doctor* (1919).

For the Roman Catholics, we are greatly indebted to the research and advice of Virginia Bowes, and see also *St Winefride's, Neston, 150 Years* (1993).

For Methodists, see F. F. Bretherton, *John Wesley's Voyages to and from Parkgate, with an account of early Methodism in Neston and Parkgate,* in *The Methodist Recorder* (Winter 1903), (the same author also tells the story of Squire Brook); E. L. Hilditch, *Little Neston Methodist Church Centenary History* (1972); and John Isherwood, *History of Willaston Methodist Church.*

For Presbyterians, see C. C. Lundie, *The Presbyterian Church of England at Neston and Parkgate* (1933), and the Sessions Minute Book kept at the United Reformed Church, Neston.

For Congregationalists, see F. J. Powicke, *Centenary History of the Cheshire Congregational Union* (1907).

The 1851 ecclesiastical census details for Cheshire are in British Parliamentary Papers 1852–53, Vol. 89, and the information for Neston parish is in the Cheshire Record Office (HO129/760).

CHAPTER SIX

THE POWERS THAT BE

As with the rest of Victorian England, Neston had to adapt to a growing population, changing expectations, new technology, such as railways and electricity, and a consequent growth in civic pride. When the principal landowner, the Mostyn family, pulled out in 1849, the townspeople were forced to look after their own affairs. Local government changed radically, in order to better deal with the growing problems associated with providing a clean and safe place to live. New systems were introduced for poor relief, maintenance of public health, street lighting, crime prevention and an efficient fire-fighting capability. Gas and electricity supply, housing and health care received the attention of both the local authority and individual townspeople. Civic confidence was reflected by the building of a town hall.

LOCAL ADMINISTRATION

Among the records of the Mostyn family are accounts of the manor courts of Neston and of Leighton and Thornton. The Mostyns, as lords of the manor since 1672, had the right to hold the ancient courts twice yearly — a court leet and court baron — relics of the old feudal system, which every tenant had a duty to attend. By doing so, he would participate in the smooth running and good order of local government by enforcing customary rules. Tenants who upset this good order by committing minor infringements of the law were punished by "fines" or "amercements" (financial penalties) paid to the lord of the manor.

Minor disputes, such as those concerning ownership of tenants' holdings, land drainage and stray animals, were dealt with, but more serious crimes were sent to the Assize or Quarter Sessions. It was also the duty of the manor court to elect various local officials, such as constables, burleymen and leavelookers. The bailiff, the lord's agent, summoned the court, which was presided over by the steward of the manor. Cases were heard by thirteen jurymen chosen from the tenants present.

In October 1840 a court was held for the manor of Leighton and Thornton on behalf of Edward Lloyd Mostyn at the house of William Parry in Leighton. The court returned two constables to ensure the Queen's peace, and two burleymen, who looked after hedges and commons.

There is a record of a court for the manor of Great Neston being held at the house of Esther Briscoe, the Mostyn Arms Hotel, in Parkgate in October 1847. The jury included shopkeepers, a physician and a headmaster. A complaint from a resident of Snig Lane (Brook Street) concerned the lack of repair of Bennets End Lane — probably the continuation of Snig Lane into the fields. The six negligent occupiers were fined the sum of £12, to be levied in goods if the repairs were not done by the following first day of January. When the jurors decided to view the place to ascertain why water washed away gravel from the lane from time to time, they decided that a wall built by one of the occupiers was an encroachment onto the lane. The people concerned agreed to make another watercourse.

Compromise and common sense brought about practical solutions to shared problems: the common good was decided by the local people.

The Mostyns' manor courts ceased with the sale and break-up of their Neston and Parkgate estate in 1849. Manor courts for Little Neston and Hargreave were held by the joint lords, the Earl of Shrewsbury and Thomas Cottingham.

Another ancient court that functioned until the 1850s, though with much less benefit to the inhabitants, was the Wirral hundred court, occasionally known as the Wirral Wapentake. Originally a right of jurisdiction belonging to the Crown, the right to hold the court and associated privileges of the lordship of the hundred were often leased by the Crown to a prominent individual or family. Very few of these hundred lordships persisted after the start of the nineteenth century, their powers being taken over by the magistrates and police.

Their concern was with minor disputes over land and boundaries, weights and measures, treasure trove and debts under forty shillings, but the hundred courts often had a reputation for extortion and injustice. Although the court could not actually impose imprisonment for debt, it could do so for contempt, though it generally imposed fines. An unscrupulous lord of the hundred could make money in this way, or use the powers to inflict revenge on particular persons.

Rather than leasing the Wirral hundred lordship when it became vacant, the Crown sold the franchise in 1820, thereby losing any control over its function. It was sold by auction to a Liverpool solicitor, John Williams. When he was convicted for forgery in 1829, it was sold to his father, Samuel Williams of Neston, who held the court in a building in Pyke's Weint, just off High Street opposite to the parish church. Samuel Williams died in 1853, and the title passed to his grandson, who sold it in 1854 to Samuel Holland Moreton, a solicitor and moneylender. Together with Robert Grace, he ran the court from the Tranmere Castle Hotel and the Shrewsbury Arms at Hinderton.

Under Moreton and Grace the hundred court became a byword for corruption and injustice, the two men using the rights afforded to them by the lordship to extort money from the public. They were typically concerned with such affairs as minor encroachments onto highways, trespass, bread weights and ale testing. Disobedience of any order was treated as contempt, and fined; packed juries of their friends were brought in by omnibus from Birkenhead; people were accosted on the street to sit on juries, and fined if they refused to co-operate. If they defaulted on their fine their property could be seized and sold.

In 1856 a dispute concerning Christopher Bushell, of the newly built Hinderton Hall, and a right of way may well have led to the demise of the Wirral hundred lordship. An 1856 Act of Parliament included a clause ending the Wirral court, although hundred courts persisted in other areas for several years.

Another important strand of local administration was the parish vestry, the rights of which included the power to collect rates for various purposes. Since at least the sixteenth century, parishioners at the annual Easter meeting, held originally in the vestry, chose parish officials, including one churchwarden (the vicar choosing the second one). From the time of the Elizabethan Poor Law the parish had been responsible for the relief of the poor, collecting a rate for that purpose, and two overseers of the poor were appointed at the annual vestry meeting. Like all the parish officials, they were under the jurisdiction of the magistrates. The overseers were probably the most important parish officials, burdened with the task of administering the Poor Law, relieving the poor, and coping with vagrancy and the poor from other parishes. The chronic problem of relieving the poor became so severe that a major new Poor Law Amendment Act appeared in 1834, totally revising the system of poor relief.

Other officials chosen by the vestry included township highway surveyors, who also had the use of a rate for maintaining the roads, and assessors of taxes responsible for the rate collection.

At the 1850 Neston vestry meeting the churchwardens were Thomas Jones and Nathaniel Grundy. Thomas Jones and Emmanuel Mallinson were the highway surveyors, and William Meacock and Robert Jones overseers. At the beginning of June the vestry minutes record that Thomas Jones was resigning as assistant overseer after eighteen years. Farmer William Rothwell was elected in his stead, at an annual salary of £16, to be paid out of the poor rate.

Under the 1855 Nuisance Removal Act — an attempt by the Government to deal with the nation's growing sanitary problems — the vestry elected a nuisance removal committee for the township. A meeting of inhabitants was summoned in November to elect the committee, and thirteen members were appointed, including the vicar, Richard Gleadowe, and other prominent Neston men, including the Thomas Jones mentioned above. By 1859 Christopher Bushell was a member of the committee. We have no record of what, if anything, the committee did, and by 1860 the responsibility for nuisance removal was transferred back to the Board of Guardians by the Government.

By the late 1850s the vestry meeting was appointing two township constables, an ancient office which in former times the manor court had elected. The vestry also elected the keeper of the pound, who collected stray animals.

The system of poor relief initiated by the 1601 Act, making the poor the responsibility of the parish, presented an ever-increasing burden as populations gradually increased. The poor rate was originally supposed to be used for materials to provide work for the able-bodied poor, or to maintain the helpless old, young and infirm, — "the impotent poor". The increasing cost of provision led to drastic changes in the system of relief with the 1834 Poor Law Amendment Act, which took away the previous independence of the parishes and formed Unions of neighbouring townships, whose ratepayers were empowered to elect one or two Guardians to form a Board.

The new Act was supposed to alter the old system, which to all intents and purposes had developed into handing out vast sums of money and imposing a high poor rate on the parishioners, by replacing it with board and keep in the workhouse in exchange for labour from the able bodied. The standard of living and comfort was supposed to be such that life and work outside the workhouse would be preferable, and it would only be regarded as a last resort. Work was to consist of such jobs as stone breaking, pig breeding, farm work, or household and nursing jobs for women. Children would also be admitted to the workhouse and attend the workhouse school up to the age of twelve years or so, and then be sent out to serve as apprentices.

And so Wirral Union was formed of 56 townships, and the Guardians first met in May 1836 at the Magistrates' Room in Birkenhead. Sir William Thomas Stanley of Hooton was the first chairman, and Richard Congreve of Burton was one of the vice-chairmen. The Board was authorized to purchase land at Clatterbridge, considered to be the centre of the peninsula, on the high road from Birkenhead to Chester, on which to construct a workhouse to accommodate 130 people, with the capability of being enlarged for 200. The builder was William Quay of Neston.

Cases of hardship were being brought before the Guardians before the workhouse was completed. In July 1836, for example, Margaret Bartley of Neston was to receive relief, but her five children were to be summoned to show cause why they or some of them should not maintain their mother. Relief for another Neston woman was to be discontinued, but a third was to be given relief with arrears.

Provisions of food and clothing were discussed by the Guardians before the workhouse opened. Girls were to be supplied with two chemises, two bed gowns, two petticoats of red flannel and two of blue flannel, two pairs of stockings, one pair of shoes and a straw bonnet. Boys had two shirts, a suit of fustian, jacket and trousers, a pair of shoes, a cap or straw hat and two neck handkerchiefs. The diet was drawn up as 1½ pints sweet milk porridge and 6 oz bread for breakfast, with a rotation of different dinners each day, such as suet pudding or 5 oz boiled beef with 1 lb potatoes, or fish scouse and potatoes. Supper every day was bread and porridge with treacle. The old and infirm were also to get tea, sugar and a little tobacco and snuff.

Further examples from 1838 show the wide variety of outdoor relief given to the poor of Neston by the Guardians: a family's rent was to be paid; a couple aged 68 and 70, sent by Guardians from Lancashire back to their home town, and now unable to work, were given 4s. a week; a paternity order was served; shoes were mended and many articles of clothing provided, such as stockings, shifts, trousers, clogs, and for a man from Ness *"a boot for the lame foot and a shoe for the other"*.

In 1844 the Neston overseer was authorized to obtain a warrant against a father who had abandoned his wife and six children; an eleven-year-old was to have his pay discontinued and to go to service; funeral expenses and shoe mending were paid for. Many of those requesting help were "offered the house" – given food and board at Clatterbridge in exchange for labouring on the farm, breaking stones or domestic work.

The early days of Clatterbridge Workhouse also saw the early days of Clatterbridge Hospital. Infectious diseases such as smallpox and typhoid fever were common, and in 1843 the Board of Guardians built a fever ward, to which the first patients from Neston came in 1844.

In 1848, under new legislation, the Guardians resolved that a general sanitary committee be appointed, decreeing that the Guardians of each township should associate themselves with the local clergy and any other interested residents, to maintain a system of

> *house to house visitation concerned with keeping the town and roads clean and also the inside of the houses of the poor and that they could if necessary call upon the assistance of the Medical and other Union officers.*

Under further legislation in the Government's campaign to improve the sanitary state of the town, as we saw previously, the local vestries were given authority to appoint a sanitary inspector and committee for Neston township, but by 1850 it was obvious that vestries nationally had managed to do very little with their powers, and the ultimate responsibility was given back to the Guardians, whereupon the Wirral Guardians appointed a sanitary inspector to the other townships of Neston parish, covering some 3,950 people.

It was another seven years before the town had the power to manage its own affairs to an effective degree, with the formation of Neston's Local Board of Health. But before we go into the details of how that came about, it is necessary to look ahead to see the outline of local government as it developed in later years.

The 1872 Local Government Act had formed urban sanitary districts of some areas, including those under Local Boards of Health, and the areas of Poor Law Unions outside the towns (i.e. the major part of Wirral) were classed as rural sanitary districts. Under the 1875 Public Health Act the Wirral Board of Guardians became the sanitary authority for these areas, with responsibility for public health issues, including control of nuisances, sewage and scavenging.

The 1894 Local Government Act made the areas urban districts and rural districts respectively, and gave them councils, thereby replacing Neston and Parkgate Local Board of Health with Neston and Parkgate Urban District Council. Surrounding areas, including Willaston, Burton, Ness, Raby and Thornton Hough, were in Wirral Rural District, whose council met in Hamilton Street, Birkenhead. Willaston and Raby had their own parish councils.

Further reorganization came about with the 1929 Local Government Act. Wirral Rural District Council was dissolved in 1933, and a large section of it was designated as a new Wirral Urban District, with the outlying parishes joining neighbouring areas. The new urban district of Neston now included Burton, Ness and most of Willaston.

The new Neston Urban District Council bought the Town Hall Company in 1934 for £4,500, and built the extension for a new council chamber the following year.

The Justices of the Peace in Quarter Sessions had a supervisory role over affairs in the county. This long-established institution was made up of landed gentry of the county — men with property qualifications and a vested interest in keeping an ordered peace. The magistrates were nominated by the Lord Lieutenant of the county, and they took on the responsibility of administering national policies. Under their auspices came poor law administration, wage and price regulation, asylums, liquor licences and maintenance of main roads and bridges.

The Local Government Act of 1888 sought to reform the system of Justices' administration over various county functions by establishing an elected

Neston & Parkgate Local Board

THE NESTON AND PARKGATE LOCAL BOARD

Neston & Parkgate Urban District Council

Neston and Parkgate Urban District Council

Neston and Parkgate Urban District Council

NESTON AND PARKGATE URBAN DISTRICT COUNCIL

Neston Urban District Council

Neston Urban District Council

Neston Urban District Council

NESTON URBAN DISTRICT COUNCIL

Fig. 73 Local government: titles and typefaces over the years.

body — the county council. Fifty-seven county electoral districts were formed in Cheshire, excluding Birkenhead, Chester and Stockport, which became county boroughs. Each district was to return an elected representative to form the new body, in place of the previous administration by the Justices. In practice many of the JPs were elected to the new body. Neston and Parkgate's first member was Duncan Graham, JP, of the Lydiate, near Willaston. He was a successful merchant and benefactor of that township, and was responsible for bringing a water supply to Willaston.

The first meeting of the provisional county council was held on 7 February 1889 in Chester Castle, and the second meeting in Knutsford, three weeks later. Nineteen aldermen were elected and Duncan Graham was nominated chairman. Council meetings were to be held quarterly. Several committees were formed, *inter alia* for finance, main roads, contagious diseases (animals), and lunatic asylums. The first statutory meeting in April 1889 set a general rate of a penny in the pound. The county council had supervisory powers over the local sanitary authorities, and could appoint a county medical officer.

An early representation came from Neston's law clerk in June 1889. The Local Board was requesting that application should be made by the county council to the Board of Trade for the creation of a Sea Fisheries District, to protect the mussel beds by establishing a close season.

The number of county council committees proliferated over the years, gradually taking over responsibilities for public services; by November 1889 there were already fourteen committees. By the 1929 Local Government Act the County itself took over responsibility for the poor, infirm and needy, replacing Guardians and the workhouse system with public assistance.

THE WATER SUPPLY AND PUBLIC HEALTH

Neston gained a Local Board of Health following the cholera epidemic and the need for a safe water supply.

One of the reasons for the position of the settlement of Neston was proximity to a stream for a water supply. Now mainly underground, in culverts, it rises in a field at the bottom of Liverpool Road, runs along the southern edge of the town via Stanney Fields, then under Bridge Street, and enters the estuary near the site of the Old Quay House at Little Neston. For hundreds of years the townspeople would have taken their water from the streams, wells, springs, pits and ponds that surround the town.

From around 1749 some houses in the town had a piped supply. The source of this private supply was a well or spring in Liverpool Road, adjacent to what is now the junction with Drake Road. This was known as the "Har", or "Ar", Well, probably a derivation from "higher" well. An estate map of 1796 calls Liverpool Road "Higher Well Lane". In a letter to the *Birkenhead Advertiser* in 1865, it was claimed that the waterworks consisted of a pit with a 1½ in. pipe inserted in it, and that no mechanical power was involved. Underground lead pipes carried the water down Liverpool Road and to a reservoir or tank built by the plumbers Laurence and Daniel Ridgate in 1749. The tank, or "lodge", was situated at the junction of Mill Lane (now Raby Road) and High Street. Water was piped to some of the houses in the town, or sold from a tap on the site, known as the lodge pipe.

It is difficult to estimate how many Neston houses had the private water pumped to them: the correspondence in the 1865 *Birkenhead Advertiser* concerning Neston's waterworks (by this time owned by Baxter's), complaining of the level of rates paid for a poor water supply, mentions cottagers and workmen as receiving supplies. During the 1866 cholera epidemic the Medical Officer of Health, Dr David Russell, claimed that "*with few exceptions the inhabitants of Neston use the water supplied by the waterworks*", though this probably includes those who bought the water from the tap at the tank.

There were difficulties with the supply in summer, in particular for the poor, who had to use streams and wells; and even those with the piped supply sometimes had to carry water from the spring (from which water still flows) at Moorside, on the edge of the river. The first edition of the 25 in. Ordnance Survey map shows many water sources around the town centre which must have predated the local authority supply. There were several private pumps, and also at least eight wells and two taps which were located in the street.

In 1861 some Neston residents had attempted to raise funds to erect a public well in the town. Christopher Bushell had offered to pay any deficiency, but nothing had happened. However, in 1865 Bushell put forward the money to sink a well in the market place — the area in front of the White Horse Inn at the Cross. Despite some opposition by a few residents who thought that the poor would cause a nuisance when fetching water, a wheel well was sunk.

Unfortunately the well water soon became contaminated by seepage through the sandstone from ashpits, middens and drainage. At the time of the 1866 cholera epidemic it was reported that the well water had not been used for drinking for several months.

In Little Neston there were public wells in Mellock Lane and Lees Lane. There was a spring and pump in Mealor's farmyard (now White House), on the Green, but the water was contaminated by drainage from the farm.

The supply from the wells was often scanty. A local writer in the 1880s said of the Little Neston wells:

> *Strings of women, boys and girls might have been seen standing patiently waiting till sufficient water had oozed up to fill their pitchers.*

Parkgate was said to be inadequately supplied by several wells.

Fig. 74 Neston Cross, *c.*1870, showing the wheel well sunk at Christopher Bushell's expense. The White Horse public house was pulled down in 1877.

There was no authority locally to raise a rate for town improvements, although the Local Government Act of 1858 would, if adopted, give power to elect a Local Board of Health and raise a rate, and to pass bye-laws for road improvements, water supply, sewerage, street lighting and cleaning.

As regards the rest of Wirral, in January 1843 the Birkenhead and Claughton Gas and Water Company sank a well and opened a public waterworks at Springhill, which in 1877 was invested in the Corporation of Birkenhead. The Wallasey Local Board commissioned a waterworks in Liscard in 1863. In 1859 the Wirral Waterworks Company was incorporated by Act of Parliament to supply most of the other parts of north Wirral, and the West Cheshire Water Company was formed in 1884 to supply most of south Wirral.

The poor conditions of Neston, particularly the water supply and drainage, moved some of the townspeople to seek to give the town responsibility for running and raising finance for its own affairs. In July 1866 a meeting of ratepayers recommended that the churchwardens should convene a meeting of parish ratepayers to discuss adoption of the Local Government Act, but before the meeting could be convened an event occurred which brought home to the people the urgency of the situation, and the need for a Local Board of Health.

In the summer and autumn of 1866 Britain was swept by the fourth major outbreak of cholera since 1831. Previous outbreaks had reached Liverpool, but Neston did not fall prey until this 1866 outbreak, which killed 12,000 people in England.

The cholera bacterium had a rapid and characteristic effect on its victims — vomiting and severe diarrhoea, then agonizing cramps and often fatal dehydration. Well over half the cases were fatal.

The disease had been raging for some weeks in Liverpool, where 2,000 people died. The first local cases occurred in Parkgate in early September. One contemporary account was that a Liverpool woman who had been suffering from the disease had come to Parkgate to recuperate, and handed her linen to a servant in the lodging house to wash, and this passed the disease to her and the landlady. Four women are recorded as dying in Parkgate, and within a few days cases were appearing in Neston. Another seven were subsequently to die in Parkgate.

Three town centre tradesmen were among the first deaths in Neston. At least eleven people were dead within one week, and the Poor Law Guardians formed a committee, which included Christopher Bushell and the vicar, Mr Gleadowe, for carrying into effect the Nuisance and Disease Prevention Acts. They had regular meetings with Dr David Russell, the Medical Officer. He was provided with an assistant, a nurse and a horse. Thomas Johnson was employed for burning infected linen, and disinfecting powder — chloride of lime — was strewn in the streets, but the disease spread for a further three weeks, eventually reaching Little Neston.

Sergeant Kearns of the county constabulary reported that burials took place at night and the people were stricken with fear. The chaplain of the Union Workhouse at Clatterbridge, the Rev. Mr Redhead, said that so great was the panic that it was difficult to get anyone to attend to the dead, and many people had left the town. It was hoped to get some nursing help from Liverpool.

The vicar, Mr Gleadowe, was said to have gone into every public house in Neston, and instructed the publican to aid him

> *by closing their houses against men sitting and soaking by the hour – to give a man a glass of ale if he needed it but not to permit tippling.*

Apparently the publicans carried out his wishes, though the ale in fact would have been safer to drink than the water!

In late September, although by this time the epidemic had begun to wane, two cottages were obtained as a hospital near the Green. This was the area off Mill Street behind the houses now facing the library, and was an area that had a high concentration of cases. It was staffed by a matron and three nurses, but was only used for a week or so. Tar barrels were burned in the town, supposedly to kill infection in the air.

Fig. 75 Cottages known as "The Green", off Mill Street, with May Cottage behind. Two cottages in the vicinity were briefly used as a hospital during the cholera epidemic of 1866.

In accordance with the Disease Prevention Act, all soiled linen and bedding used by people suffering from the disease was destroyed, and compensation in kind or money was made by the Board of Guardians. William Edwards, a Parkgate farm labourer, who lost his wife, received two blankets, three sheets and a quilt, and money for a bolster, a chaff bed and a mattress. James Gleave, a bootmaker of High Street who also lost his wife, was given bedding and the cost of three yards of carpet. Richard Price of Golden Lion Yard was given bedding and the cost of a linsey petticoat and two shawls. His two-year-old son had died. Samuel Pace, their neighbour, a blacksmith, had also died, and his widow was given sheets and money for bedding. John McCumsky, having lost one of his eight children, was recompensed with bedding and money to a total of 9s. 2d. Peter Campbell, an Irish tinker, of the Green, was given a quilt and money for a cradle and a pair of trousers. Two of his children, George (seven years old) and Anne (three years old), died within two days. Two years later Neston's Health Committee served a notice that tenants should cease using the donkey shed and two middens at the side of his door, as they were in an offensive state.

The meeting of the Disease Prevention Committee that recommended these compensations resolved to pay Dr Russell £50,

> *to compensate him for his extra labour in attending upon the cholera patients at Neston and also in consideration of the loss he has sustained in his private practice.*

It was still incorrectly believed by many people, expert and layman, that the cholera bacterium floated in air and could be inhaled. The true facts, that the disease was contracted through the ingestion of water polluted with human sewage from cholera victims, or food and drink contaminated with the disease, for example by flies that had been on infected sewage, were by no means universally accepted. The bacterium was particularly hardy, and could live for weeks in water or bedding.

The Medical Officer of Health was reluctant to blame the water supply specifically. In a letter to the *Birkenhead Advertiser* he claimed that it was coincidence that there were no new cases in Neston town centre since the time the public well was closed, that its water had not been used for drinking anyway, and that everyone in Neston infected thus far had used the water ("*tested and found pure*") supplied by the private waterworks – presumably bought from the tap by many people, rather than being connected to the piped supply.

Approximately fifty people eventually died within the month that the disease raged, but it finally persuaded Neston of the necessity of adopting the Local Government Act and doing something to banish the filth and squalor which existed.

By late October a meeting was organized, chaired by Richard Gleadowe. Christopher Bushell spoke strongly in favour of forming a Local Board, pointing out that the vicar and others had in fact made efforts some years previously to do so. At the end of February 1867 another public meeting was held, but the proposal was out-voted by the agent of the landowner of much of Little Neston, the Earl of Shrewsbury, and friends. But a poll of the townships was demanded, and the Act was adopted on 2 July 1867.

Twelve members were elected for the Neston and Parkgate Local Board of Health, representing Great Neston, Leighton and Little Neston. The first members included Christopher Bushell, Dr David Russell, A. S. Grenfell, Joseph Mealor and William Pritchard. Six of the members had been (to little effect) on the nuisance removal committee under the auspices of the Poor Law Guardians.

A water supply was one of the first subjects discussed by the new Local Board of Health. The chairman, Christopher Bushell, was authorized to ask Mr Duncan, Liverpool's water engineer, to report on the best system of water supply, and prepare an estimate for his scheme. By May 1868 there was an agreement to purchase land for a waterworks, off Lees Lane in Little Neston, from the Earl of Shrewsbury, and in June Charles H. Beloe, water engineer, presented detailed plans for the water supply. In October the Local Board doubled the rate to one shilling in the pound.

By January 1869 advertisements for tenders for water pipes were published, and in February an inspector from the Local Government Board in London reported on the poor sanitary state of the district. However, by this time, payment of rates was being resisted, and feelings were running high concerning the cost of the proposed waterworks. At the request of the Neston Local Board, the Local Government Board held an Inquiry, but the Home Secretary refused to rescind the Local Board. However, by the end of the year, the town's leading figures — Duncan Graham, Christopher Bushell, Dr Russell and Richard Gleadowe — had resigned from the Board.

In December 1869 two reports from two further water engineers were considered, one utilizing the spring at Moorside. Two months later the owner of the private waterworks, Mrs Ann Baxter, offered to sell the works to the Board; it would not entertain the offer, but did consider using the "Ar" well in Liverpool Road as the source for the Board's supply.

In March 1870 the Board decided to dispense with Charles Beloe's services, and over the next few months tried to reach an agreement over payment, but in October he was again asked to take charge, and the Board surveyor's short spell as engineer was rescinded. The tender of Ebenezer Timmins of Runcorn was accepted, and the well was sunk 150 feet into the New Red Sandstone off Lees Lane. In March 1871 tenders were accepted for the engine house and cottage for the waterworks, and Robert Jackson was appointed engineer, filling the post for the next six years. Permission for a further loan was obtained from the Government, a further rate increase was declared, and it was resolved to issue placards recommending the inhabitants to order their water services in advance, so that time and confusion would be saved.

The pump began filling the reservoir in October 1871. Water was raised to the surface by a double-acting bucket pump, via a cast iron rising main, to the brick-built reservoir (now disused). Power was from a reciprocating steam engine, with steam supplied from a Lancashire-type boiler fuelled with coal from Little Neston, about the quality of which there were complaints from time to time. Pumping took place two days a week.

At this time the practicalities of using water in a suitable form for fire fighting were important, and Neston's public water supply was first used for this purpose against a fire at the Royal Oak Inn in Little Neston on 23 December 1871. Hydrants were installed in Parkgate Road and Park Street in 1876.

In 1871 Mrs Ann Baxter, who owned the original supply from the Higher Well, threatened

> *as a waterworks company able and willing to lay on water proper and sufficient for all reasonable purposes to which it may be required*

to apply for an injunction against the Local Board, in expectation of compensation according to the Sanitary Acts. Nothing came of this threat, however, and Baxter's waterworks, still supplying water in July 1875, was eventually sold in 1876 to a local builder, William Grocott.

Neston did not seem to particularly appreciate its water supply; in May 1872, in response to a questionnaire from the Poor Law Inspector, it was reported that

> *at the present time only about one fifth of the inhabitants have availed themselves of this supply, which has been available for the last six months. Otherwise the water supply is bad in quality.*

Notices were sent to property owners requiring them to do necessary works to obtain the proper water supply.

By October 1875 nearly 12,000 gallons a day were being drawn from the reservoir – about six gallons a day for each person using the water. Many people were supplied from communal stand pipes, sometimes for up to ten cottages, and a reward was offered by the Board for information that assisted in convicting anyone using the water who did not pay for it. In January 1875 quotations for water to Moorside were sought, but this supply was not completed until October 1879. The well in Chester Road was filled in in 1872, and the one in Mellock Lane in 1877.

Charges were made for the use of water by builders: Joseph Stafford was charged £1 when he built two cottages in Brook Street in 1878, and William Grocott was charged ten shillings each when he built four cottages in Parkgate Road near the Cross. In 1879 it was decided to charge for water for slaking lime. In fact all persons using the Board's water for purposes other than domestic were to be charged extra, including farmers for horses and cattle. In 1878 William Prince became water engineer, and held the post until his death in 1920.

NESTON and PARKGATE URBAN DISTRICT COUNCIL.

NOTICE IS HEREBY GIVEN

That the following Special Charges for Water supplied from the works and mains belonging to this Council will be made from this date to all persons who require it for other than domestic purposes at the following scale, viz.:

	Per annum.
For Horses (other than Farm Horses)	5/- each.
,, Farm Horses - - - -	2/6 ,,
,, Carriages (Two or Four Wheels)	4/- ,,
,, Cows - - - - - -	1/6 ,,
,, Gardens - - - - -	8/- ,,
,, Bakehouses - - - - -	10/- ,,
,, Slaughterhouses - - - -	20/- ,,
,, Livery Stables - - - -	20/- ,,

Dated May 7th, 1895.

(Signed) WILLS HARPER,

Clerk to the Council.

Fig. 76 Water charges were still being levied at many different levels for different applications in 1895.

In 1883 discussions commenced on a water supply for the Hinderton area, which necessitated the building of a water tower on land donated by Christopher Bushell. He had pointed out the iniquities in the financing of the water supply system: water rates did not cover the cost of producing the water, and the deficiency was made up from the general district rate, which could be considered unjust, as many ratepayers on the outskirts of the town, including Hinderton, could not get the water. A total of 44,000 gallons a day were being consumed in Neston, Parkgate and Little Neston at this time. Bushell wanted a round water tower, and called in Alfred Waterhouse (the architect of Hinderton Hall over twenty years earlier) to design it. It was built in 1884, using stone from Bushell's quarry. An auxiliary pump drove water from the reservoir to the tower, and the depth of water was monitored from the waterworks by a telescope directed at an external gauge on the tower.

Fig. 77 The Hinderton water tower. In 1976, the iron water tank and surrounding stonework on its top were removed, and it was converted to a dwelling, as depicted here.

Duncan Graham of the Lydiate in Willaston financed the extension of the water supply from Hinderton to Willaston (not then within the Neston Local Board's jurisdiction), which was completed in 1885. After 1895 most of Willaston was served from the Hooton boreholes.

In June 1889 Captain Congreve of Burton Hall, as Burton Manor was then called, was enquiring if water could be supplied to Burton through the pipes at Willaston; the Local Board resolved to supply Burton at one shilling per 1,000 gallons via a meter fixed by Congreve and subject to approval by Duncan Graham, who had paid for the Willaston supply.

By 1888 water was sold to the biggest customers by meter. In six months the gasworks used 30,000 gallons, the railway station used 20,000, and the colliery used 377,000 gallons. One potential customer took measures to get his own supply: A. G. Grenfell of Mostyn House was being charged what he considered to be an exorbitant rate for the Board's water to fill his swimming bath, and so he sank his own artesian well, employing the same engineer as had sunk a well for the cable company in Old Quay Lane, a water supply subsequently used by the laundry on the same site. By 1897 Grenfell had sunk three artesian wells, the third of which still supplies the school with all its water.

By 1925 there were 80 cottages still using standpipes. In 1927 a new 21 in. borehole was sunk 300 feet deep at Lees Lane. The steam plant was replaced with a diesel-driven, 120 h.p., vertical shaft, borehole pump. There were technical problems with this new machinery, reportedly because the Government refused to sanction a loan for the recommended Swiss pump, and insisted on a British one. The new Gorstons reservoir was built with a capacity of 360,000 gallons — more than double the former one. An electrically driven pump was installed in 1929 in the old well in case of emergencies. The next year a second stand-by pump was added, and these two pumps supplied all the water for nearly a year while the diesel engine was reconditioned.

By 1939 there were fears over the bacterial quality of the water. Housing development with cesspools, a nearby sewer and the disused mine shafts being used for dumping trade refuse all contributed to the contamination. Both well and borehole were being used at this time, and chlorination was begun in August 1938. In 1941 it was recommended that the old well be closed completely, but it was decided to keep it open for the duration of the war.

The original aim of the Local Board of Health that had provided the water supply was to clean up Neston, and this task involved an efficient drainage system. Unlike the modern town, the population of nineteenth-century Neston was concentrated into small areas in and around the town centre.

Fig. 78 The waterworks at Lees Lane, Little Neston: sinking the new borehole through the sandstone in 1927. From left to right, posing for the photographer, are E. J. Lewis, G. Norman, P. McCumsky, W. Norman and A. Briscoe.

Ashpits, middens, donkey sheds, and pigsties existed in close proximity to the cottages, with no organized sewerage system. Waste and sewage ran along channels at the side of the road. Groups of houses often shared the same midden and privy — usually a board over a shallow pit, the contents of which were sprinkled with ashes from the adjacent ashpit, and periodically dug out. As late as 1869 a Government inspector reported on bad conditions, particularly mentioning Little Neston as dirty and untidy.

An 1876 report on Ledsham township, part of the rural sanitary district of Wirral Union, told of a privy connected to a large open cesspool which contained an enormous amount of filth. To this a drain led from a cellar window, where there was a funnel, into which water draining into the cellar was ladled. Diphtheria was reported in the house.

Sanitary conditions in Raby and Thornton Hough were said to be satisfactory. In Thornton Hough the manager for the landowner, Joseph Hirst, enforced conditions on his tenants which kept the village clean.

Various legislative attempts to regulate sanitary conditions from the 1840s appear to have had little or no effect in Neston. In July 1867 the Board of Guardians is recorded as giving orders to clean the gutters in Neston after a long drought and an outbreak of diarrhoea, this being the year following the cholera epidemic, but major action had to wait for the formation of the Local Board of Health in October of 1867. The Board's first concern was to establish a proper water supply, but by October 1868 the members of the Board's nuisance removal committee took themselves on a tour of the town and instigated weekly cleaning, with a horse and cart. Several landlords were served with notices to clean their properties.

In 1870 a new sewer was provided for Parkgate, and residents were served notices to drain their houses into it. Finance was insufficient to complete the sewerage of the whole district, and a £4,000 loan was authorized by the Local Government Board. The following year the Board decided to buy a field (now Tanks Field) in Church Lane for its sewage precipitation tanks, and by 1878 the majority of Neston and Parkgate houses were connected to the sewer.

Disraeli's 1875 Public Health Act was an important landmark of this era, enabling numerous bye-laws to be drawn up: for example, every new dwelling had to have its own sanitary facility.

An 1881 bye-law limited the hours that privies could be emptied of nightsoil to between midnight and 8 a.m. from March to September, and between 11 p.m. and 9 a.m. from September to March. By the early 1880s there were complaints that landlords would not empty ashpits and privies, some contending that it was the duty of the Board to do so. By 1885 the Board was recommending residents to convert their facilities to water closets. They were totally opposed to the advice of the Medical Officer of Health that they should adopt some method of emptying the ashpits and privies. They refused to do so for several years, and in 1888 claimed that farmers were happy to take away the contents of the middens, that employment of a horse, cart and man would cost over £100 a year, and that a policy of encouraging gradual conversion to water closets was therefore preferred. They did, however, agree to carry out the emptying for tenants who could not get it done (the tenant paying if he could afford to do so), and by 1892 they were being called upon almost daily to do so.

The sewerage of Little Neston was begun in 1894.

In 1900 a report required by the Local Government Board called for a new sewage works nearer the Dee, and the works was started in 1902. The treated sewage was discharged via an outlet at Parkgate, which had to be extended in 1909.

In that same year Dr Yeoman, Medical Officer of Health, reported some difficulty in persuading people to convert from privy middens to WCs.

Otherwise well-informed residents of Neston claimed that there had been no infectious diseases in Neston until it was sewered. During the previous year only four conversions had been carried out. By 1923 conversions were still far from complete, and orders were served on 83 houses to carry out conversions. It was by this time becoming obvious that the current sewage disposal methods and the receding tides were becoming inadequate to cope with the waste from a growing population. A 1927 surveyor's report said that

> *the whole of the foreshore from the Urban District boundary at the Colliery is rapidly becoming polluted with stagnant sewage ...* [it is] *more and more difficult for sewage to escape as even the high tides only just reach the polluted area.*

Major works were carried out in the early 1930s to ensure a cleaner effluent. The disposal works was modernized, with enlarged tanks and sludge lagoons. Parkgate's sewage was now piped to the works to be dealt with alongside that of the rest of the district.

Finding sites for dumping "dry refuse" was a problem for the council into the 1930s. In 1900 the disused quarry at Park Street was being used, but there were complaints that "wet refuse" was being deposited there and causing obnoxious smells. There were problems in finding land for tipping within easy reach of the town, but the council decided against purchasing a destructor. They also refused to sanction the use of galvanized iron bins to replace ash pits, because of the problem of having to empty them once a week. It was made clear that people were responsible for emptying their own bins if they had them.

By 1914, however, people were being encouraged to substitute bins for ashpits. The council also installed iron bins in the streets to replace the wheelbarrows that had previously served. So gradual replacement of the old ashpits and middens by dustbins began, and by 1931 all new houses had to have iron bins. A circular in 1934 suggested that people should use the old ashpits as coal houses.

In the 1930s household refuse from outlying areas — Ness, Willaston and Burton — was collected by private contractors.

STREET LIGHTING

The provision of clean water and safe waste disposal were the first priorities of the Local Board of Health. Another objective was to enhance the safety of the roads by providing street lighting, which was first achieved by oil lamps, then by gas and, eventually, electricity.

Neston had no public street lighting until 1876, when one lamp was installed in Station Road, which ran from Bridge Street to the old Neston railway station on the Hooton line. Another lamp was fixed in Park Street. They were both oil lamps fixed to buildings, and in the spring they were taken down, painted and stored in a cellar until the autumn.

The exercise in public lighting was generally agreed to have been a success, and so during the following winter lamps were installed at Windle Hill, the junction of Raby Road and High Street, the Cross, Liverpool Road, Little Neston, and Boathouse Lane and three on the Parade at Parkgate — sixteen in all. Two men already working for the Local Board were delegated to light the lamps, one getting 2s. a week for Little Neston, and the other 6s. a week for Neston and Parkgate, working his dinner hour and leaving work at 3.30 p.m. to light the lamps.

These lamps too were only lit over the winter months, and then only on dark nights. For example, in February 1878 they were lit for twenty days. For the lighter months they were taken out of the pillars and stored at the waterworks. Lighting in the latter part of March was left to the discretion of the surveyor, and in fact no lamps were lit after 8 March.

One elderly Nestonian questioned the need for street lighting; while drinking in a local hostelry he was quoted in the *Chester Chronicle* as saying

> *Oi don't see t'use on it ... until two or three years ago there never were no lights in town and we had allus done vera weel wi'out 'em. When Oi went a sweet-hearting in the lanes with wenches we never wanted no loights to go courting wi.*

In 1882 gas came to Neston, and the lamp over the newly constructed Bushell fountain was gas lit. Gas street lamps were charged by the gas company at 16s. a lamp for supplying gas for five hours a night for six months. A decision was taken to light the lamps every night, irrespective of moonlight, but it had to be rescinded as it would have disturbed the contract arranged with the gas company.

There were complaints of the *"miserable flickering lights"* in Station Road. The new Bushell Road, which Christopher Bushell had paid for as access to Neston Station from Hinderton Road, could not be lit by gas as it was too far from the mains. Some oil lamps were being gradually replaced with gas as the new pipes were laid. In 1891 one of the Board members claimed the gas lighting was poor because of "bad gas", but the directors had it tested and it was said to give up to 15 candle power, and frequently up to 17. They suggested the Board should change the burners.

A public electricity supply was not available in Neston until 1928, and electric street lighting was then gradually introduced. The gas lamps on Parkgate Parade were not converted to electricity until 1965, and some residents then complained that the brighter light would require them to fit bedroom curtains.

GAS AND ELECTRICITY

The first gas company in Britain had been founded in London in 1812; Birkenhead's gasworks opened in 1841; there had been a serious attempt to start a gas company in Neston in the early 1860s which had come to nothing, but in 1881 the Neston and Parkgate Gas Company was formed after a public meeting, addressed by a representative of Dempster and Son, Yorkshire gas engineers. The Neston and Parkgate Local Board passed Dempster's plans, and W. Pritchard of Little Neston was given the contract to build the gasworks on a site in Church Lane near to the sewage tanks. The manager's house and the retort house can still be seen.

The first gas holder was in a well 36 feet across and twelve feet deep from the top of the surrounding wall, containing 10,000 cubic feet of gas. Fifteen men were employed in the construction, and work was completed by November 1882.

A brief ceremony was held at the Cross, when Dr Russell, chairman of the Local Board, had the honour of flaring up the lantern on the recently installed Bushell fountain — and the glass broke, much to the delight of the watching crowds. Several shops took immediate advantage of the new fuel, including Molyneux the baker (now Briscoe's) in Park Street; Oakes and Griffiths, drapers, in Parkgate Road (now the building with the pillars on its front); and Woodall's, the chemist (now the barber's shop) in Parkgate Road. On the inauguration of Neston's new gas, the *Chester Chronicle* offered hints on safe usage, including regulating the supply at the meter, and never delegating the duty of checking that the gas was off to a servant or child; if a pipe burst, thick brown paper smeared with tallow would serve as a temporary seal.

By the end of 1882, 33 customers used the gas. Profit on the first two months was considered satisfactory at £15. The gas company obviously saw profit in the use of their fuel for street lighting instead of the oil then used. The lamps were still only lit in winter, the lanterns being taken out of the pillars in the summer months. The company soon came under criticism for ruts and trenches left in the roads after pipe laying. By 1885 the company was paying a dividend of 3½% on the 792 £5 shares. Expenses had included £20 on storm damage, but £470 had been made from the sale of coke and tar.

There had been a disappointing take-up of gas, with still fewer than 50 consumers. Colonel Richard Lacy, who lived in Moorside at the house now called Springvale, was made managing director, and the Rev. Richard Gleadowe was chairman of the company. He said that the cost of gas being greater than oil was only apparent, taking into consideration cleaning and trimming oil lamps and the constant breakage of glass. Landlords were not installing gas fittings; Gladstone Road had just been built with no provision for gas. Gleadowe admitted that some people wanted gas illumination in church because it was dark, but he confessed he thought the present "*calm and tender light*" was preferable to naked gas flames. He had, incidentally, caused gas pipes to be installed in his new vicarage, built in 1859, so now felt the benefit of it. Many people said they did not want gas because of the low pitch of the ceilings.

The number of users gradually increased to 50, and a second, larger gas holder, and new tar and liquor tanks were built in 1887. A third holder, however, planned in 1889, was not constructed. In 1931 Birkenhead Corporation acquired the Neston and Parkgate Gas Company. The Neston works was kept in operation by the corporation until a trunk main, giving direct supply from Birkenhead, was laid.

Although Neston did not get a public electricity supply until 1928, there had been an attempt made by A. G. Grenfell to interest the town in a public electric lighting scheme as early as 1896. Grenfell had an electric plant installed in Mostyn House School in 1894, and two years later, as a member of the district council, he organized a public meeting after 715 questionnaires had been sent out, with 110 returned, 78 of which were in favour of electric public lighting. The vast majority of residents, however, were not interested in the proposals, and so Grenfell resigned his position on the council. A private works, built for the Hinderton Electric Supply Company, was established to serve the large houses being built in Hinderton Road in 1908, with its plant at the top of Blackey's Lane. The council declined the offer of entering into an agreement for a town supply.

Some premises had their own plants for many years before a public supply was available. As early as 1898, Joseph Johnson made electricity with a gas engine used for his woodworking machinery. The current lit his High Street premises.

In 1928 Neston finally got a public supply, at the same time as Heswall, from Birkenhead Corporation. On Saturday 11 February, a switching-on ceremony was performed by H. F. Russell, chairman of the urban district council: a brilliant sign declaring "Use Electricity" lit up High Street, and 40 houses and shops were illuminated by the new supply.

POLICE AND FIRE BRIGADE

One of the functions of local government was to appoint constables to keep order, and in the mid-nineteenth century a police force was developed. The provision of a mains water supply greatly improved the ability to fight fires, so that a fire brigade was also formed.

The office of constable was an ancient one, its holder originally being chosen by the manor court, and then confirmed by and responsible to the magistrates in Quarter Sessions. From 1842 the parish vestries could select the township constable, though the magistrates were still responsible for them. The position of constable was unpaid, and it was an unpopular office, mainly assisting the overseer in the execution of the Poor Law, rather than preventing crime.

With all the changes in society, and large concentrations of population in industrial areas, a reformed system of policing was called for. In 1829 the Cheshire Constabulary Act enabled the magistrates to appoint a High Constable for each hundred or division, and an Assistant Petty Constable for each township or group of townships. The old township constable system continued alongside. The new constables were to be paid by the overseers out of the poor rate, and it was only after 1852 that they could levy an additional rate for policing.

The 1852 Act also amended the 1829 Act to allow the appointment of as many Petty Constables as the JPs wanted. In 1856 a further Act made the establishment of a paid police force compulsory. In that year the Quarter Sessions appointed a police committee to implement the Act, and Wirral was designated District No. 6, with one superintendent, one inspector, two sergeants and 25 constables. Birkenhead maintained its own force.

With the advent of the county council after the 1888 Local Government Act, responsibility passed to a standing joint committee of JPs and elected county councillors.

Neston's lock-up was in Park Street, to the rear of what is now the site of the Methodist church. A building with two small cells was constructed in 1827, financed by subscription. The cells were reported to be damp, and inefficient, except for the confinement of a prisoner for a short period. In 1865 a new police station and magistrates' room was built on the same site, becoming the Cheshire Public Assistance Office in 1939, when the new Section Headquarters was built in Hinderton Road.

In the early days of the Cheshire constabulary, the chief constables worked hard to create a disciplined force. Nevertheless dismissal of an officer for being drunk was a regular event. In 1857 the chief constable issued an order that

> *warns the Constabulary against entering Public Houses when on duty except for the purpose of duty and cautions them against drinking in public houses even when off duty, it being far better for the Constable to send for what drink he requires when practicable than to sit drinking in such places.*

There were reminders, too, such as the chief constable's edict of 1880 that

> *Of all qualifications of a constable none are of greater importance than perfect sobriety and perfect truthfulness.*

There were numerous regulations about uniform, such as these from 1879, that

> *Spikes will be worn on helmets when attending Divine Service.*

and

> *All members of Constabulary are hereby prohibited from wearing spectacles in Public while in uniform.*

In that same year, Sergeant Warwick at Neston received a stern reproof. The chief constable had visited the town and examined the lock-up book, finding that the sergeant had neglected his duty by keeping the book in a very slovenly and irregular way, the heading on each page having been omitted and not properly indented. It was only in consideration of his long service that the chief constable did not deprive him of his merit badge. Four months later Sergeant O'Donnell of Neston and a constable were deprived of their merit badges, because of the improper and illegal use of firearms while on duty.

The 1880 General Election created a great deal of extra work for the force throughout the county. Superintendents were warned to see that on the day of nomination or election, all heaps of stones or other similar missiles were removed from the neighbourhood where these events would take place. Contingency plans were made for many towns, and trouble erupted, including at Neston (as described in Chapter One). In the early 1880s Neston police were often employed in controlling the many navvies who were working on the West Kirby extension to the Hooton–Parkgate railway line.

By 1886 Wirral Division had one superintendent, two inspectors, seven sergeants and 42 constables, with two extra for New Brighton in the summer. Sergeant Davern at Neston was paid 31s. 6d. a week, and Sergeant O'Donnell, by now an inspector, received £95 a year.

The work required of the police in Neston was probably typical of a town well endowed with pubs. The newspapers reported relatively few cases of theft, like the occasion in 1879 when three women from the notorious Pyke's Weint went into Foster's drapery shop with a horde of children. While the children chased about, one of the women stole some shawls. They were found in her house the next day, and she was sent for trial at the Quarter Sessions.

The police were required by the local magistrates to improve Neston's image, and in the two years from 1898 to 1900 there was a campaign to discourage bad language, for which Pyke's Weint in particular was well known. There were also cases of violent death to deal with. There was the young fisherman, said to be love-sick, who in 1889 climbed over the wall surrounding the disused and flooded quarry at the top of Mill Street and drowned himself. The quarry was filled in four years later. There was the man who went shooting rabbits in 1919; he wounded a rabbit and then struck at it with the butt of his gun, which discharged and wounded him fatally in the stomach. There was the young man convicted of murdering his brother in 1925, but he was found to be insane. But it was in 1900 that the perseverance of the Neston police was really put to the test. Constable James Ross had been in the Plough Inn in Park Street, leaving his bicycle outside. When he came out, he saw someone riding off on the bicycle, but he pursued the thief on foot and caught him.

A public water supply was regarded as a great asset as far as fire fighting was concerned, compared with earlier methods of carrying water from pits and wells. The water from the Local Board works was first used in a case of fire in 1871, at the Royal Oak in Little Neston. In 1879 the Local Board bought a fire hose from the Royal Insurance Company, to attach to the hydrants installed in some roads. Neston's police sergeant was keeper of the Board's hose, but there was no organized brigade at this time.

Nearby villages called on the assistance of the larger towns. For example, in 1867 Chester's volunteer fire brigade had been called to the fire that destroyed Puddington Hall, and in 1890, in the case of a serious fire at a farm shed in Ness, a messenger had been sent to Neston to telegraph to Birkenhead for assistance. Birkenhead's brigade was run by the police until 1895, by which time they had a steam fire engine and dealt with 95 calls, eight outside the borough.

In 1896 Neston UDC bought, with voluntary subscriptions, a manual fire engine from Liverpool Corporation. A brigade of eight men and a captain were appointed, with helmets – brass for the men and plated for the captain and deputy. The council's surveyor, John Morris, was captain for a while, until he left to take up a new appointment and was succeeded by Hutton Wright, a farmer, of Leighton Hall. William Fleming, a builder, was his deputy, and later became captain. Most of the men were employed in local building trades, and gave their services voluntarily except when actually attending a fire. The engine's two horses were provided by William Jones of the Letters Hotel (opposite the town hall), and he was the driver. The first fire attended was probably one at Burton Hall, when the Congreve family lived there. This original pumping engine was rediscovered in the town hall basement, but has since been lost.

Neston's brigade obviously had its limitations: Birkenhead's brigade had to be called in 1901, when a house and shop suffered a serious fire after the upsetting of an oil lamp, and the adjacent premises were also affected. In 1902 the urban district council took over responsibility for the fire brigade, with four council employees available and practised in running the engine.

Much of Wirral, including Neston, was covered by Birkenhead fire brigade in later years. Burton was served by Lever Brothers' brigade from Port Sunlight until 1933. By 1940 Neston, Burton and Willaston were the only areas covered by Birkenhead's brigade. Wirral Urban District Council established its own fire brigade and ambulance service in place of the arrangements with Birkenhead, and built a new fire station at Heswall, which opened in May 1940.

In the Second World War Neston had its own auxiliary fire service, stationed in the old property at the Cross that had been Hancock's, the butchers. After bombing ceased it had little to do, and closed down. In 1947 the county council became responsible for providing a fire service, and Neston was served from Heswall, then still in the county of Cheshire.

HOUSING

In the early days of the nineteenth century, people lived in the town and village centres; in Great Neston houses were built along the main street, with small courts and weints leading off it. Parkgate's, Little Neston's and Willaston's populations were similarly concentrated, and there were small settlements at Leighton and Moorside.

Fig. 79 Houses formerly in Brook Street, near the Brown Horse.

In the early nineteenth century most of the houses in Neston's main street had three storeys; there were still some single-storey thatched cottages at the junction of Liverpool Road and Park Street, at the Cross on the site of the old White Horse and adjacent shops, and on the corner of Raby Road and High Street. There were several small groups of two-storey brick cottages, in Liverpool Road beyond the Malt Shovel, on the south side of Brook Street, along a weint off the main street near the site of the town hall, and at Golden Lion Yard on the other side of the main street.

Several terraces of sandstone cottages were constructed around the middle of the nineteenth century – Poplar Weint, Pear Tree Crescent, off Bridge Street, and on the Green at Little Neston.

The typical Victorian brick terrace appeared from the mid-1870s, when the colliery in Little Neston was taken over by the Neston Colliery Company, and a street (New Street) of terraced houses was built and rented to the company. In the 1880s the row looking towards the estuary was called Sea View, and included a shop.

A national boom in speculative house building occurred towards the end of the 1870s, and this was reflected in Neston. A typical brick terrace of four-roomed houses was built in Brook Street in 1879–80 by the proprietor of the Brown Horse Inn. A virtually identical terrace was built in Badger Bait a few years later, and similar brick terraces were built off Bridge Street (Eldon Terrace and Woodward's Yard), Raby Road and Town Lane in Little Neston. The terraces were usually constructed in sections over several years, as finance became available.

Three pieces of land in Chester Road were bought by James Thompson of Liverpool in 1880, and he planned an extensive scheme of 96 plots, including several new streets. In the event he only built Gladstone Road and the "villas" in Hinderton Road. Mr Thompson seems to have been a less than conscientious builder: it was reported to the Local Board that he was constructing the outside walls of the villas nine inches instead of fourteen inches in thickness, and a few years later a crack appeared in one of the gables.

The Local Board of Health was enabled by various Public Health Acts, including that of 1875 to regulate house building as regards the health and sanitary aspects, and the Board's surveyor kept a check on the progress of building. Bye-laws covered such matters as "air-space" at the rear of the buildings, the size of windows, scullery waste pipes and the height of rooms. No house was allowed to be occupied before a certificate of occupation was supplied by the Board's surveyor.

Landowners hoped that the railway, built from Hooton to Parkgate in 1866 and extended to West Kirby in 1886, would bring with them a demand for housing, but the demand from commuters was slow to materialize, because, it was claimed, the railway fares were too high. Certainly some developments were very slow to take off: N. A. Earle laid out Earle Drive in 1902, but only two houses were built before the First World War.

In 1900 the UDC was offering loans of four-fifths of the cost, up to £300, for working men to build their own houses. In these early years of the twentieth century, houses on the north side of Raby Road, and several in Liverpool Road and Olive Drive, were built, as well as some larger properties by A. G. Grenfell in Parkgate.

In 1913 plans were submitted by Sir Percy Bates of Hinderton Hall and Mr J. L. Barber, in the name of Neston Cottage Company, to build houses in Chapel Field, Burton Road. They eventually built houses at the entrance to Cottage Close in 1914.

There was a shortage of housing both nationally and locally at this time that was not being addressed with any success. Slum clearance was encouraged and carried out in the town centre in 1912, in Pyke's Weint, off High Street opposite to the church. The Medical Officer of Health reported that in one of these properties there lived two adults and six children, floorboards were rotten and dangerous to walk on, and it was verminous. Twenty-five houses were reported as being unfit for habitation, but there was a shortage of property to rehouse people. In response to an enquiry from the County Medical Officer of Health as to what the UDC was doing to provide more cottages for the working class, the council clerk was directed to consult the Neston Cottage Company.

In 1917 the Local Government Board was attempting to encourage house building by offering substantial assistance from public funds for the construction of 100 workmen's cottages at the end of the war. By 1919 the UDC had formed plans to build 70 cottages on 12½ acres between the station in Mellock Lane and Cottage Close off Burton Road, purchasing some of the land from the Neston Cottage Company, together with 30 cottages at Parkgate, between what is now the Wirral Way and Station Road. No progress was made, however, and after three years the scheme was abandoned, despite the post-war housing shortage. The local authority blamed the Government's lack of action for the failure of the scheme, on the planning of which a considerable amount of time and public money had been expended.

The 1921 census showed the need for new housing in the town. There were 274 houses with two families to each, and three or more families lived in 69 houses. In the worst 28 cases of overcrowding, 207 people shared 42 bedrooms – an average of almost five people to a bedroom.

Under the 1923 Housing Act, which gave subsidies, several properties were built, including four cottages for Albert Fleming on the site of the old quarry in Mill Street.

The Ministry of Health approved a scheme in 1925 for the local authority to build houses, and consequently eight were built on land in Raby Road (Raby Gardens) and sixteen at Parkgate (Mostyn Gardens); in 1927 30 local authority houses were built in Burton Road (Talbot Gardens).

Much of Neston's housing was still in poor condition, but shortage of replacement housing prevented further demolition. About 40 cottages were condemned but still inhabited in 1927. Neston Council of Social Service, concerned at the lack of affordable housing, founded the Neston and Parkgate Housing Society Ltd, a public utility housing society. Under the Housing Acts, the council could grant subsidies or pass on Government subsidies; in addition, ordinary shares and loan stock were issued. The trustees were William Jackson, E. Lees Evans, John Larden Williams, Mrs Troughton and Lionel Barber. A six-acre site was bought from Albert Fleming in Liverpool Road, and by December 1928 40 bungalows were ready, and were named Mayfield Gardens. Twenty were let to ex-servicemen and ten to tenants of condemned houses. By May 1929 30 houses were also completed, and there were 240 applications for them.

In 1931 the housing society built eighteen houses on the west side of Burton Road and sold the freehold for £340, at fifteen shillings a week. Two years later it built twenty houses in Cottage Close, and in 1933 it bought the last section of the colliery site, and demolished the chimney. Eight pairs of semi-detached houses, each with half an acre of land, were built and let to tenants prepared to use them as smallholdings. The site was known as Homecroft. In 1957 the gardens were reduced to a quarter of an acre, and the remainder of the land was sold. A proposed scheme for four blocks of four houses in Burton Road in 1937 did not come to fruition as the UDC would not lend the finance.

Private speculative building flourished in the 1930s: Brookland Road, Parkgate, for example, and the Bendee and Mellock estates (Badger Bait) in Little Neston come into this category.

In 1935, under the Housing Act 1930 (Slum Clearance Sites), there were closing orders on many properties, such as Swift's Weint in Parkgate, cottages in Golden Lion Yard, Liverpool Road, Pennington's Weint at the junction of High Street and Chester Road, Pritchard's Weint in Little Neston, and several in Ness and Willaston.

The 1935 Housing Act was concerned with overcrowding. From 1937 the local authority could enter a house in order to measure rooms and calculate the acceptable number of residents. In certain cases the occupier could be served notice to abate the overcrowding. Thirty-four houses were reported as being overcrowded. Twenty-eight houses in Rocklee Gardens were built for the UDC in 1936, and Mellock Estates built eleven pairs of semi-detached houses, with a further seven pairs in Talbot Avenue in 1938.

Fig. 80 Typical slum dwellings: condemned cottages at the entrance to Golden Lion Yard, just off High Street.

In November 1938 the Ministry of Health wrote to the council, pointing out that 78 unfit houses had been vacated and only 28 built to replace them. The Ministry was concerned that the council was not planning to build any more properties itself, but was relying on private enterprise. It was important, said the Ministry, that housing accommodation should be within the means of the persons to be rehoused. The council expressed its confidence that needs could be met.

HOSPITALS

In the 1840s smallpox and typhoid fever were prevalent in Wirral, and in 1843 the Board of Guardians built a fever ward at the Wirral Union Workhouse at Clatterbridge, at a cost of £90. The first patients, who were from Neston, were admitted in 1844.

The Wirral Joint Hospital Board was formed in 1888, and was responsible for the provision of an infectious diseases hospital. It bought land from the Guardians at Clatterbridge for the purpose, and the hospital gradually developed over the years. By the early 1920s the fever hospital had 50 beds for scarlet fever, twelve for diphtheria and twelve for enteric fever. Patients not requiring isolation were sent to Birkenhead and Liverpool hospitals or Chester Royal Infirmary. In 1933, 36 Neston patients were treated at Clatterbridge, 29 suffering from diphtheria.

The old workhouse and infirmary, redundant after the passing of the 1929 Local Government Act, were taken over by the county council and became Clatterbridge (County) General Hospital, with 300 beds by 1935, with much new building taking place in the 1930s. During the Second World War there was a Ministry of Health emergency hospital ("the huts") on the site, and an American military hospital. The various aspects all merged, and in 1948 the Hospital Management Committee succeeded the Wirral Joint Hospital Board.

A convalescent home for Chester Royal Infirmary was opened at Parkgate in 1882, the ceremony performed by the Duke of Westminster. Situated near the Watch House, where flats have been built in recent years, the home accommodated 25 patients to convalesce in the healthy air, for up to three weeks, financed by subscription. The house was bought with funds from the Parkgate Sea Bathing Charity, established in 1790, which enabled poor invalids to stay in Parkgate to benefit from the sea bathing.

Fig. 81 The convalescent home at Parkgate belonged to the Chester Royal Infirmary from 1882 until it was sold in 1923.

The home was taken over as a Red Cross hospital, as was Neston Institute in Hinderton Road, from 1914 to 1919. Maud Gladstone, the wife of Henry Neville Gladstone of Burton Manor, took a great personal interest in the welfare of the convalescing troops. The house was returned to Chester Infirmary in 1919, but was sold in 1923. The property was bought with funds forming part of the estate of Frank Rigby. It was named Rigby House, and in summer months was used as a holiday home for poor children, and for local charities in winter.

When the Red Cross hospital in Neston Institute closed after the First World War, the balance of funds was used towards buying Dee View, a large sandstone house next to the Green at Little Neston, built by William Pritchard as his own residence. A local committee organized the purchase, and Lord Leverhulme opened Neston War Memorial Hospital in June 1920. Miss Bell, the district nurse, was appointed matron, and there were five trained nurses and two probationary nurses.

Fig. 82 Neston War Memorial Hospital, *c.*1940, showing the extension to the right of the original house.

The hospital had 21 beds, and patients were attended by their own doctors and visiting specialist medical officers. People who were not compulsorily insured under the National Health Insurance Acts could become subscribers at thirteen shillings a year. Fifteen shillings a week was the minimum charge, which covered nursing, board and care, and four guineas a week was charged for the private ward.

In addition to the subscriptions, a lot of fund raising took place, including firework displays organized by Mr Grenfell at Parkgate in the 1930s. There was also a workmen's contributory scheme, and collecting boxes around the district.

In 1948 the hospital management, after several difficult years financially, relinquished their responsibilities to the new National Health Service. The hospital remained open until 1964, and its closure is still regretted by many older residents.

District nursing was introduced to Neston in 1900, when the Neston and Parkgate Nursing Society was formed, with Nurse Scott as its first district nurse. The society needed £100 annually, and was funded by subscription. The district nursing scheme had originated in Liverpool, founded by the philanthropist William Rathbone, to train and organize nurses to attend the sick poor in their homes. By the mid-1930s Neston's Nurse Barber was carrying out nearly 2,500 visits a year, supported by local subscribers and donations from local businesses. The Neston organizing committee included such well-known local names as Mrs Troughton, Mrs Jackson and Mrs Larden Williams. In 1948 the Nursing Society was absorbed into the Ministry of Health.

The county council ran an Infant Welfare Centre in the 1920s, every Thursday at the Methodist Church Sunday School. Organized by a committee, welfare workers and lady helpers weighed the children every week, while the doctor saw them monthly, keeping a check on rickets and tubercular problems. The county council also ran a maternity clinic with two midwives.

The 1890 Local Board minutes tell us that 17s. 6d. was paid to John Wilding for use of the ambulance for a patient taken to Chester General Infirmary, and was to be claimed from the Guardians – presumably a "horse ambulance carriage", such as Birkenhead had from 1896.

In 1918 E. C. Whineray from Leighton Court donated a motor ambulance to the council. It was decided in 1920 to put the ambulance under the control of the council's surveyor, and Mr Hacking, a Voluntary Aid Detachment man, was to assist when taking patients to hospital. Mr Chrimes, the driver, was to be paid two shillings an hour. The ambulance was only to go out after a deposit had been paid (£1 in Wirral, or £2 across the Mersey), but allowances were given by the council. In all cases other than in extreme urgency the surveyor was to be applied to before the ambulance could be taken from the shed.

By 1925 an agreement was made with the ambulance service of Birkenhead Corporation's fire brigade, in consideration of payment by the council of the equivalent of a penny rate. The ambulance could be used for accidents and emergencies at no cost to the patient, and was available for removal of "private" cases for a fee. The old ambulance was offered to the secretary of the cottage hospital.

Neston did not seem to make much use of the Birkenhead ambulance: it was called three times in 1931, five times in 1932 and six times in 1934. In the mid-1930s the Birkenhead ambulance was serving the "protected areas" of Wirral and Neston UDCs, but by 1940 Wirral had its own service.

An ambulance donated under the will of A. B. Earle of Puddington was available for the duration of the war for the routine use of the people of Neston, in addition to transporting injured and wounded to and from hospitals. It was manned by the local Red Cross detachment under its commandant, Miss Pamela Jackson. Willaston had similar use of an ambulance for the war years, donated by Geoffrey Boston.

THE TOWN HALL

The building of a public hall for the town was suggested at a meeting of Neston and Parkgate Local Board in early 1887 as a commemoration of Queen Victoria's Golden Jubilee to be celebrated that year. The town was certainly in need of a hall, the only premises for social events and meetings being the Liverpool Road schoolrooms. And the Local Board needed office accommodation and a suitable place to hold its meetings, which at that time were taking place in the courthouse in Park Street.

A public meeting was called in March 1887, when the Local Board member Mr John G. Churton, of the Manor House, Moorside, proposed that

> *an effort should be made to erect a public hall suitable for public meetings, festive occasions, entertainments, concerts and such like assemblies as a recognition of Her Majesty's Jubilee Year.*

An initial attempt was made to establish a Jubilee Hall fund by public subscription. But the response was poor, and so the idea of building the hall as a Jubilee commemoration was dropped, and it was decided to form a limited liability company selling shares to finance the scheme. The chairman of the directors was John Churton, who also became the major shareholder, and the secretary was John Morris, surveyor to the Local Board, who had designed the Bushell fountain five years previously.

Architects were invited to submit plans, and the various designs were exhibited. Sites considered for the building included a field off Buggen Lane, the site of Church House, where the parish hall now stands, and the Brewer's Arms yard. The site eventually purchased at a cost of £500 was a garden on which stood the old drill shed used by the Rifle Volunteer Corps — a building which was previously the old National School.

The architect of the chosen design was David Walker (whose work includes churches in Liverpool and Birkenhead), although a number of modifications were necessary to reduce the cost. It featured a concert, or assembly, hall, a drill hall, a boardroom, two ground-floor offices, a kitchen and a "lavatory" (for washing, the WC being outside the building).

In August 1887 the promoters made a formal application to establish a limited liability company, issuing 3,000 shares at £1 each. The Neston Town Hall Company was registered in October. By March 1888, 1,383 shares had been subscribed and 245 promised, but some people refused to participate as they objected to the chosen site, located among the public houses in the town centre.

Tenders were invited for the building of the hall, and that of William Pritchard, from Little Neston, was accepted. He had built several properties in Little Neston, including his own house, later to be used as the Neston cottage hospital. The design was described as being

> *a free adaptation of Queen Anne period in brick and terracotta with sparse use of red stone and internally red deal and yellow pine with pitch pine flooring.*

The roof was supposedly designed to secure perfect acoustic effects.

On the evening of Thursday 6 September 1888, the ceremony to lay the foundation stone took place. A procession was led from the school in Liverpool Road by the Volunteer Corps, headed by its band, followed by the schoolchildren, then the Neston Lodge of the Order of Druids, and finally the directors and friends. A substantial crowd gathered to hear the speeches and to watch Mrs Churton lay the stone. She was presented with an engraved silver trowel with ivory handle to spread the mortar. Beneath the stone were placed copies of *The Times*, the *Chester Chronicle* and the *Birkenhead Advertiser*, and some coins. There were various speeches, and the ceremony ended with the National Anthem. Some of the younger people of the town indulged in the old Neston custom of dancing on the Green behind the Golden Lion Hotel almost opposite to the town hall site.

By the end of October the roof timbers were being positioned, but some delay was expected in getting the terracotta bricks for the facade. By mid-December the outside walls and top stones were completed, and two months later the building was ready for occupation. The basement drill hall and armoury were rented by the Volunteers, an office and boardroom by the Local Board, and the North and South Wales Bank leased an office.

The first function to take place in the town hall was a ball for the Neston Rifle Volunteers in February 1889.

After the Neston Urban District Council had been formed in 1933, it bought the town hall from the company in June 1934 for £4,500.

SOURCES

This chapter was written by Susan Chambers.

The manor court records of the Mostyn estate can be found in the Mostyn Mss. (6250), at Bangor University. For the Wapentake, see R. Stewart-Brown, *The Wapentake of Wirral* (1907).

The vestry minutes are in the Cheshire Record Office (P/149), as are the records of the workhouse at Clatterbridge (LGW).

The minute books of Neston Local Board of Health and Urban District Council are kept in Neston Town Hall. Public health records for the old Rural Sanitary Authority of Wirral and Wirral Rural District Council are in Birkenhead Central Library (A/HH).

For Police, see A. W. James, *To the Best of our Skill and Knowledge, a Short History of the Cheshire Constabulary* (1957), and Police Committee minutes in the Cheshire Record Office (CJP).

For Buildings, planning applications are in the Cheshire Record Office (LUNe 2004).

For Hospitals, see Central Wirral Hospitals Management Committee, *A Short History of Clatterbridge Hospitals* (1966), in Bebington Central Library (CWB362), and minutes of the Wirral Joint Hospital Board from 1889 in Birkenhead Central Library.

Cheshire County Council minutes are in the Cheshire Record Office (CCC).

Much information has been derived from newspapers, especially the *Chester Chronicle* and *Birkenhead Advertiser*.

CHAPTER SEVEN

OFF DUTY: NESTON AT LEISURE

For men, the centre of social life, until the second half of the nineteenth century, was the public house. The inn was much more than the bar, where friends would meet for a drink. It was the natural meeting place for public affairs, like the meetings called by the tithe commissioners in 1843 and 1848; for the Dee Yacht Club which met at the Mostyn Arms in Parkgate; for the Freemasons who met at the Union; for the Foresters who met at the Nag's Head; for the Druids who met at the Golden Lion. The larger inns were also an important point of contact with the outside world, for their landlords organized the coaching services. The coach, and later the horse omnibus, for Tranmere Ferry ran, in 1850, from the Golden Lion or the Ship. Until the railway came in 1866, a coach for Hooton would run from the Pengwern Arms. In the 1840s the coach to Chester, which had earlier run from the Mostyn Arms, was running from the Pengwern Arms in Parkgate via the Black Bull in Neston. Similarly, the pubs were often the centres for sport. For example, the bowling green behind the Golden Lion was celebrated as the place for the Ladies' Club dance every year. There were also bowling greens at the Pengwern Arms and the Nag's Head. Quoits, which takes up less room, was a very popular pub sport. The object was to pitch a heavy iron ring over an iron stake. In the 1970s a quoit was found beside the Coach and Horses. The customers at the Malt Shovel seemed particularly keen on sport: there was a shooting gallery there, and boxing matches were held in a cottage next door known as the Office. In 1883 a contest there turned into a general fight. In Willaston, both quoits and bowls were played at the Nag's Head.

Neston was renowned for the number of its pubs, and they were supported by the Neston brewery. At one time innkeepers would brew their own beer, but in the eighteenth century Neston contained two "common brewers" — that is, wholesale brewers who supplied inns. One of these, Joseph Hayes, ran his brewery in High Street, just below the church. In 1857 Thomas Parry bought his brewery and ran it until the 1880s. A little earlier, in the 1850s, Charles and Nathaniel Cooke, whose firm was later to become the Birkenhead Brewery, owned the Neston works, and an encyclopaedia of chemistry described their beer thus:

> *Some very excellent bitter ale is now brewed in Birkenhead by Messrs. Cook Bros. Some of the ales they manufacture, especially those at their Neston works, are very similar to Burton. The Editor believes that the secret of this superior*

product is chiefly to be found in the composition of the water which he analysed with some care, and found to contain large quantities of earthy carbonates and sulphate of lime, without any organic matter, which, when existing in any amount, is decidedly deleterious.

Fig. 83 Quoits, an ancient game of considerable skill, with rules similar to those of bowls, was (and in some places still is) played on a pitch 21 yards long, having a "prob" — a peg in a circular target area of clay, as shown here — at each end. A flanged metal ring, or quoit, weighing up to 6 lb was thrown the length of the pitch towards the opposite prob, the winner being the player whose quoit landed nearest to it.

The generous provision of pubs in Neston, and perhaps the growing population, gave the place an unsavoury reputation. In the 1870s, particularly, there were many drunk and disorderly cases before the magistrates, and in 1878 people complained of the rowdy youths who congregated on the street corners and intimidated passers-by. The vicar, R. W. Gleadowe, demanded action from the Justices. They certainly tried, but longstanding Neston attitudes could not be changed overnight. In 1886 it was written that the only recreation that many young men took was "*lounging around odd corners, giving annoyance to passers-by by ribald remarks and unseemly attempts at jocularity*". More seriously, in 1888 a baby was found dead, "*having been suffocated accidentally in bed by its mother*". It was her sixth illegitimate child. The report went on to say that such suffocation often seemed to occur on Saturday nights or Sunday mornings.

The efforts to combat drunkenness and improve the moral reputation of Neston took two forms: one was the temperance campaign, and the other the encouragement of sporting and social societies.

Nationally, the British and Foreign Temperance Society was founded in 1831, and the Band of Hope, a temperance association for children, was founded in 1842. Although the movement was originated by, and remained strongest among, the nonconformist denominations, the Church of England formed a Total Abstinence Society in 1862 which became the largest of them. Several temperance organizations worked in Neston. The first reference we have is for 1848, when the Rechabites provided tea for 300 in Parkgate.

Many temperance meetings were held in the mission hall at the head of High Street. There, in 1877, the Parkgate and Neston Temperance Society was addressed by Matthew Webb, the first man to swim the English Channel, who was later drowned while trying to swim across the foot of Niagara Falls. Captain H. J. Ward, who had built the mission hall, was Webb's uncle. The Free Gospellers at Neston Colliery formed in 1882 a Temperance Band of Hope, with its own drum and fife band.

In Neston, as indeed nationally, the movement began to show results. In 1888 it was reported that, thanks to the temperance societies, there were six times fewer drunkenness cases before the Neston court than there had used to be, *"but from all accounts the vicious indulgences which were the crime of Babylon are as active as ever"*. Just what this severe reproof refers to is uncertain. If it refers to prostitution, then the indulgences continued, for in 1902 a woman and her two daughters were convicted of keeping a brothel in Pyke's Weint.

These three girls were commemorated in a Neston rhyme:

Talk about Pyke's Weint,
We have the best of any,
We have got the best three girls,
Et, Kit and Nelly.

Another way of tackling the drink problem was to cut down the number of licensed premises. A highly unpopular Licensing Act had been passed in 1872, which restricted the hours that pubs could be open. It was opposed in some surprising quarters: the Bishop of Peterborough said that he would like to see *"England free better than England sober"*. For years after this, it was uncertain whether a liquor licence could be withdrawn without compensation, and when it was decided in 1891 that compensation was not necessary, most Justices felt that withdrawal of a licence without compensation was unfair. The debate was resolved by the Balfour Act of 1902, which provided compensation from a fund levied on the brewers. In 1904, therefore, following a petition from the vicar, Turner, all eighteen of the local licences were objected to. It was pointed out that there were nine licensed houses within 320 yards of Neston Cross. These were the Malt Shovel, the Brewer's Arms, the Plough, the Neston Hotel, the Golden Lion, the Brown Horse, the White Horse, the Greenland Fishery, and the Coach and Horses. The Greenland Fishery had already been amalgamated with its next-door neighbour, the Black Bull, when the same brewery acquired both in 1892, giving rise to this rhyme:

Black Bull chucked and stranded,
Green fish safely landed,
"One licence less," the Bench exclaim,
"But drinking space just the same,
Temperance not advanced one jot,
Time wasted, twaddle, cant and rot."

In 1904, only the licence for the Coach and Horses was refused, and that was granted on appeal. A year later, by agreement with the brewers, three licences were withdrawn permanently — the Golden Lion, the Nag's Head, and the Sawyer's Arms in Parkgate.

Fig. 84 The Sawyer's Arms, a small beerhouse in Parkgate, was named after Richard Bartley, a sawyer and the original landlord. It was closed in 1905 as part of the national campaign to reduce the number of drinking licences, and has now been a private house for many years. It adjoins the large house, Pengwern, on one side, and has Dee Cottages on the other.

Of the remaining pubs in Neston, the Plough, a small inn in Park Street, closed in the First World War; and the Neston Hotel closed in 1931.

Fig. 85 The Neston Hotel, once known as the Vaults, and between 1891 and 1902 as the Letters, was next to the Golden Lion, opposite the town hall.

Another means of tackling the drink problem was to provide alternatives to the public house as a meeting place. To this end, a cocoa-house opened in Mostyn Square, Parkgate, in 1876, at "*the late watch house of the coastguards*". It was originally called the British Workmen Public House and Fisherman's Rest, and was set up by a company which had established sixteen such houses in the previous six months. There had been an earlier venture on the same lines which closed in 1873. The Parkgate cocoa-house continued for at least ten years.

It was at this point that some curates of the "muscular Christian" type tried to follow the advice of Sidney Smith, that "*the true way to attack vice is by setting up something else against it*". In the 1880s the curate was the Rev. K. Kempston, who helped to found cricket and football clubs. In the 1890s it was the Rev. William Barrett. He founded a new quoits club in 1890, separate from the public houses; he also promoted bowls and football.

Neston Quoits Club had a pitch behind the houses in Raby Road, and there was a Parkgate Quoits Club, active since about 1884, which was given a new ground by Reginald Haigh, in 1892, next to his lawn at Leighton Banastre. In 1910 there was a Little Neston quoits ground by Victoria Road. But this ancient game died away entirely after the First World War.

Bowls went out of fashion for many years before a new Neston club was formed on the Golden Lion ground in 1892. A new bowling green was opened at the Liberal Club, of which more presently, in 1904.

Fig. 86 The bowling green behind the Neston Hotel.

The present Neston Cricket Club started in 1895, but it had several short-lived predecessors. The inauspicious start was in 1874, when a Chester team came to Parkgate, but only seven players turned up for the home team and were ignominiously defeated. Mr Kempston's club lasted some years, but a new one was founded in 1890; however, like its predecessor, it probably suffered from having no ground of its own. Reginald Haigh, a keen sportsman and resident of Parkgate, had a private cricket ground, and he had thrown this open to the navvies who came to build the railway to Hoylake in 1886, so that they could play "*football, quoits and many other games*". He was stimulated to start a new club, renting its present ground,

Fig. 87 Dr H. M. Speechly keeping wicket at Neston Cricket Club's Parkgate ground in 1895.

Fig. 88 Neston and District Cricket Club's First Eleven, 1927.

by the arrival of Dr Harry Speechly, a good cricketer. Haigh was president and Speechly the captain of the club, founded in September 1894, but playing its first season in 1895.

All this sporting activity encouraged many other such ventures.

The Football Club, which played on a ground near the old Neston railway station, organized a sports day in Parks Field in 1886 which *"stirred up the stagnant blood of the young fellows in the neighbourhood"*. As well as running races, there were also a sack race, a donkey race, a greasy pole and a tug of war. Running was popular locally. In 1881 two well-known Neston runners staged a race along the Chester High Road which attracted 500 spectators. It also attracted the local policeman, who charged them with obstructing the highway. They were fined 2s. 6d. each. In 1901 and some subsequent years, the Liverpool cross-country championships were held in Parks Field, with the runners making seven circuits of the old steeplechase course on the race ground.

Fig. 89 The Neston Comrades Football Club proudly displays its trophies in the 1920–21 season.

The oldest of the local societies were the friendly societies, whose members subscribed for future benefits which would, at the simplest level, pay their funeral expenses. This provision was particularly attractive after the Anatomy Act was passed in 1832, permitting surgeons to dissect the unclaimed bodies of paupers. The first benefit society in Neston was founded before this, in 1814, but the Neston Female Friendly Society is described separately, below. The others were exclusively for men. The oldest of these, formed in 1839, was the Foresters – the Court Stanley Lodge of the Order of Foresters –, which marched in July. Next came the Neston Independent Brotherly Society, formed in 1841 and marching on Whit Monday. In 1858 the Neston Lodge of Druids was set up. The Oddfellows had a flourishing branch – the Loyal Habah Lodge – nominally in Burton, though covering a wider area. Finally, there was the Neston Victoria Jubilee Lodge (which suggests it was formed in 1887) of Ancient Shepherds. Like the Ladies' Club, the men's societies met once a year, marched to a service in church, and often called at the houses of local gentry, to pay their respects and, no doubt, solicit subscriptions.

Fig. 90 Members of the Order of Oddfellows at Mill Lane corner, Ness, *en route* from the Little Neston Working Men's Institute to Burton church for their Whit Monday service, *c.*1910.

A more exalted kind of friendly society was the Freemasons. There had been two lodges locally in the eighteenth century, but they had died away. A new branch, the Dee Lodge, was formed in 1875 and met at the Union Hotel, Parkgate, where one of its founder-members, John Acton, was the landlord. The Dee Lodge still exists, but it moved from Parkgate in 1922, first to Heswall and in 1941 to Port Sunlight. A separate Neston Lodge was formed about 1948.

Another early society, which had considerable influence in Neston, was the Volunteers. In 1859, largely because Napoleon III was making warlike noises in France, volunteer rifle corps and rifle clubs were formed all over the country. The 11th Cheshire (Neston) Rifle Volunteers (reorganized in 1882 as No. 5 Company, 1st Cheshire Rifle Corps) were founded in 1860 with three officers and 70 men. They used to meet in the old National school on the site of the town hall, and from 1889 in the basement of the new town hall. They staged an annual shooting competition near the Old Quay House, for which in 1878 some very practical prizes were donated by local tradesmen, such as port, beef, boots and coal. Later they were holding monthly, and in 1892 fortnightly, shooting competitions.

Fig. 91 The Neston Volunteers (No. 5 Company, 1st Cheshire Rifle Corps), *c.*1900.

The pride of the Neston Volunteers was their band, mustering fourteen players in 1888. The band played at many local celebrations, especially the annual marches of the friendly societies. Less has been reported of the Neston Volunteers after 1900, when there was a shooting accident in which one of their men lost an eye. All Volunteer forces were disbanded in 1908, when the Territorial Army was formed in their place. A semi-official

"Home Guard", then called Volunteers, was set up in the First World War, and B Company of the 10th (Wirral) Battalion included Neston.

Between 1900 and 1921, Parks Field was the scene of annual summer camps of artillerymen, who used to fire their field guns across the estuary, from the field now occupied by the North Parade. Although local people were not involved, it was a popular spectator sport. Children would try to retrieve the brass shell cases and sell them as scrap metal. In 1904 a boy was injured when he picked up a live shell; the fuse exploded, but luckily not the shell. In 1960 a live twelve-pounder shell, discarded or perhaps hidden in about 1900, was dug up at Parkgate. The artillery range was condemned in 1922, and the summer camps came to an end.

Fig. 92 Artillery practice in 1903. Men of the 1st Worcester Royal Garrison Artillery (Volunteers) fire field guns across the Dee.

Shooting continued as a civilian sport after the Volunteers were disbanded, through the Parkgate Rifle Club, formed in 1905 for both men and women. Their range in Manorial Road was built on in the 1920s.

The most ambitious sporting enterprise before the First World War was the Liberal Club. This was the brainchild of A. G. Grenfell of Mostyn House and William Lever, who was elected Liberal MP for Wirral in 1906. The intention was to provide Neston with a social centre, while advancing the Liberal cause. Some £50 shares were sold, but most of the cost was met by a bank loan of £2,500 guaranteed by Lever. The club offered bowls, billiards, shooting and a football team, as well as social events and a bar,

Fig. 93 Members of the Parkgate Rifle Club outside their clubhouse in Manorial Road in 1905.

Fig. 94 The Liberal Club later became the Neston Institute, and is now known as the Civic Hall.

when it opened in 1902. But the bar was soon to be the cause of trouble. A. G. Grenfell had suddenly (and temporarily), under the influence of his missionary brother Wilfred, become a teetotaller. He shocked a meeting of the Church of England Temperance Society, which favoured moderation, by castigating the society for not pressing for total abstinence. One of the first public debates in the Liberal Club was on this issue. At the end of the same year, December 1903, an argument in the club led to a fight outside, after which one of the fighters died from a fractured skull and the other cut his own throat. A few months later, the Temperance Association, led by Grenfell, was presenting to the magistrates a petition to reduce the number of licensed premises, when it was remarked that the Liberal Club had a licence. In 1905 the club went dry and, since there was no prospect of paying off the debt, Lever paid the loan and so became owner of the club; but without a licence it was much less popular. In 1908 Lever opened a Liberal party office elsewhere in Neston, and the old club was named the Neston Institute, and leased to the Congregational Union, after being offered to the Methodists. The building became a Red Cross hospital during the First World War, and afterwards reverted to the control of the Congregational Union, which sold it in 1947 to Neston Council.

At much the same period that sports clubs began to grow in Neston, there also developed societies for other activities. These were stimulated by the opening of the school in Liverpool Road, which was always intended to serve for adult meetings in the evening. The first such society to be recorded there was the Floral and Horticultural Society, which held its show in the schoolroom in 1867.

THE NESTON & DISTRICT
Food Economy & Horticultural Committee.
SECOND ANNUAL
Vegetable, Fruit & Flower Show.
Held at Neston Institute, Saturday, August 23rd, 1919.
THIRD PRIZE
FOR
12
7 Class. Awarded to C. Norman

Fig. 95 A Flower Show certificate awarded in 1919.

The first mention of music, other than the Volunteers' band, recorded in the newspapers, was a Musical Society formed in 1877, followed by the first concert of the Neston Vocal Society the next year. These two societies were separate, as each held concerts in 1881. Reginald Haigh, already mentioned as a promoter of sport, put on concerts in Parkgate for the fishermen during the 1880s, and also for the railway navvies. One performer who is remembered from the days before the First World War was Ithiel Lloyd, who did female impersonations. For example, he and his friends from Parkgate put on a show at the town hall in 1910. Such concerts were very popular, if only because *"there was nothing else"*.

In 1905 the Neston Concord Society was formed, and for 50 years staged Gilbert and Sullivan operas and similar light musical plays. Between the Wars these performances were even more popular. The Concord Society was renamed the Neston Amateur Operatic Society in 1920, and its shows ran for five or six days. The society's last show was *Tom Jones,* in 1955.

A social focus of a different kind developed after the First World War, in the British Legion. It was reported in 1919 that 841 officers and men from Neston had served in the war, of whom 91 were killed (and are named on the war memorial erected in 1920). One of the fallen was Lt.-Col. Christopher Bushell, who was posthumously awarded the Victoria Cross in 1918, and was a grandson of the Bushell whose memorial fountain stands at Neston Cross. Many of the returning soldiers became Comrades of the Great War — one of several associations which merged in 1921 to form the British Legion. They were launched financially by Colonel Harrison of Denna Hall, who provided them with a hut on the field next to the parish church, hitherto known as Church Field, but then to be known as Comrades Field. Col. Harrison sold the field to the church in 1919, but it remained as a football field for the Comrades. In due course the Legion established itself near the Institute, where the present Royal British Legion building stands.

Behind the field belonging to the Institute lay Stanney Fields, presented to Neston Urban District Council in 1935 by the second Viscount Leverhulme, whose father, ennobled in 1917, had died ten years earlier. The fields became a public recreation ground, *"particularly for use as a playing field for children of 14 years of age or under"*.

Parkgate was involved in the leisure business throughout our period. In 1840 its days as a seaside resort were numbered, owing to the rise of New Brighton, but it was still being developed as a resort, by extending the sea wall, for example, until its landlords, the Mostyn family, sold the whole village in 1849. People still came to Parkgate for a seaside holiday, and would rent rooms or houses until 1939, but the numbers were small. More

Fig. 96 Staged by the Neston Amateur Operatic Society in 1931, *Ruddigore* was typical of the society's popular productions during the inter-war years.

significant were the day-trippers, encouraged by the coming of the railway in 1866, but particularly by the establishment of Bank Holidays in 1871. After a few years, thousands would flock to Parkgate on these days. It was then that the donkeys, normally employed in pulling carts loaded with shellfish across the sands, waited on that projection of the sea wall known as the "Donkey Stand", to take children for rides along the Parade. These visitors were probably not from Neston, but local people flocked to Parkgate for the races on Parks Field and the regattas, both of which are described more fully later. Sports were held in Parks Field to mark public occasions. To mark Queen Victoria's Golden Jubilee in 1887, a procession of the local societies, led by the Volunteers' band, walked from the Cross to Mostyn Square, sang the National Anthem and went for sports to Parks Field. The peace celebrations in 1919 followed a similar programme.

A more patrician sport at Parkgate was yachting. This began with the foundation of the Dee Yacht Club at Parkgate in 1843. Three years later, "*The view on the promenade is now enlivened by the pretty vessels of the Dee Yacht Club being moored in line*". The club lapsed for a while, and was revived as the Royal Dee Yacht Club in 1863. Its members met at the Pengwern Arms, but the club is not heard of again at Parkgate after 1872, although an attempt to bring it back was made in 1908. Some sand-yachting, however, was tried on the shore from about 1912, though chiefly by Mostyn House boys in the 1920s.

Fig. 97 Pupils from Mostyn House School sand-yachting, *c.*1930, when Parkgate still had a firm, sandy beach for seaside activities.

Sarah Ann Brazenell was the landlady of a lodging house in the 1920s at Balcony House, where the assembly room at the back was divided into cubicles for the summer visitors. They would buy their own food and hand it in to Mrs Brazenell's kitchen to be cooked for them.

A fillip to Parkgate's bathing reputation was given by the opening in 1923 of the open-air swimming bath, beyond North Parade. The bath was 335 feet long, and, instead of having deep and shallow ends, had deep and shallow sides. Hilda James, who had swum in the 1920 Olympic Games, aged 15, and whose father was manager of the baths, gave swimming lessons. In 1930 a second bath was built, 220 feet long and very shallow, intended for non-swimmers. For the first time, swimming appeared on the timetable of the local schools, not only in Neston but in Heswall.

Fig. 98 The Parkgate swimming baths being well used in 1925.

The baths had been designed to fill and empty with the tide twice a day, but after a few years the water had to be pumped in. By 1939 the supply of water was becoming a problem owing to silting in the river, and so A. M. D. Grenfell, whose father had built the baths, sold them to pay for an air raid shelter for Mostyn House. The baths reopened in 1941 for a couple of seasons, but the site then became derelict for many years.

On the estuary itself, wildfowlers would stalk the geese, with shoulder guns or punt guns. The first of these were the Kemp family of Burton. In 1898 the Cheshire Wild Birds Order imposed a shooting season on the estuary, preventing the shooting of birds between 1 March and 12 August. The year before, two wildfowlers, including Joseph Grundy, a Neston grocer, were badly injured when their punt gun exploded.

Fig. 99 A wildfowler and his duck punt, silhouetted against the river: Tom Evans *"along the Main Bank"* in 1907.

It was a great occasion in the nineteenth century when outside entertainers visited Neston. Wombwell's Menagerie came in 1885, and in 1915 most of the children at Liverpool Road skipped school to see Bostock's Animal Show. The fair that had become traditional on Ladies' Day was held in a field off Raby Road that is now a car park. The field was owned by Mrs Collins, who owned the fair, and when it was sold to Neston Council, the sale included a covenant which gave the fair proprietors the right to return there for a week each year. A show with local animals, though organized from outside, was the donkey competition, which ran for several years from 1887. This was an attempt by the Society for the Prevention of Cruelty to Animals (not Royal in those days) to improve the lot of the donkeys, used largely by the Parkgate fishermen. On the first occasion,

1,000 people came to watch 25 donkeys being judged. The next year, however, the competition was described as "*disorganized and chaotic*". In 1893 the Wirral sheepdog trials were held in Parks Field, with 139 entries.

But the most invasive of the outside entertainments was the cinema, which signalled the end of the close-knit, inward-looking world of old Neston. Films were first shown at the Institute in about 1912 by J. W. Maxwell, who owned one film of his own – "Diana of Dobsons". If the film he expected failed to arrive, the audience had to accept "Diana of Dobsons" once again. In 1915 he advertised that he showed

> *the world's best pictures at 7.45 p.m. every Wednesday and Saturday, seats 3d. and 6d., at the Neston Electric Picturedrome.*

Fig. 100 A poster from outside Neston's New Cinema in 1936.

When the Institute became a hospital during the War, Maxwell showed films in the town hall. Neston's New Cinema opened in April 1921 with the film *A Temporary Gentleman*. There was seating for about 400, and the arrangements were considered very modern for their time. Balcony seats were 2s., and the stalls seats ranged from 5d. to 1s. The films were accompanied by a pianist, but there was a small orchestra between about 1925 and 1928. A hazard to the musicians during the children's Saturday matinées was that the children did not bother to visit the toilets, and streams of urine would run down the sloping floor. When talkies arrived in 1930, a musician was kept for a while to play between films. The New Cinema closed in 1960, reopened with a new management in 1961 as the Royal Cinema, but soon closed for ever.

Children's organizations appeared in the years before the First World War, first as temperance organizations and then under the influence of Baden Powell's scouting movement. A Parkgate branch of the Liverpool Society for the Protection of Young Girls was formed in 1900, and a branch of the Girls' Friendly Society was run by Mrs Whineray at Leighton Court. The first Boy Scout troop was formed in Neston in 1908, with fifteen members, led by Arthur Williams. Girl Guides were first started in 1914 at Miss Richardson's Moorside School, but this company was closed to the school. In 1920 the 2nd Neston Guides was formed. Like many Scout and Guide companies, it was denominational in character, being attached to the Church of England. Similarly, the 3rd and 4th Neston Guides were attached to the Presbyterians and Methodists respectively.

Miss Barber used to take the Guides to camp in the 1930s, and remembers that the railways used to carry their equipment free of charge.

Neston Sea Scouts were in a dormant and leaderless condition when they were revived in 1935 by Tom Browne. He was the headmaster of HMS Conway at Anglesey, but had a house in Old Quay Lane. The Sea Scouts then met in the old Comrades Hut behind the parish church hall, but after several moves they settled in the barn of the former Pengwern Arms in Parkgate, next to the Boat House, until the barn was demolished to make a car park in 1973.

THE PUBLIC CEREMONIES

In the Neston of the nineteenth century, each year was punctuated by great outdoor occasions in which most people would take part, if only as spectators. Some of these occasions had their origins in the festivals of the Church — particularly the Easter ceremonies, such as "lifting". Others were wholly secular, such as the races, the regattas at Parkgate and the greatest and most enduring of them all, Ladies' Day. These festive occasions helped to bind the people of Neston into a community. The sense of community was very marked before the First World War, but most of the great public occasions had withered away by 1920.

The most popular, or in some quarters unpopular, of the Easter customs was "lifting", said to commemorate the raising and lowering of Jesus from the cross. Arthur Watson, curate of Neston, and schoolmaster in Parkgate in 1860, gave this account of it:

> *There was an odious custom prevailing, when the cockle-women &c used to "lift" the men, when they could catch them. They would even stop carriages, and the male occupants were forced to pay blackmail, or submit to being dragged out and "lifted". I think on the Tuesday the compliment was returned by the sterner sex.*
>
> *I remember a Mr Gleadowe , rather an irritable man, being intercepted. I being young and active, somehow eluded them and escaped the ignominy.*

The custom had once been widespread in the north of England, and had been trenchantly described by an indignant citizen of Chester in 1771:

> *... a nuisance, I mean the practice of Lifting; or rather, the assembling in a riotous manner of a considerable number (I am sorry to say) of females, at all the gates and other thoroughfares of this city, to extort money from every man whose business may oblige him to pass that way.*

George Gleave, a resident of Neston who recalled the custom in 1891, after it had died out, had more sympathetic memories.

> *Lifting in Neston was not considered a nuisance. The assailants were mostly young men, while at their approach, watch and ward were strictly kept by the opposite sex. In speaking to an octogenarian in Neston a few years ago, who had lived as a domestic servant at the Mostyn Arms Hotel, I asked her if she remembered Ryley* [the actor who lived at Parkgate]. *"Yes," she answered, "we lifted him, and also some other gentlemen at the hotel, and he gave us half a sovereign."*

Easter was much more than a religious festival. Marking, as it does, the arrival of spring, people would wear new clothes if they could, and would celebrate the holiday joyously. Like "lifting", most of the Easter celebrations had a decidedly secular air, whatever their origins might have been. The Crow, for example, on Easter Sunday was appointed the official censor of dress, and "*that sable official*" would show his disapproval if he spotted anyone who was not wearing something new.

Easter Monday began with the grotesque custom of "riding the lord". In this, a man was paid to ride on a donkey from the top of High Street to Chester Lane, and on the way would be jeered and pelted with rotten eggs. Then came "lifting", which began to be disapproved of towards the end of the century. In 1883 a Heswall man was summoned for assault after he entered a house unbidden in pursuit of "lifting". After "lifting", people would retire to drink egged ale and to eat egg pudding. Another Easter observance was said by George Gleave to be cock-fighting, performed chiefly at Ness, but also in Neston and Little Neston. Of one Easter custom often found elsewhere, the performing of plays called pace-egg (from "Pasque" egg) plays, Gleave had *"but faint recollection in Neston"*. As near as Thurstaston, though, "paste-egg" plays were being performed by children about 1880.

These customs, involving riotous behaviour, as well, no doubt, as a good deal of drinking, were frowned on by Gleadowe, the vicar. They came to be replaced, without his help, by a genuinely decorous and religious outdoor custom — that of ushering in the New Year. From the 1860s until his death in 1910, Colonel Lloyd addressed a meeting at Neston Cross on New Year's Eve. His congregation came principally from the non-conformist churches. A similar outdoor ceremony emerged after the First World War on Armistice Day.

THE RACES

It was a cause of further regret to R. W. Gleadowe that another Church festival, Whitsuntide, was connected in the popular mind with Neston races. These races, held annually at Whitsun, began in 1728 and originally coincided with the spring fair, which lingered until the 1850s. The racecourse was at first on Windle Hill (a place-name which has mysteriously moved half a mile southwards in recent years). On Windle Hill there is a large field on the inland side of Hinderton Hall. The first edition of the Ordnance Survey map for the area, made about 1840, showed the course and the race-stand on this field, and James Stonehouse recorded that he remembered the Windle Hill course in use about 1845. Before then, though, the races were being held, at least in some years, in Parks Field in Parkgate, and Bryant's map of Cheshire, published in 1831, shows the racecourse in Parkgate. Indeed, Stonehouse also remembered that the Smith family of Wood House in Wood Lane used to provide refreshments for visitors to the races in the 1840s.

The Chester newspapers carried advertisements for the Neston races until 1846, but no further mention of them has been found before 1881. It seems likely that the decline of the Neston fairs (said to be "nearly obsolete" in 1850) caused the races to fall into abeyance for some thirty years, until they were revived by the Wirral Hunt. In 1881 the Wirral Hunt Club steeplechase, *"the gala of the Wirral Harriers, charmingly situated in the meadows below Leighton Hall"*, was the occasion of six races. Parks Field is not actually in Leighton, but the chairman of the race committee was Johnson Houghton of Leighton Hall. The six races were the Wirral Hunt, Wirral farmers' and Wirral open steeplechases, the Wirral Hunt members' cup, the Leighton open steeplechase and the Consolation stakes. On this first occasion, two horses were killed in falls.

Under the auspices of the Hunt, Neston races were run annually for about sixteen years. The character of this regular festival was remembered in two ways — the informal atmosphere, and the heavy police presence. Harry Neilson recalled:

> *In the old days the race meeting at Parkgate was like a jolly old-fashioned picnic. There were no inclosures, and people from Birkenhead, Claughton, Oxton and round about made up family parties and big tuck hampers, and drove to the course in all sorts of conveyances, 'buses, wagonettes, open hired cabs etc. Two or three slap-up coaches and four-in-hand drags gave an old-time touch to the scene.*

In 1889 the *Chester Chronicle* recorded that *"all the best families of the district had picnic parties made up for the occasion"*.

Not everybody viewed the races in this favourable light. Fifty or sixty policemen were drafted in for the occasion in some years, and their arrests of pickpockets and illegal gamblers, such as three-card trick men and those running gambling games at which the customer could not win, were regular items in the press reports. The vicar preached against the immorality of the races. However, his opposition to this popular festival did not go down well. In 1879 he rashly arranged the annual vestry meeting on the afternoon of Easter Monday, which also happened to be the race day. He was asked to change the date of the meeting, and refused; but the legality of his action was successfully challenged because he had not given the precise notice required by law. After about 1886 the magistrates refused to grant an occasional licence to sell alcohol at the races, and public behaviour improved accordingly, although arrests for illegal gambling would continue.

The prizes were in cash. In 1888 they ranged from £30 to £50. Spectators were charged to enter Parks Field, and one year all the gate money, some £50, was stolen after the cashier left it in a leather bag in an empty carriage.

In 1889 the Neston races were mentioned in the national press, through the fate of one of the visitors. He was called James Maybrick, a Liverpool cotton broker, who set out on horseback for the Neston races, although he was not feeling well. He had told his parlourmaid that he had taken an overdose of medicine. It was a very wet day, and Maybrick was drenched. Despite being so wet, he rode from Parkgate to Bromborough to dine with some friends, where he became ill. After his death, his wife was charged with his murder; she was accused of extracting arsenic from flypaper. She was convicted and sentenced to death, but was reprieved and served fifteen years in prison.

The races at Parkgate survived a number of threats in the 1880s. They survived the vicar's wrath and the loss of the occasional licence. They even survived the loss of the bottom strip of Parks Field, when the railway was extended from West Kirby to Parkgate in 1886: the route of the railway included *"that part of the race-ground called the water-leap"*. The races continued well into the 1890s, and the last mention of them that has been found was in 1895, when a jockey was seriously injured while riding in one of the steeplechases.

When soldiers were reported to be camping in Parks Field in 1900, it was described as *"formerly used by the Wirral Hunt steeplechases"*.

THE REGATTAS

In 1824 the editor of the *Chester Chronicle* listed a number of ideas which might improve Parkgate in the eyes of its seabathing visitors, such as a library, music and a regatta. It was possibly in answer to this appeal that a regatta was organized in 1827. Whether they were an annual feature from then on is uncertain. They were regularly mentioned in the 1830s and were well established in 1842, when the Parkgate Regatta was organized for the benefit of the village's boatmen. A band (Stubbs' Royal Harmonic Band) played during the afternoon of 22 September, and there were six races: for schooner-rigged boats, two for jigger-rigged boats, for small boats, and two for four-oared boats, one of them open only to women rowers. There was dinner afterwards at Mr Williams's of the Ship Inn, and at Mrs Briscoe's of the Mostyn Arms Hotel. A straw in the wind, though, on this occasion may have been the presence of Mr John Rigby, who brought *"his beautiful new steamer the Lapwing to anchor opposite the hotel"*, and invited the regatta committee on board for wine. The following year, 1843, the Dee Yacht Club was formed at Parkgate, as we have seen. However, the yacht club sank into inactivity, and so may have the regattas, in that the records of them in the newspapers faded away for twenty years. In 1863 the yacht club was refounded, and the following year the Parkgate regatta was revived, by the yacht club, as a mixed social occasion. There were races for yachts and for boats rowed by gentlemen, several sailing races for fishermen, and a race for boats rowed by *"mechanics"*. There was a trophy for the yacht race and cash prizes for the rest. In the late 1860s, however, the conditions at Parkgate were ceasing to be favourable to yachts, and the yacht races began taking place off Heswall, while in 1872 the club left Parkgate for Hilbre.

The regattas continued, though how regularly is uncertain. The races in 1903 were described as the Heswall and Parkgate regatta. The programme for the last of the traditional regattas, held on 11 July 1914, describes the afternoon firmly as Parkgate Fishermen's Regatta. There were races for both sails and oars; for nobbies, yawls and punts; rowing and sculling races for fishermen and for all others; and a tug of war between rowing boats. To finish the afternoon there were races, for old men, and for young girls whose winner was given a child's tea set. The final event was a tug of war. In earlier years this had been between Neston fishermen and Parkgate fishermen, but in 1914 the team of eight Parkgate fishermen was challenged by a team of seven ironworkers from Ellesmere Port. Just as Parkgate seemed to be losing, a score of wives and girl friends seized the end of the rope and pulled the Port men to defeat. The umpire started to protest, but was told that the Port men should have brought their own women! Afterwards there was dancing on the Green, a piece of ground behind the houses, on which Holywell Close has since been built.

Fig. 101 The Parkgate Regatta, as photographed in 1903.

The war prevented any more regattas until 1920, but when the day came, there was no wind and therefore no sailing. The prize money was divided equally between all the entrants. The crowds adjourned to the Green to dance to a band from Heswall, but after a very short time a downpour of rain sent the band fleeing for shelter. That inauspicious day was 2 October, so in 1921 a more usual date was fixed, at the end of July. The rain poured down, and a lack of wind was followed by half a gale. But the races did take place (although in the race for nobbies, only one boat finished), the band of the Liverpool Orphanage somehow managed to play on the Donkey Stand, and there were races afterwards. But the old spirit, not to mention the old weather, was judged to have gone, and the regatta was never revived.

LADIES' DAY

Ladies' Day, the annual procession of the Neston Female Friendly Society, has been much written about; indeed, the local newspapers usually contain an account of the society every year, before or after its meeting on the first Thursday in June, when Neston's streets continue to be brought to a halt for the afternoon.

The society was founded in 1814, although its rules were not approved until three years later. Friendly societies for women were quite common at the time. A Women's Society was formed in the Mendips in the 1790s, of which the writer Hannah More was a member; this society had a rule, as did the Neston ladies, that any member who had an illegitimate child should be expelled. But the Mendips Society's rules went on to say, *"this rule shall not apply if she has twins as her first misfortune"*. There were similar friendly societies for women at several other places in Cheshire in the nineteenth century: at Farndon, Malpas and Tattenhall, for example. And at Gresford, in Flintshire, a Ladies' Club flourished between 1840 and 1930.

When the Neston Society celebrated its fiftieth anniversary, in 1864, the *Chester Chronicle* published a very full account.

> *The members of the club assembled in the National Schoolroom at half past two o'clock where they formed into procession. There were 28 honorary and 80 benefit members present. The procession was made up of the leading ladies of the district as well as the wives and daughters of the most humble working men. All were dressed in a neat and becoming manner, there being no attempt on the part of the honorary members to outvie in style and appearance their poorer sisters.*

The distinctive badge of membership, then as now, was the white wand, a staff dressed with flowers:

> *Each member carried a white wand with a large bouquet of flowers and a rose on the breast.*

Some years later, these flowers were the cause of some awkwardness:

> *A pretty and singular sight it is to behold the forest of wands, beautifully, chastely and profusely decorated with flowers coming up the middle aisle, and in some cases so large and broad were these decorations that some of the ladies seemed at a loss for the moment what to do with their graceful signs and tokens of membership. It would be a good arrangement to have a ring attached to the end of the pews to receive those pretty staves.*

This suggestion was later put into practice.

In 1864 the procession was led from the schoolhouse in Liverpool Road to the church by the band of the Cheshire Militia. It had been the custom before this, as it was later, to invite the band of the local Neston Volunteers

Fig. 102 The decorated wands are proudly displayed in this scene during Ladies' Day, *c.*1890.

to play, but in this year they were rejected, and their protest at the rebuff was made very publicly.

> *During the delivery of the sermon, the conduct of the Neston band was very reprehensible. It seemed the managers of the club did not think the musical ability of the Neston band to be of a sufficiently high character to warrant their being engaged and accordingly they made arrangements with the band of the 1st Cheshire militia. This gave umbrage to the Neston musicians who, considering they had not been well treated, assembled opposite the church and* [during the sermon] *they poured forth music of a most discordant character, much to the annoyance of the congregation; and it was not until the Rev. Coxon* [of Heswall] *went out of the church and remonstrated with them that they left and proceeded to another part of Neston.*

On that occasion the procession of ladies, having re-formed after the church service, went straight back to the schoolroom. In later years, however, it was the custom to pause at Neston Cross. In 1888, for example, the procession again formed at the church door, and proceeded via Church Lane and Parkgate Road to the Bushell fountain, where a halt was made and a circle formed with the band in the centre, the National Anthem being played by the band.

Fig. 103 Ladies' Day centenary, 1914: the scene at Neston Cross, with the centenarian Mrs Turner among the spectators.

When the members of the club returned to the schoolroom, they found tea prepared — in 1864 by the landlady of the Golden Lion, in 1888 by caterers from Parkgate Road; and the annual report and accounts of the Society were read out.

The contributions of members depended on the age at which they joined — from 8d. a month to 1s. 6d. For this subscription, members received sickness benefit, stated in 1887 to be 5s. a week; a benefit of 10s. at the birth of a child; a superannuation, or pension, of 2s. 6d. a week after the age of 65; and an allowance for funeral expenses. But the funds relied on the generosity of honorary members, who would not seek to draw benefits:

> *It is much to the credit of the gentry of Neston and Parkgate that since its formation they have taken a lively interest in its prosperity, many of the influential ladies residing there having become honorary members.*

These dignified proceedings had their less dignified side, and in the early years, there were scenes of carnival all along High Street. The reporter in 1883 took a very jaundiced view of such things:

> *There are some, and those not a few, that give the utmost support to the society, that would be glad to see the adjuncts attendant upon its celebration done away*

Neston Female Friendly Society.

(Registered under Friendly Societies' Act.)

BENEFITS:

Medical Attendance.
Relief in Sickness, &c.
Old Age Pensions.
Funeral Allowance.

Several Thousand Pounds have been paid for these objects.

Honorary Subscriptions, Half-a-Guinea

ESTABLISHED JANUARY 1ST, 1814.

Capital invested and in hand over £2,000.

Lady Patroness—MRS. TROUGHTON.

Treasurer—MISS ROBERTS.

Assist. Treasurer—MRS. LIVERMORE.

Trustees:

J. PEMBERTON, ESQ. R. L. PRICE, ESQ.

REV. WALTER BIDLAKE.

Medical Officers:

LEWIS GRANT, M.A., M.D. H. G. CARLISLE, M.D.

G. GUNN, M.D., F.R.C.S. (Edin).

Honorary Stewardesses

MISS ROBERTS AND MRS L. GRANT.

Benefit Stewardesses:

MRS. BUSHELL AND MISS HENDERSON.

Committee Room, Neston,

26th May, 1926.

Dear Madam,

The Annual Gathering will be held on Thursday, the 3rd June, 1926. The procession will start from the National Schools at 2 p.m. Members will attend Divine Service at the Parish Church, when the Vicar of Neston (Rev. Walter Bidlake) will preach. Afterwards the Annual Meeting will be held in the Town Hall. Tea will be provided.

Yours faithfully,

DICK WHARAM, Secretary.

To..

Fig. 104 The Neston Female Friendly Society in 1926.

with, such as the dangerous and exciting swinging boats and perilous hobby horses and roundabouts as well as the tribes of nut barrows, cake stalls and such like indigestible commodities, as well as the noisy shooting galleries that are to be found congregating in the public house yards in the vicinity of the town.

Notice how the word "exciting" was used as a reproach. The reporter wanted such things banned from the town altogether, but the police managed to shepherd the stalls and sideshows to a field in Raby Road, thus starting the custom, still observed, of having a fair on that ground on Ladies' Day.

Much more worrying for the puritans of Neston was the dancing that took place on the Green behind the Golden Lion.

Here, according to the annual custom, old and young engaged in dancing, non-members being charged a shilling each for admission, the amount raised being given to the funds of the club. The lady patroness was present, as was the Rev. Mr Coxon, the Rev. Mr Gleadowe and other influential gentlemen of the neighbourhood. No drink was allowed to be brought on the Green and the greatest decorum was observed.

On this occasion there were some 700 dancers, so that a considerable sum of money, perhaps £30, would have come to the society's funds from the entrance money. Despite the offer, reported in 1883, by some local gentlemen to reimburse the society with the lost gate money if the dancing were done away with, the custom persisted:

The dancing on the green itself cannot, perhaps, be considered objectionable but it is the proceedings afterwards that often bring ruin and misery to many.

The dancing survived, nevertheless, possibly until the Golden Lion closed in 1905, and then it transferred to the more decorous surroundings of the Neston Institute.

Between the two World Wars, Ladies' Day was remembered for its fine weather, although it did rain in 1928. In 1938 there was not merely heavy rain, but gales and hailstones as well:

It was unfortunate that the children and girls, as well as the older members who took part in the procession, had to protect their summer dresses with coats and mackintoshes because of the wind and rain. Filmy hats suffered damage.

Some of the sermons delivered to a captive audience of women in the nineteenth century would make the congregation cringe today. The Rev. Mr Gleadowe, former headmaster that he was, delivered a blunt lecture in 1864: he told mothers that they should be orderly, tidy and frugal and make their husbands' wages go as far as possible, that they should deal for ready money and find out where the cheapest and best things to be got, and much more in the same vein. In 1888 the Rev. William Barrett urged that wives should adopt, in the words of St Paul, *"the ornament of a meek and quiet spirit"*.

The vicar's sermon in 1938, by contrast, acknowledged the wider public that he addressed:

> *Let us see that Neston is a living entity with a life of its own, and let it be our duty to make the fullest contribution to that life.*

But the clouds of war were gathering. The vicar also referred to air raid precautions and advised that everyone should volunteer for these duties.

Fig. 105 Messing about in boats at Parkgate in the 1930s.

SOURCES

This chapter was written by Geoffrey Place.

A great deal of the information has been derived from newspapers, principally the *Chester Chronicle.*

The analysis of the water from Neston Brewery is in J. Sheridan Muspratt, *Chemistry, theoretical, practical, analytical (part 9)* (1853–61).

The rhyme about "Et, Kit and Nelly" was remembered by Mrs Oxton in a taped interview in Neston Library. For the rhyme about the closure of the Black Bull, see *The Birkenhead Wasp* (1, 5, 30 September 1892) supplied by Ian Boumphrey.

The origins of Neston cricket are mentioned in J. H. Gilling, *50 Years of Neston Cricket* (1947).

Freemasons are recorded in John Armstrong, *The History of Freemasonry in Cheshire* (1901) and J. D. Dale, *The Dee Lodge No. 1576* (1976).

Memories of retrieving the artillery shells at Parkgate were recorded by Mrs E. M. Hough in an essay, *"Early Days in my Village"*.

The rules of the Dee Yacht Club in 1843 can be found in the Cheshire Record Office (DDX 24/29). A copy of the programme for the 1914 regatta was provided by J. Pearson.

For the cinema, a good account can be found in P. A. Carson and C. R. Garnett, *The Silver Screen* (1990), but that book was published after our own research, which is indebted to the recollections of Thomas Johnson and Flo Dodd.

Miss Barber provided information about the Guides.

The information about the Easter ceremonies and "lifting" comes from a letter by Arthur Watson in *The Griffin*, magazine of Mostyn House School (September 1899); and see the *Cheshire Sheaf* for April and May 1891.

Harry B. Neilson, *"Auld-Lang-Syne"* (1935), was the source of the quotation about travelling to Neston Races.

Aspects of Ladies' Day and the Neston Female Friendly Society were researched by Susan Chambers.

We acknowledge the help of Norman Cullen in preparing this chapter.

CHAPTER EIGHT

KEEPING IN TOUCH

We tend to think nowadays that before the day of the train and the car, people used to travel on horseback. This is not really true. The majority of people probably never rode a horse, and there are plenty of references to people who were alarmed at the prospect of having to ride a horse or who fell off one. If you were not in a position to ride in a horse-drawn carriage, trap or cart, you walked. The pace of life was accordingly slow.

The railways changed all that. Once you could reach a railway station you could travel far, fast and cheaply. Railways ran to a timetable, and the precise time began to matter as it had never mattered before. The invention of the postage stamp had a similar effect on correspondence. The pace of life quickened to accommodate an emphasis on change. The car and the telephone continued the same process in the twentieth century. By all these means Neston's links with the outside world were forged.

ROADS AND FERRIES

The most direct route to Wales was straight across the Dee estuary. There was a ferry service from the Boat House Inn to Flint in the 1830s, but many people travelled on foot from Wales to Neston market. Bob Craig, a visitor to Parkgate at this time, decided to buy a horse in Holywell after seeing an advertisement in a local paper. He borrowed a horse and rode across the estuary. He wrote

> *But the screaming gulls and whistling curlews were put to flight before I had half crossed the river's bed, by cheerful chatter, laughter and fragments of Welsh airs sung in chorus by a hearty crowd of cockle and mussel gatherers, fishermen and farmers' wives on their way to market on the Cheshire side – men, women (they were the majority) and children, on foot, on ponies and donkeys, and in little carts. At the ford I met a second detachment of Welsh peasantry preparing to cross, by making bundles of shoes and stockings and tucking up petticoats very deftly. Having passed the channel, the wheels and footmarks formed a plain direction for a safe road ... brought me to the centre of Flint without any need of a guide.*

All this shows that crossing the Dee on foot at that time took place regularly. It was still dangerous, though, as the return journey proved. He bought the horse and hired a guide who saw him across the ford of the main channel, and told him to make for Neston windmill. A storm was brewing and thunderheads darkened the sky. He lost his way, and knowing the tide was coming in, galloped furiously in what he hoped was the direction of safety. At last he saw a light which brought him to the shore. It was a cottage window, and peering in he saw two rushlights burning at each end of a young child's coffin. *"I owed my life to death."*

The *Chester Chronicle* for 5 May 1846 reported another incident:

> *On Saturday morning last, as the carriage of the Hon. Mr Mostyn was crossing the estuary of the River Dee from Parkgate to Flint, under the charge of a guide, the horses got into deep water. The coachman somehow or other lost his seat and was carried down the stream, and was drowned. The carriage and horses and the guide were saved.*

The ferry service ran regularly and connected with a coach at Parkgate for those who wished to travel to Liverpool. In 1843 Matthew Coates had the following advertisement in the Birkenhead Directory:

> *The North Wales Ferry boat house Parkgate. Boats to Flint, Bagillt and the opposite shores of Wales and for marine excursions always ready at the Ferry House with able and experienced crews.*

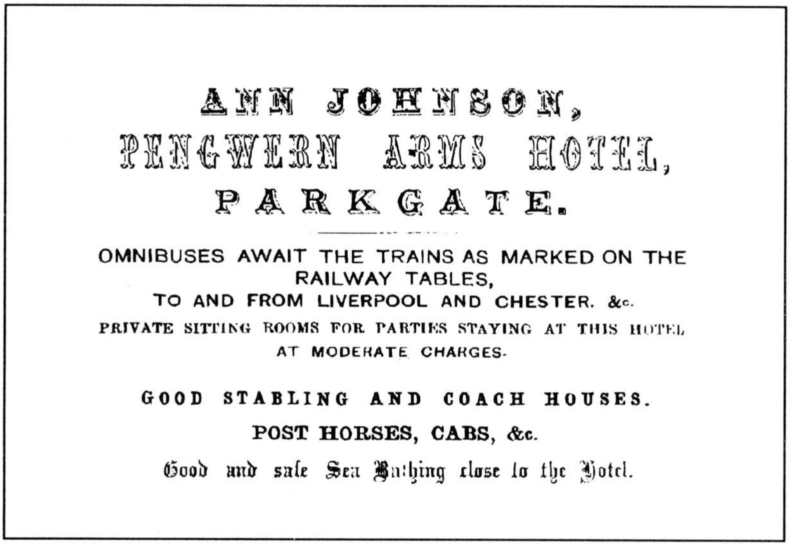
ANN JOHNSON,
PENGWERN ARMS HOTEL,
PARKGATE.

OMNIBUSES AWAIT THE TRAINS AS MARKED ON THE RAILWAY TABLES,
TO AND FROM LIVERPOOL AND CHESTER, &c.
PRIVATE SITTING ROOMS FOR PARTIES STAYING AT THIS HOTEL AT MODERATE CHARGES.

GOOD STABLING AND COACH HOUSES.
POST HORSES, CABS, &c.
Good and safe Sea Bathing close to the Hotel.

Fig. 106 Mrs Ann Johnson was the landlady of the Pengwern Arms, Parkgate, from 1864 until *c.*1872. The inn was severely damaged by a storm in October 1881, and closed, before being demolished a few years later.

Other evidence from a timetable of 1847 states that the ferry sailed from Parkgate once every day and left Bagillt on the return journey about two hours later. Departures from Parkgate varied from 5 a.m. to 5.30 p.m., according to the state of the tide. Sale particulars of 1849 refer to the Pengwern Arms as *"that old-established inn and Ferry House"*. When the Chester–Birkenhead railway opened in 1840, the coaches for Liverpool ran to Hooton station rather than to Tranmere.

The last year in which the directories mention the ferry is in 1860. Joseph Railton owned the ferry boats and Thomas Johnson owned the inn and the omnibus *"which leaves the Boat House twice a day during the summer season for Hooton station"*. On 20 May 1864 Thomas Johnson and his brother Joseph took three men who were carrying out a survey of the Dee in a ferry boat. They were becalmed and when they were able to return at 10 p.m. there was a heavy swell. After waiting an hour they tried to land in a punt, which capsized. Joseph drowned and his body was washed ashore at Heswall. Thomas managed to get ashore but died from exhaustion. That was the end of the ferry, and the inn was demolished in the mid-1880s. The Boathouse Café was built on the site in 1926.

The coach services referred to above relied on a good road system. Tradition, reinforced by an Act of 1555, required that roads should be maintained by the people living locally. Justices of the Peace had to supervise maintenance, using unpaid compulsory labour. The work was unpopular and few people had the relevant skills. However, the system worked to some extent while demands on the road network were limited. When trade grew in the seventeenth century, and with the onset of the Industrial Revolution in the eighteenth century, this system was inadequate, and a solution was found in turnpikes. Travellers were charged a toll which provided funds to maintain and improve the roads. Road engineers such as Telford and McAdam showed how road surfaces could be improved if the funds were available. Trustees had to obtain an Act of Parliament to charge the tolls and to set up toll gates. The first turnpike for Wirral was set up by Act of Parliament in 1787, which empowered trustees for

> *amending and widening the roads from the City of Chester ... to the Assembly rooms in Parkgate ... and from Great Neston to the Woodside Ferry.*

Another Turnpike Act was passed in 1826. The book of reference to the map of the route refers to

> *the present Turnpike Road between the City of Chester and Parkgate in the county of Chester at or near a certain dwelling house known by the name or sign of the Shrewsbury Arms and now in the occupation of John Robinson*

situate at a place called Hinderton in the township of Little Neston ... by way of Upton to the township of Hoose [Hoylake] *in the same county.*

The two trusts were merged in 1833. On the road from Chester to Parkgate there were two toll bars, at Woodbank and Badger's Rake. The accounts of the trust give a guide to the traffic levels in different parts of Wirral. A study by Geoff Dodd states the very much higher toll gate rents (these were farmed out by the trust) at Moston and Hooton, averaging £600 a year in the 1830s, compared with about £100 and £20 at Woodbank and Badger's Rake respectively, which is evidence of the light traffic along the Parkgate Road. Bates's Directory of Stage Coaches stated for 1836 that the stage coach for Chester to Parkgate was one return journey on Wednesdays and Saturdays only, with twelve seats. This compared with three return journeys daily between Chester and Birkenhead with 39 seats. Coach travel was very expensive. In 1846 the return coach fare from Parkgate to Chester was 2s. inside and 1s. 6d. outside.

The surfaces of these turnpiked roads were well maintained. Henry Aspinall, in his publication *Coaching Memories,* stated the roads were in perfect condition, as every loose stone was picked up. The turnpike trusts had men stationed at the turnpikes, each responsible for a certain section of the roads being kept in perfect order. These roads did not have a tarred surface, as originally a macadamized road was one made of small stones which were compacted together by traffic to form a natural cement. In contrast to the turnpikes, Ormerod in 1819 described other roads which

are proportionally bad ... cattle driven along the lanes which are seldom composed of any material other than the natural clay or soft red sandstone.

In 1888 the newly formed county councils took charge of the main roads, and in 1894 secondary roads were handed over to the urban and rural district councils.

Before the councils were established, the 1862 Highways Act had made provision for Highways Boards to be set up, although towns with a Local Board of Health were exempt. The desirability of returning Neston's roads to local control was one of the reasons advanced for forming Neston's Local Board in 1867. The Highways Board for the Hundred of Wirral reported on the state of the roads in 1863: two problems in Neston were the theft of road materials, and a nuisance in Snig Lane (now Brook Street) caused by Thomas Lloyd's tanyard.

The Highways Board took over responsibility for local pounds, which were pens to hold stray animals. To recover an animal which had been impounded, the owner had to pay 1s. 6d. for a horse, 1s. for an ass, 6d. for a pig. There was trouble in Little Neston in 1865, when the "pinner" was charged with stealing an ass. The pound in Little Neston was by the Green in front of White House Farm. The Neston pound was originally in Raby Road, but was moved in 1867 to Cross Street.

The Neston Local Board was in dispute with Lord Talbot's agent in 1890, about stone taken from the quarry at Hinderton for the roads, apparently for the previous twenty years. In the 1890s, stones were being collected from the shore at Parkgate to be broken up for roads: Mrs Cunningham and her young daughter were paid 5s. for a load of five hundredweight. Earlier, stone for roads had been imported from Wales: in 1877 a flat with stone from Penmaenmawr was unloaded at Moorside.

The centre of Neston is built on solid sandstone which in places formed the roadway, as it still does beside the Green in Little Neston. Neston's original market place was on the bare, uneven rock between the old White Horse and the north-west side of the Cross, and the area was known as "On the Rock". The rock surface was lowered, flattened and given a top dressing in 1887, and the same was done in 1900 at the junction of Liverpool Road and Park Street, by the Methodist chapel. The first use of asphalt recorded in the Local Board minutes was in 1881, but roads generally were not tarred until much later. The chief reason for tarring roads was the dust created by motor cars. Even by 1906 the expense of providing water carts to lay the dust on roads was causing worry to Neston Council, which advocated a motor vehicle tax to pay for it. The County Council was similarly alarmed in 1908 at the cost of laying the dust on its entire network of roads. The tarring of roads did not, however, become general until after the First World War.

The Council often widened roads when the opportunity arose. In 1895 it tried to buy the Watch House in order to widen the Parkgate Parade, but fortunately the owner asked more than the Council would pay. New roads were rare. Bushell Road had been made in 1885 with a gift of £400 from Christopher Bushell to provide better access to the station, and in 1902, as already mentioned (Chapter Six), a Manchester property developer, N. A. Earle, laid out Earle Drive in Parkgate in order to sell building plots, but only two houses were built there before the First World War.

The modern safety bicycle greatly increased people's ability to travel. J. K. Starley of Coventry first produced a bicycle where the power was taken to the back wheel by a chain from the pedals, and the development of the pneumatic tyre by Dunlop in 1888 led to a cycling craze in the late 1890s. Cycling clubs were set up all over the country, and the *Chester Chronicle* reported that the Neston and Parkgate Cycling Club organized a parade, including fancy dress, to raise funds for a Parkgate pier. This was an abortive attempt to put a new deck on the old posts of the disused ferry landing stage by the north slip. A new cycling club was formed in 1899, and an expedition to Ellesmere Port was reported the next year. And Neston could boast its very own brand of bicycle, called *The Nestonian*,

Fig. 107 An 1889 calendar advertises William Lawton's wares.

manufactured by William Lawton at his works — a large shed at the corner of Bridge Street and Station Road. Lawton made this bicycle, probably assembled from ready-made parts, between 1888 and 1905. Thomas Chrimes also assembled bicycles at Neston.

And just as cycling became popular in the last years of the nineteenth century, so did walking for pleasure. This interest was marked in 1888 by the formation of the Wirral Footpaths and Open Spaces Preservation Society, which set out to map, mark and keep open the footpaths. The book *Walks in Wirral* was published in 1907. It gave a route to Parkgate from the Woodside ferry to Prenton by tram, thence to Storeton, Brimstage, New Hall, Boathouse Lane and Wood Lane to Parkgate. Later ramblers' books gave other walks, including Neston and Parkgate, sometimes linked with bus or train journeys. The heyday of walking for pleasure was probably the 1930s.

The development of the motor car in England was hampered by the law which required any horseless carriage to be preceded by a man with a red flag. The purpose of the law was to protect the droves of sheep and cattle and to prevent horses from bolting. The law was repealed in 1896, and a speed limit of 12 m.p.h. was imposed on "light locomotives". The 1903 Motor Car Act raised the limit to 20 m.p.h. and introduced car registration and drivers' licences. In prosecutions, driving at more than 20 m.p.h. was known as "scorching".

In 1904 there were six cars and six motor cycles registered in the Neston Urban District area. Examples were the Neston and Parkgate Hygienic Laundry, with a 10 h.p. Wolseley van in chocolate and yellow, and Dr Lewis Grant's 8 h.p. de Dion Bouton in dark green. For the county of Cheshire the number of licensed vehicles rose from 4,297 in 1910–11 to 124,857 in 1940–1.

The papers began to report road accidents. For example, in March 1906 the *Echo* reported that Mr A. G. Grenfell and Mr Hodgson were travelling in a motor car along the Chester and Parkgate road when a pin came out of the steering gear, causing the driver to lose all control of the car, which was wrecked against a telegraph pole. The occupants were flung out but escaped without injury.

As cars became more common, services for them were developed. The first licence in Neston to keep petrol was granted to A. D. Prentice, the ironmonger in High Street, in 1905. In the 1914 Directory, Edward Chrimes, a cycle dealer in 1910, had a motor garage in Brook Street. The same directory refers to G. W. Bridson with the Neston and District Motor and Taxi Car Garage.

Fig. 108 A car outside Chicken Corner Farm, Raby. It is thought to be a Delahaye, built *c.*1905.

George Tilley, who has already (Chapter Three) described some of his early experiences, drove a blue Dodge baker's van for Evans of Liverpool Road, between 1926 and 1935. He remembers how he learnt to drive and what road conditions were like.

> **I worked in Neston station yard as a coal agent for Wirral Colliery. The company bought some Austin wagons and I learnt on those. I asked how the gears worked and was told to think of them as a letter H with neutral in the centre. "Before you change gear you put in the clutch which is on the left side of the pedals. Be careful of the accelerator", which in those days was the middle pedal. I backed wagons up to the weighbridge, which was a tight fit. I could drive and there was no test, and I went to the bakehouse with no trouble at all. Driving was easy as only the odd toff had a car. The bakery had three rounds with a van for each.**
>
> **One round was Neston, Little Neston, Ness, Willaston and Hooton, with deliveries mainly to houses. You had to watch out for cyclists and keep six feet away from them. The petrol for the van could be bought from a garage down Chester Road run by George Hill. There**

was also Leeman's at Parkgate, and Mealors' had a pump in Ness. Petrol was 1s. 4d. a gallon and Benzol was 1s. 5d., which was what we bought as it gave more miles per gallon.

Fig. 109 E. G. Davis's garage along the Chester High Road, opposite Boathouse Lane, *c.*1910. The site is now occupied by Leighton Motors.

Neston roads were very quiet in the nineteenth century, but there were a few automotive vehicles about. The Bridson family had steam engines from 1870 to 1967.

The founder of the business was Robert Bridson, who started with threshing machines in 1870. His son, George Weir Bridson, worked on steam engines in gold mines in South Africa, returned to England and then took over the business from his father about 1898. He died in 1932 and was succeeded by his son Thomas Bridson, who sold the business in 1967.

Robert Bridson not only had threshing machines but also steam ploughing engines. These were traction engines which were driven to the opposite sides of a field, and a plough attached to a wire rope was pulled between them. The company branched out into other work, particularly in North Wales, where it hauled lead from the Halkyn mine to Greenfield station.

The traction engines (or, more accurately, steam road locomotives) were also used to pull furniture vans.

Business expanded, and between 1908 and 1919 the company had ten engines – a combination of Marshall, Aveling, Burrell and Fowler machines. Only three remained at the end of 1919, though the Fowler engine had been purchased new during the year. The slump in the 1920s led to diversification into tar spraying, for which the company had contracts with Cheshire County Council.

Fig. 110 A Fowler 1919 steam road locomotive, owned by Robert Bridson and Son, Neston.

George Bridson, the great-grandson of the founder, recalled that an engine driver had to start work at 5 a.m. to get steam up ready to move off one and a half to two hours later. The engine could travel at about 10 m.p.h., and before 1914 to get to Wales they had to go via Chester, as the Queensferry bridge was not strong enough. The spraying outfit consisted of a traction engine pulling two tar tanks and a living van. The steamroller pulled two gritting machines and a living van. The foreman, engine drivers and second men came from Neston and lived in the vans during the week. They returned home at weekends. Other labour was recruited in the area they worked.

Tar spraying was a summer activity, and the outfit returned to Neston at the end of August. The Burrell was used as a threshing machine during the winter. It was converted to this role by changing the back rubber-tyred wheels for cross-bar wheels to give more grip. The company threshed grain for farmers in a radius of about ten miles. After 1925 there was only one set of threshing equipment operated by Bridson's. Its local competitor was Charles Gray, who had a business based at the mill in Leighton Road, and he had more sets of machines.

Bridson's also undertook engineering work in its premises at Neston, such as replating bin wagons and servicing steam road rollers. During the Second World War it undertook heavy haulage as well.

BUS SERVICES

Crosville has been the principal operator of bus services over the years in the Neston area. The company was incorporated in May 1906 as a motor manufacturer and engineering business. It was the idea of George Crosland Taylor, who had made a name for himself in electrical engineering (see Chapter Three). His associate was Georges Ville, a French motor engineer. The name Crosville is a combination of their surnames. The company intended to build cars to Ville's design at Crane Wharf, Chester. Between 1908 and 1911 five cars were assembled, all of different designs. The company also undertook general engineering work, and in 1911 it acquired a charabanc and started a bus service between Chester and Ellesmere Port.

A second bus operator in the area was John Pye, and in 1916 he ran a motor vehicle (probably a lorry with removable seats) from Heswall to a munitions factory in Queensferry. Soon after the First World War, subsidized by his uncle, he started to run a bus service from Heswall to Birkenhead. A factor in this development was a long railway strike at the time. He also started another service, which ran from Parkgate via Neston and Thornton Hough to Birkenhead. These services did not go to Woodside, but only to the outskirts of Birkenhead, as the Corporation wanted to protect its own tram services from bus competition.

At this time Crosville was expanding its services into Wirral. In 1921 the Chester–West Kirby via Puddington service was started. A timetable dated 1 June 1922 shows two services — Chester–Meols, via Puddington, Burton, Ness, Neston, Parkgate, Boathouse Lane, Heswall, etc.; and

Chester–Meols, via Shrewsbury Arms, Neston, Parkgate, Neston, Thornton Lane Ends, Heswall, etc. Both services had two trips each way each day.

Crosland Taylor explained how new routes were started:

> *First of all we travelled over it by car and decided the places of the fare stages and their mileage. Then we worked out the timetable and fare table for one bus, say three or four trips on a weekday and a late one on Saturdays, allowing for time for meals by the crew. Handbills were printed announcing the date of starting and details of the services. These were distributed to every house within half a mile of the route.*

Crosville was seeking to develop its services, and Crosland Taylor's view of its decisive move, about November 1923, was as follows:

> *I was having lunch with Claude* [his brother] *at Crane house on a Thursday as usual when he said "Johnny Pye's in the market". This news was electrifying. For a long time we had looked on his main service from Heswall to Birkenhead with some envy. There it was – bang in the middle of the place where the money came from – and Johnny Pye himself – what a character! – not to speak of the invisible uncle who backed him financially and was pressing him to sell. "How do you know?" I asked. Claude winked an eye, "Never mind about that," he said, "The point is the terms."*

After a long discussion about the terms, a board meeting of Crosville's was called, and Crosland Taylor continued:

> *The price was to be £25,000 including £7,500 in shares. Date of taking over to be 1st January 1924. I went down there and stayed at the Victoria Hotel in Heswall to get the bus and duty schedules in some sort of order ... and still more difficult to make the old buses run, but the route was good and more than worth the money – even then.*

Jack Barlow recalled that

> *his fourteen buses were kept for a short while by Crosville, but being a mixture of makes and non-standard they were replaced within a year by Crosville vehicles. All had solid tyres and a nominal legal maximum speed of 12 m.p.h. They were known to exceed this! I remember journeys on such vehicles on very poor road surfaces were distinctly bumpy!*

Crosville continued the Parkgate–Prenton route, and added an extra summer service between the same places via Clatterbridge, Raby village, Willaston and Burton. But this was not a great success, and the extra service was abandoned in September 1926. The Parkgate–Prenton service was diverted to Woodside following an agreement with Birkenhead Corporation in October 1930. In 1924 the 8.30 a.m. bus from Parkgate was due to arrive at Prenton Road tram terminus at 9.10. The fare was 1s.

The growth of bus services led to more traffic on the roads of Neston, and the local council wrote to Crosville in November 1928. It asked if drivers could be instructed to proceed slowly through Neston and down to the front, thereby setting a salutary example to other motorists. The reply from Crosville said the speed of omnibuses would be attended to. However, in the following year there were further complaints about the speed of buses.

In 1928, the Railway (Road Powers) Act gave the big four railway companies powers to operate their own bus services. The London Midland and Scottish Railway made an outright bid for Crosville, which was accepted in May 1929. Crosville buses were originally painted grey with red lettering. After the takeover they were painted maroon, in the same style as the LMS railway carriages.

RAILWAYS

Neston was influenced by railway development before it was connected to the national system. The Chester and Birkenhead Railway was opened in September 1840, and coaches ran from Parkgate and Neston to the nearest station at Hooton.

Fig. 111 Neston (South) Station, *c.*1900. No doubt the ploughs on the platform are from Mealors' works at Ness.

In the mid-1840s many schemes for railways all over the country were proposed. The period 1844–47 is known as that of "the railway mania", which ended in a financial crisis in 1847. Work was interrupted, and many proposed lines were completed later. A sale of land in Parkgate in 1849 refers to a railway which was projected but never built:

A railway is now in course of formation to unite the whole of these estates with Liverpool, Manchester, etc. by joining the Chester and Birkenhead Railway at Spital Station.

In 1852 it was stated that the line was to be called the *"Parkgate, Birkenhead and Chester Junction Railway, now before Parliament"*. The station was shown on the scale plan as being on the south-east corner of Buggen Lane.

Another scheme was the 1847 Parkgate, Chester and Birkenhead Railway, which had

capital of £50,000 in shares of £10 each with power to borrow in mortgage or bond, £20,000 as soon as the whole of the capital is subscribed for and half thereof taken up.

The time limit for compulsory purchase of the land was four years, and five years to complete the work from the passing of the Act. Railways were expensive to build, and the average cost was £40,000 per mile. Therefore the figures quoted in the Parliamentary Bill are not likely to have been the full cost of a five-mile railway.

In 1864 a Mr Everitt, the chairman of the Wrexham, Mold and Connah's Quay Railway, proposed building a railway from Hooton to Mostyn on an embankment across the River Dee. Although this idea failed, owing to Admiralty opposition, permission was given for a line from Hooton to Parkgate. The famous railway contractor, Thomas Brassey, had the contract for the line, with Mackay as agent and Johnson as engineer.

The *Chester Chronicle* reported in June 1866 that William Jones, a navvy, was killed at Little Neston, run over by a wagon while making the new railway. The line was opened on Monday, 1 October 1866, and the next issue of the *Chester Chronicle* reported the event as follows:

Opening of the Parkgate Railway. This new branch line of railway has been constructed by the Birkenhead Joint Railway companies to connect Hooton and Parkgate, and was opened for traffic on Monday. It is a single line of rail and is nearly six miles in length, passing from Hooton on the Birkenhead and Chester railway through the villages of Willaston, Little Neston and Great Neston, terminating at Parkgate. According to the timetable there will be six trains each weekday to and from Parkgate, communicating with Birkenhead and Chester, and three trains each way on Sundays. This new branch line cannot fail to confer immense advantages upon the several districts through which it passes and must greatly develop this portion of the Hundred of Wirral.

Fig. 112 The first passenger train passing under Moorside Bridge following the opening of the Parkgate Railway.

One development linked to the railway was the sinking of a new shaft at Neston Colliery in 1874. A mineral branch line was built from the colliery to join the Hooton–Parkgate line just before Moorside Bridge. Nothing is known of the first locomotive, which was sold in 1882, but the colliery had a Black Hawthorn Company Limited 060 tank engine which was built in 1881 and called *Lord Talbot.* It hauled coal trucks from the colliery to the sidings at Parkgate. Coal was also sent to Lever's at Port Sunlight. A photograph of about 1890 shows two Wirral Colliery Company wagons at the soap works. An estimate of coal traffic in 1926 was about ten wagon loads a day. This was when the mine was in decline, and coal traffic on the railway would have been much greater in earlier years.

In 1882 there were plans to extend the railway from Parkgate, and two routes were proposed by different companies – the London and North Western, and the Seacombe, Hoylake and Deeside line. The former company was successful, and the first pegs for the route were put in a field by Cheltenham Walk (now the Rope Walk) in January 1883. Railway construction required a great deal of labour, and the *Chester Chronicle* on 24 April 1886 referred to some 300-400 working in the vicinity of Neston, and their withdrawal having a serious effect on local trade. The paper also mentioned a missionary, Mr Tyrell, and a Mrs Garrett. She had founded the Christian Excavators' Union, which was a national organization. A room had been set aside for the mission in Parkgate Road. Other activities were available for navvies, as the *Chester Chronicle* for 13 February 1886 reported that a concert had been given by Reginald Haigh. He was thanked for having thrown open his football field to them for football, quoits and many other games.

Navvies in 1838 were referred to as *"the terror of the surrounding country"*, but conditions had improved greatly by 1886. The *Chester Chronicle* said

> *It should be stated in justice to these men, that they have conducted themselves with great decorum during their stay in the vicinity, and it is worthy of note how rarely have the real navvy men had to appear before the magistrates at their monthly sessions ... whenever a delinquent has been obliged to appear in court who has designated himself as a "navvy", nine times out of ten the delinquent has turned out to be a Liverpool, Birkenhead or Chester loafer ...*

However, the influx of so many labourers undoubtedly caused problems in Neston, and not every account was as glowing as that one.

Fig. 113 In 1886, Parkgate's final station, on the Heswall side of Parkgate Road, replaced the original one which had been built on the Neston side twenty years previously. With its stretch of double track, this station was one of the places on the single-track line where trains could pass each other.

The *Chester Chronicle* reported the opening of the extension as follows:

> *The new extension line of railway which has been constructed by the London and North Western and Great Western Railway companies to connect Birkenhead with West Kirby via Hooton was opened for traffic on Monday morning without any kind of formality or demonstration ... At Parkgate a new station has been created at a short distance east of the old station. The new station is large and commodious, there being two platforms, each 340 yards long. On the down side* [to Hooton], *there is a general waiting room, a ladies' waiting room and other conveniences, whilst on the up side there are booking offices and waiting rooms for the Public. The approaches to the station are wide and convenient, and for the safety of passengers there is a subway leading from one platform to the other with a very easy gradient ... The opening of this new line will afford the public an opportunity during the approaching holiday season of visiting the beautiful district which it traverses.*

The route was a single track, with passing places at Willaston, Parkgate, Heswall and Thurstaston. Each was controlled by a section which was based on the stations with passing places. The driver was given a "staff", which had to be handed in to the signalman at the next crossing station. The train could not proceed to the next section until the driver had the staff. A traveller in 1913 refers to this at Hadlow Road:

> *Driver, Stationmaster and Guard, with prodigious silver watch in hand, having leisurely discussed the weather and the haymaking outlook while awaiting "time", we were off again.*

When the line was built there were six trains a day, but by 1937 there were more than three times that number. Some trains had a carriage which was added to the Birkenhead–London train at Hooton. At Hooton you could catch an express train to Brighton and Hastings or Bournemouth and Portsmouth. In 1937, too, First and Third Class from Neston or Parkgate to Liverpool were 2s. 3d. and 1s. 6d. respectively.

Charles Gillett worked as a relief porter on the line in the late 1930s, and he recalled that

> *Neston Station was in Station Road, and there were two clerks and two porters employed. Parkgate had the same number of people, but also a signalman and a stationmaster who was responsible for both. A porter booked on before the first train, the 6.45 from Hooton. He had to light the station gas lamps in the winter and issue the tickets. The first train was a busy one, with usually about one hundred passengers, mainly men going to Cammell Laird's or Shell. The clerk used to come on at 7.20 to book for the next train at 7.35. The 8.06 train had many school children on it. The rolling stock was GWR, four sets pulled by a tank engine. Only the small tank engines could turn round on the turntable at West Kirby.*

The porter had to collect parcels from the trains, and anything perishable had to be delivered immediately. The 10.31 train from Hooton was important as it carried Palethorpe's sausages, and they had to be taken to the shopkeepers. If the sausages did not come on that train, the shopkeepers would not accept them as they would not have time to sell them. There was a two-wheeled handcart to carry them in as well as other local parcels.

The parcels were everything you could think of. Mealors' sent ploughs, but these went goods traffic. There was a pick-up by a large goods train. It went down about 11.30 and back about 1.30. It would shunt at all stations, but at Neston the goods had to be unloaded onto the platform from the vans. Then you put the goods in and a road wagon from Birkenhead would come and deliver them locally. The porter would deliver within a mile of the station, but it was a long way to push a barrow up to the Shrewsbury Arms.

There was still fish trade from Parkgate. Mussels and shrimps, etc. were brought in a lorry, and the porter had to weigh them and help load them into the vans in the siding. They went to Bury, Bolton and Manchester. By the late 1930s the tonnage was falling, and so the fish was loaded on to the passenger trains as parcels traffic. It was seasonal and also depended on the tide how much was loaded.

Reg Chrimes travelled on the train to Calday Grange Grammar School in the late 1930s:

I lived in Gladstone Road and went across Stanney fields to the station [a park is there now]. *It was a well kept, busy station. The trains were GWR rolling stock, with cream and brown carriages. On the journey to West Kirby the girls were in the first carriage and the boys in the last one. Each boy was allocated a seat, and a fifth- or sixth-former was in charge of each compartment. There were boys already on the train, as some came from Ellesmere Port, Bebington and Port Sunlight. Some homework was done on the train and there were some rumbustious goings-on. It depended how conscientious the fifth- or sixth-former was. It was a long walk from Kirby Park to school.*

By the late 1930s the line was beginning to decline, the colliery had closed, and there was competition from cars and buses.

Neston was served, not only by the Hooton–Parkgate–West Kirby railway, but also by the line from Bidston to Wrexham, which still operates.

The Wirral railway from Birkenhead to West Kirby had proposed a line down the middle of the Wirral peninsula to Hawarden Bridge. When it could not raise the necessary capital, two other companies took over — the Manchester, Sheffield and Lincolnshire Railway, and the Wrexham, Mold and Connah's Quay Railway. The operation was called the Wirral Railways Joint Committee, and the first sod was cut by the Prime Minister, William Ewart Gladstone. The railway committee changed its name twice, as the Wrexham, Mold and Connah's Quay Company had financial problems. These led to it selling out its share to the Manchester, Sheffield and Lincolnshire Railway, which later became the Great Central Railway. When the line was opened in 1896 it was called the North Wales and Liverpool Railway. The line was built by Monk and Newell of Bootle, and was fourteen and three-quarter miles from Bidston to Hawarden Bridge.

By this time mechanisation had come to railway building, with steam excavators, known as steam navvies, being used. An old photograph shows them at work near Burton Station. It was opened on 16 March 1896 for goods traffic. Mr Gladstone travelled on the railway on 4 April, and it was opened for passengers on 18 May. The *Chester Chronicle* recorded an account of the first day for passengers in its issue of 23 May 1896:

> *THE NEW RAILWAY ACROSS WIRRAL. The new North Wales and Liverpool Railway was opened for passenger traffic on Monday morning. The first train to travel on the new line was the 7 a.m. from Chester which travelled direct to Seacombe the terminus, where it was timed to arrive at 7.41 a.m. The first train from Liverpool was the 8.10 a.m. for Chester and North Wales. These times, however, it should be stated, are quoted from the timetable, but as the day wore on the service became somewhat irregular. This, however, is not remarkable for the first day, and no doubt before long the times for arrival and departure will be marked by greater punctuality. The new railway was freely patronised during the day and the service will evidently become a highly popular one, placing as it does the people of Wirral as well as Liverpool within easy reach of Chester, Wrexham and North Wales. The carriages, it may be added, are those of the Manchester, Sheffield and Lincolnshire Railway.*
>
> *Our Neston correspondent writes 'a large number of persons from this district availed themselves of the opportunity of having a ride on the line on the opening day. At Neston station there was a display of flags, Mr West, the new stationmaster and his employees, having decorated the station and bridge close by with bunting kindly lent by Mr W. Chambers. In the evening a number of residents in Neston and the immediate vicinity visited the station and patrolled the roomy platform. A good service of trains is provided and there is every reason to assume that a prosperous future is in store for the latest venture of the Manchester, Sheffield and Lincolnshire. It is to be hoped, however, that through communication to the Mersey tunnel will soon be provided. At present the trains run to the Seacombe Ferry.'*

This line did not carry as many passengers in the 1930s as the Hooton–West Kirby line, largely because connections to Liverpool were better from the other line. Eric Gillett, who worked at Heswall Hills in the mid-1930s, remembered that the passenger trains were short, with two coaches, though there were five on a Saturday if necessary. The line ran

LNER cattle specials at night. Ships from Ireland brought the cattle into Birkenhead, and they were taken in trains of 18-20 trucks to York.

After the Second World War, this line received a welcome boost with the construction of the iron ore terminal at Bidston for John Summers. In the 1930s the steelworks had relied on scrap steel, some of which was transported on the Bidston–Shotton works line.

THE POST OFFICE

1840 was a watershed in postal history, when Sir Rowland Hill introduced the prepaid adhesive postage stamp and a uniform charge of one penny for letters up to half an ounce.

Since 1789, letters had been carried on mail coaches, superseding the slower system of postboys on horseback. Charges went by distance: up to eight miles for 2d; but 6d. for twenty miles, and that for a single sheet only. A letter from London could cost several shillings and so was expensive.

The first post office in Neston of which we have any information was run by John Wolstenholme in 1822. The Post Office listed towns by their distance from London, and Neston's mileage mark was 201. Senders would have to hand in their letters at the post office and the recipient would often have to collect them, paying the postage on receipt, although it is known that a letter-carrier might take letters from Neston to Parkgate. In the 1830s the new railway lines began to carry letters, but the following letter shows that in 1838 all was not well with Neston's mail:

> *There is certainly just grounds for complaint, as to the delay, generally speaking, of the mails – there can hardly be any so irregular, as to time, as the Chester and London. I live in Neston, and by the arrangements of the Post Office the mail should be at Sutton by half past five p.m., thence a foot messenger is despatched to this place, but owing to the delay of the mail, the messenger has not been able to leave Sutton before eight or nine o'clock at night during the winter, by which we are prevented having our letters and papers from London till noon the next day, as the delivery of letters takes place here only once a day after the arrival of the messenger at eleven o'clock in the morning with the letter bag from Liverpool and Chester. It is impossible for me to know the cause of the delay but I am told it is owing to bad working of the mail coach and the non-interference of the proper officer, who no doubt has a most liberal salary for his work, and who ought to see that the Chester and London mail coach is better timed than being from two to four hours daily behind time. I did not know till lately that the London letters for Neston come by the railway to Chester at eleven o'clock in the morning; but I am not so unreasonable as to suppose that they can be forwarded before the mail coach*

passes through from London to Woodside, which should be, I am informed, at four o'clock in the afternoon. Instead it is six, seven or eight o'clock.

This letter, signed by "A Nestonian", was printed in the *Chester Chronicle* on 26 January 1838.

The result of the penny postage and distribution by train was a rapid increase in the number of letters posted, from 72 million in 1839 to 208 million in 1841 and to 5,000 million by 1910. (By comparison, the figure for 1992 was 22 thousand million.) The old mileage mark was replaced by a number, and from 1844 Neston's number was 184, which appeared on the cancellation stamp.

The position of the post office in Neston varied according to who the postmaster was, but it was usually at or near the Cross. One of the longest-serving postmasters was George Jackson, from at least 1890 to 1912, after which his wife Ada took over. He built the tower, in bright red Ruabon brick, at the Cross. Parkgate had its own post office in 1850, and in 1890 Little Neston also gained a post office. Its need was described by James Stonehouse, who acted for many years as the Neston correspondent for the *Chester Chronicle*:

The writer of these lines was the cause of a postal service being established at Little Neston.

There had been no delivery of letters to houses in Little Neston, and the letters were left at the Williams family's farm, the buildings of which can still be seen at the corner of Mellock Lane and Talbot Avenue. The letters were placed on the kitchen window ledge and were exposed to the mercy of anyone who chose to take them, turn them over or read their contents. Postcards were especially the object of curiosity. It was with the utmost difficulty that half a dozen signatures were collected for an appeal to the Post Office, but eventually a box was inserted in Maylor's barn. A post office was established at Mealor's the tailor, and he was appointed letter-carrier.

In 1887 the *Birkenhead Advertiser* reported the memories of an old postman, Joseph Woodward. His route was originally Broadlake, Ashfield Hall, Five Lane Ends, Thornton Hough, Raby, Lydiate, Willaston mill and Willaston, twice a day, with about a dozen letters each time.

Neston post office became a telegraph office by 1874 so that telegrams could be sent. Photographs of the Cross show boys loitering round the Bushell fountain: these were often telegraph boys waiting to be sent to deliver a telegram. The parcel post started in 1883.

In 1894 the Post Office rather unwillingly permitted pictures to appear on postcards, the plain version of which had been introduced twenty years earlier. The picture postcard became very popular and is a useful source of information. Local photographers whose work appeared on postcards include Arthur Maycock of Parkgate, Harold Hurst and Vincent Crook.

Postcards, which cost ½d. to send, were often used where now we would use the telephone. By 1914 there were up to five deliveries a day in some places, and orders could be sent to shops by post for goods to be delivered the same day.

THE TELEPHONE

The telephone was invented by Alexander Graham Bell in 1876, and was demonstrated in Philadelphia, USA. Development took place very rapidly, and one of the earliest public telephone services in England was in Liverpool three and a half years later.

In the early 1880s a number of telephone companies were set up in the North West, and these merged with companies in other areas to form the National Telephone Company. This was the company which asked the Local Board in Neston for permission to bring its poles into the town. Permission was granted in 1890, provided that the poles were not placed in front of any house (as far as practicable). Two years later the Local Board asked the telephone company to provide a call office in Neston. In reply the company stated they had not received a single order from Neston and had met with nothing but obstruction. One problem was that the Local Board had suggested ornamental telephone poles. The company argued that these were too expensive, being dearer than standard poles. By the end of 1893 the Local Board agreed to ask the company to erect standard poles in Little Neston, Parkgate and Neston. An exchange was set up at Mrs Youds's premises (next to the Brown Horse) at Neston Cross. This was moved to a building opposite Neston Methodist Church in 1902.

The first directory listing for Neston was produced in 1899, when there were 31 subscribers. By 1906 the number had risen to 64. Analysis of subscribers shows examples of doctors (e.g. Blunden and Yeoman, No. 17); the police, No. 12; companies such as Wirral Colliery, No. 8; the Neston and Parkgate Hygienic Laundry, No. 26; and William Fleming, Builder and Contractor, No. 33. Wealthy people in the area were on the telephone, such as Duncan Graham of the Lydiate, Willaston, No. 1; and A. K. Bulley, Cotton Broker, Ness, No. 35 (this is still part of the Ness Gardens number).

Today we are used to automatic dialling, but the following extract explains the significance of the operator:

> *When you take down the receiver of a telephone, a tiny light glows on the switchboard in front of which an operator sits, in the control office or "exchange". This light is placed under the number of your telephone. The operator sees it, takes up one of a pair of brass plugs connected by means of a*

cord, inside which is an electric wire. She pushes the plug into a little round hole, or "jack", above the little light and says "Number please". When you have given the number, she takes up the companion plug and with it touches the edge of the hole bearing the number you have asked for. If she hears a clicking sound she knows the line is in use and tells you "Line engaged". If no sound is heard, she presses the plug into the hole and presses a button which causes the bell on the telephone to ring. When the person at that end of the wire takes down the receiver you can begin to talk.

In 1879 the Post Office prosecuted telephone companies on the grounds that the telephone was a telegraph under the Acts of 1863 and 1869, and thus infringed the Post Office's monopoly. The Post Office won the case, but the telephone companies were confident of reversing the decision on appeal. Before this was heard a compromise was reached whereby the telephone companies operated under licence from the Post Office. However, after giving six years' notice, the Post Office withdrew the licence in December 1911, and took over the telephone companies by paying compensation.

The period of notice meant that the National Telephone Company had had less incentive to modernize, and a major redevelopment programme was needed. The First World War delayed progress, and in 1922 Neston had only 154 lines. A new exchange was built in Leighton Road and opened in 1926. The exchange equipment was listed as being of the magneto type at the end of September 1930, and of the CB (Central Battery) 10 type by March 1931. It can be assumed that the new exchange took over between these two dates. Central Battery is a manual system, but the exchange provided the power for ringing and transmission. Telephones no longer had a crank (magneto) handle, and subscribers would have simply lifted the receiver and waited for the operator to answer.

The number of telephone calls started to grow rapidly, and a number of proposals were made in the 1920s and 1930s to convert the Liverpool area to automatic working. Plans produced in 1938 envisaged Neston as one of the last areas for automatic exchanges planned for 1942. The Second World War delayed this programme, however, and after 1945 the demand for telephone connections rose very rapidly. Older exchanges were kept in use to add to capacity, and Neston's exchange eventually became automatic in January 1968.

AIRCRAFT

Neston has not had an airfield within its boundaries, but Hooton Park and Sealand are not very far away, and Neston residents would have seen aircraft flying to these places.

Hooton Park airfield is now the site of the Vauxhall car factory in Ellesmere Port. Before the First World War the site was used as a race course. The Government took over the land for Army training, and in 1917 three hangars were built on what had previously been the paddock. The airfield was taken over by 4 Training Depot Station, which moved from Tern Hill on 19 September 1917 with a collection of Sopwith Scouts and Dolphins. In January 1918 there were 37 aircraft based there, with others temporarily there at the aircraft repair centre. After the end of the War the airfield was unused until 1927, when a local businessman acquired the land with the aim of turning it into a major airport. In 1930 it was designated the official airport for Liverpool, and commercial services were run until 1933, when it was replaced by Speke.

Sealand airfield was started by an engineer, T. Murray Dutton, who started a flying school and built his own aircraft in 1916. His airfield was close to the river. The following year the aerodrome was inspected by officers of the Royal Flying Corps, who later decided to take it over. RFC inspection led to the development of two airfields sited side by side, divided by the roadway. The area to the north of the road was called Shotwick, and this became a training station. Aircraft based there included Sopwith Pups, Camels and Dolphins, and Avro 504s. The second site at Queensferry was planned as an acceptance park for American aircraft, but had not been completed by the time the War ended.

Before Neston residents saw aircraft flying to and from Hooton and Sealand, they had had the chance to see planes which landed at Parkgate. On 16 July 1912, a Mr King flew from New Brighton to show his plane to the boys of Mostyn House School. He landed on the sand, but had to delay his take-off by one hour to let the sand dry.

Henri Salmet was an aircraft mechanic at the Bleriot works in Hendon. In 1911 he learned to fly, and in the following years he undertook flying tours for the *Daily Mail.* On 8 July 1914 his Bleriot monoplane arrived, by lorry, at Parkgate in Parks Field. He was there for three days, and on the first one he took his host, A. G. Grenfell, the headmaster of Mostyn House, for a flight. Grenfell is said to have thrown a bottle of champagne out of the plane, to the danger of Territorials camped below in Parks Field, during their summer camp. Salmet made two other flights on 8 July. On the 9th he had nineteen flights, but engine trouble limited his activity on the 10th. His engine was an 80 h.p. seven-cylinder Gnome, and he had to seek help from the mechanic at Mostyn House, named Ellis, who normally ran the school's electric light plant.

Other aircraft known to have landed on the Parkgate sands included G-EBIU, — an Avro 548A, a three-seater biplane registered in October 1934, and owned by Williams and Company of Blackpool until 1939.

Fig. 114 Henri Salmet and his youngest passenger in front of his Bleriot monoplane, at Parkgate in 1914.

Fig. 115 This Avro 548A biplane attracts interest on the sands at Parkgate, *c.*1934.

SOURCES

Most of this chapter was written by Edward Hilditch.

In the section on Roads and Ferries, the description of crossing the Dee estuary comes from a book, ostensibly fiction but clearly based on observation, by Samuel Sidney, *Gallops and Gossips in the Bush of Australia*, (1854). For turnpikes, see Geoff Dodd, *The Turnpikes of Wirral*, in *Journal of the North West Society of Industrial and Archaeological History* (1977). Some Wirral Turnpike accounts are in the Cheshire Record Office (QDT), and see A. Bates, *Directory of Stage Coach Services* (1836). Henry Aspinall discussed coach travel in *Birkenhead and its Environs* (1903). Susan Chambers analysed the Highways Board records. Jim Clarke provided information about walkers, and Charles Swanborough about the Nestonian bicycle. Early car licences are discussed by R. C. A. Chesterman in *Laughter in the House* (1978), and the Motor Vehicle Register is in the Cheshire Record Office. We are grateful for the memories of George Tilley and the Bridson family.

For Bus Services we are grateful for help from Jack Barlow and T. B. Maund, and have quoted from W. J. Crosland-Taylor, *Crosville, the Sowing and the Harvest* (1948).

For Railways, see Charles Walker, *Thomas Brassey, Railway Builder* (1968), and the Merseyside Railway History Group, *Hooton and West Kirby Branch Line and the Wirral Way* (1982). We are grateful to Charles Gillett, Eric Gillett and Reg Chrimes for their memories.

For the Post Office we are grateful for Geoff Topp's help, and see *The Post Office and its Story*, by Edward Bennett (1912).

For Telephones we are grateful to Stan Roberts for his personal help and for his book, *Telephone Service in the Liverpool Telephone Area* (1981). Our thanks also go to the British Telecommunications Museum and its archives, Queen Victoria Street, London.

The section on Aircraft was compiled by Bryan Heatley.

CHAPTER NINE

WARS AND CHANGE

Although the First World War changed the face of England in so many ways, it was the Second World War and its aftermath that radically changed Neston. Between the wars, the insularity of the Neston area, and indeed the insularity of the smaller areas that made up the parish, was still evident, but was being eroded by the radio, the cinema and the motor car. The main sources of employment were changing too, most obviously with the end of the colliery, which was run down after 1924 and closed in 1928. And the tide began to desert Parkgate in the 1930s, so that the fishing industry could not revive after the Second World War.

The most telling effect on Neston of the First World War was the loss of 91 of its men, who were killed. The wounded were in evidence, in their bright blue uniforms and red ties, at the two military hospitals set up by the Red Cross at the Institute in Neston and the convalescent home in Parkgate. The first patients received at Parkgate in October 1914 were twelve Belgian soldiers, and the hospital admitted 897 patients before it closed in February 1919. During those years, the weapons of war were also evident, for a munitions factory was set up by W. E. Whineray in some huts in the garden of his house, Leighton Court. Some people went by bus to Queensferry to work at a munitions factory there.

A recruiting office was opened at the town hall in November 1915, the year before compulsory conscription was started. Workers in occupations deemed essential to war industries and food production, known as "reserved occupations", were not called up, and George Tilley remembers that several men with businesses locally managed to avoid conscription by claiming to work on the farms of relatives in Little Neston and Ness. Shortly after the war ended, there was a Victory Ball at the town hall, and some of those who had avoided military service, perhaps four or five men, were active in organising it. By this time many soldiers had returned home still wearing their khaki, since they were not given civilian clothes as they would be in 1945. Tom Smith of Little Neston, who had been a sergeant, gathered all the ex-servicemen in uniform and had them lined up at attention outside the town hall on either side of the High Street. Then a group went into the hall and dragged out those who had avoided conscription. They were kicked down the town hall steps and had to run down the High Street like scared rabbits. Behind the ranks of soldiers were groups of women, who jeered and shouted insults. All this was very embarrassing for the victims and their businesses.

Fig. 116 "The owner (pretending to work)": W. E. Whineray at one of the lathes in his munitions factory at Leighton Court.

One of the striking differences between post-1918 Neston and the decades before the First World War was the decline in the influence of the wealthy families. The Bushells of Hinderton, and the Grahams of Willaston, had exercised an almost seigneurial sway that was not matched in the 1920s and 1930s. The role of the public-spirited but paternalistic, wealthy individual was replaced by the committee. The spirit of concern for the welfare of one's fellow Nestonians was to be embodied in the Council of Social Service (CSS).

In the early 1920s a group of Neston residents organized a social welfare committee, with the aim of improving social conditions in the town. The first recorded meeting was held in December 1924, with Hugh Gamon, solicitor, as chairman, and James Hacking, teacher at Neston Council School in Burton Road, as honorary secretary, and a committee that included three local clergymen.

Much of the time in these early months was spent discussing employment opportunities for various young men. They also tried to deal with unrest at the colliery, giving the men the opportunity to air their views, but to no avail. Another concern of the committee was finding land for a children's playground in the town.

In October 1926 the members established a Council of Social Service and Unemployment Relief — a Charities Trust Fund — to be funded by public subscription. Committee members included well-known local residents such as William Jackson of Leighton Court, Mrs Bulley from Ness, Lionel Barber and John Larden Williams. At various times their committees included a clothing committee which supplied second-hand clothes and footwear to the poor for a nominal amount, and an emigration committee which was funded by Sir Percy Bates of Hinderton Hall, chairman of the Cunard Company, to assist people wishing to emigrate to the colonies. There were also a savings association, allotments, playing fields, and amenities committees.

The Council of Social Service wished to channel all local charitable needs and donations through its auspices, as it felt that much charity was directed inappropriately. It stated that it wished to serve, support and handle the funds of existing agencies. The Wirral Colliery Relief Fund handed over its management to the CSS, as did the Horticultural Society. The Flower Show was resurrected, and developed within a few years into a big Neston Show, with horses and cattle in addition to the rabbit, pigeon, flower and vegetable sections.

The Council of Social Service was most active in the 1930s. The aid committee discussed needy cases to which it could offer financial help and advice. Nicholls's Dairy provided free milk in cases of sickness or distress. Pupils with grammar school scholarships were helped with the extra cost of sports clothing and books.

There was an occupational centre off Burton Road, now a builder's yard in West Vale. As the Unemployed Work Centre, it consisted of a joiner's workshop on the ground floor, with a boot repair shop on the first floor. It provided materials at reduced prices for making and repairing furniture, garden equipment and beehives.

Gymnastic classes were held in the Institute, using apparatus bought from the old Congregational church, which was on the site of the present British Legion building.

The Council of Social Service was also the body responsible for establishing the Neston and Parkgate Housing Society in 1927. The activities of this society, which is still active in providing housing today, have already been described in Chapter Six.

Neston & District Council of Social Service.

THE LIBRARY,
PARKGATE ROAD,
NESTON,
March, 1927

Dear Sir (or Madam),

You are asked to consider the claims of the Neston Council of Social Service and, if you are in sympathy with its objects, to become a Member and Subscriber.

As its name denotes, the Neston and District Council of Social Service is an Association of those who are devoting themselves to the interest of the Community irrespective of creed or politics. With this main object in view it seeks:—

(1) To work in close touch with public departments, religious and Social authorities and Societies, and persons engaged in Social work, to endeavour to secure co-operation, and to prevent overlapping.

(2) To promote personal service.

(3) To investigate individual cases of hardship and to give assistance and advice in proper cases.

(4) To assist young people in the organization of their work and play and to provide playing fields.

(5) To assist those desirous of emigrating.

Although the Council has only been formed a short time it has not been inactive. The Juvenile Organization Committee has already secured two playing fields, one lent by a member for a football ground for the Boy Scouts, Boys' Brigade and Wolf Cubs and another rented as a general playing ground for young children up to the age of 14 years, this latter ground is being fenced and equipped with shelters, seats, goal posts, &c. the gift of a member of the Council.

A Play Centre is being formed for small children under experienced supervision.

Several Lectures for boys and girls upon interesting and instructive topics have been arranged.

Efforts are being made to obtain suitable employment for boys and girls and the question of emigration is being thoroughly gone into.

Through the generosity of a member of the Community a fund of £50 per annum has been put at the service of the Committee to assist emigration within the Empire.

A Gymnasium class and dramatic entertainments are projected.

The endeavour of this Committee is to draw more boys and girls into the various Clubs and Organizations which are proving of such great value in developing character and citizenship.

Fig. 117 Six months after its foundation, the Council of Social Service lays out its objectives and solicits subscriptions from the people of Neston.

NESTON UNEMPLOYMENT COMMITTEE.

CULTIVATE AN ALLOTMENT.
GROW YOUR OWN FOOD.

The Committee will provide further allotments rent free to unemployed and supply seeds, tools, fertilizer, etc. at about half prices.

Make your own own garden frames, seats and sheds at the occupation centre in Burton Road.

Tools and benches free.

Materials at cost price.

Particulars from
A. TILLY
A. BOOTH
or
J. HACKING, Hon. Secretary

Fig. 118 People were encouraged to cultivate allotments. Three allotment sites were run by the CSS, on one of which trees and shrubs were grown and sold cheaply. Some of them were used by the district improvement committee to improve areas of the town, such as the railway embankment.

The activities of the CSS were curtailed to a great extent by the outbreak of war in 1939, but it organized a Citizens' Advice Bureau and a branch of the Soldiers', Sailors' and Airmen's Families Association, both of which served Neston people throughout the war years.

Before the Second World War, the different parts of Neston were separated by fields, and were conscious of a separate identity. Doreen Chrimes, who came to live in Mayfield Gardens as a child in 1937, knew nothing of Little Neston or anywhere beyond the railway bridge in Burton Road, because she never went there. She felt an outsider at first, among people who spoke with a distinctive accent, because few strangers came to Neston. Her future husband, Reg, who lived in Gladstone Road, first remembers going to Little Neston in his teens, to play cricket. Some who lived in Little Neston considered their weekly walk into Neston to shop to be quite an expedition. These local differences were evident at the annual church fête on Comrades Field. As well as maypole dancing, there were races between the local schools, contested with intense rivalry and displaying an almost "death or glory" attitude.

The 1930s seem to have been years of little change in Neston, and the great changes came after the War, and particularly in the 1960s. That is why this book has concentrated on the hundred years between 1840 and 1940. However, a brief look at the years after 1940 may explain what these changes were going to be.

The Second World War made much more impact on the town than the First had done, because the bombing of Liverpool made the danger immediate. Several local buildings had their cellars strengthened with massive wooden beams for use as public air raid shelters. One of these was Balcony House in Parkgate, where the beams are still in place today. The headmaster of Mostyn House School had the foresight to sell Parkgate's open-air swimming bath in March 1939, and to build with the proceeds a huge air raid shelter in which all his pupils could sleep in bunks, as they did during the blitz of Liverpool.

The undulating wail of the siren (one on top of Mostyn House, another on the police station in Neston, and others elsewhere) gave warning of enemy planes. A few stray bombs fell harmlessly in the neighbourhood, and the local schools opened their doors late, marking their registers at 10 a.m., if the previous night had been disturbed by an air raid. The authorities feared that the enemy might land airborne troops on the Dee estuary, and there were defences at Parkgate and the Old Quay. But only one German airman baled out on this side of the estuary, and he was arrested, as he walked ashore, by Cyril Cambridge, the optician. There are 61 names on Neston's war memorial for the Second World War.

The first of the great changes which came after 1945 was the advent of the Welfare State. Despite its many advantages, it also had the effect of dismantling the sense of private social responsibility which had led the "gentry" to look after their neighbours before 1914, and which had inspired the Council of Social Service between the wars. Although the CSS survived for another 45 years, most of its *raison d'être* had gone.

Similarly, the benefits of the National Health Service also led to the closure of Neston's cottage hospital in 1964. Ten years later, in 1974, Neston lost the control of its own affairs when the borough council was merged with that of Ellesmere Port. However, these various losses of local identity were balanced by the opening of Neston County High School, at first as a secondary modern school, in 1959. One effect of secondary education in Neston was to break down the barriers between the local districts.

We have seen that the old jobs had gone. In 1920 the principal employment in Neston had been at the colliery, in the building trades and in fishing, with agriculture in the outlying villages. In the 1960s, by contrast, there was employment at Morgan Refractories in Liverpool Road and Leeman's Printers in Leighton Road, with an ever-growing number of commuters who worked outside the immediate area. A rapid increase in housing, off Liverpool Road for example, and in the West Vale area of Little Neston, brought in so many new residents that they began to outnumber the natives. Buildings filled the spaces between districts, and Neston's sense of being different had diminished.

One theme that has run through much of the hundred years of this survey is the desire to clean up Neston by improving the plumbing. This too was not achieved until the 1950s. All the people concerned about Neston's health and welfare in the nineteenth century, from Christopher Bushell and the Rev. R. W. Gleadowe, to the Local Board of Health and the Urban District Council, had striven since the 1860s to provide running water and good drains. But the improvements were slow to reach every house. There are still people who remember the earth privies with their open middens, and the fearful, smelly job that it was for the night-soil men, when they shovelled out the contents and sprinkled everything with chloride of lime. By 1945 nobody wanted the job of emptying middens. Andrew Prince, who was Public Health Officer for Neston, recalls that the last houses to be built without bathrooms were at Cottage Close in 1914, and the last houses with privy middens were in New Street, Little Neston. But it was not until 1949 that grants became available to equip every house with an indoor WC, a hot water system and a bathroom.

The final decade of our survey was experienced as a child by David Scott. The book ends with his lyrical account of his childhood memories.

Childhood memories are all I can recall from my birth in 1930 to our closing date in 1940. We have heard that the local industries were declining, and only the building trade seemed to be one of the few steady occupations. Many a local field was sold as building land, as pre-War development was slowly taking shape: West Vale, Leighton Road, Parkgate Road, and fields at Little Neston and on the road to that old-world gem, Burton, now grew bricks and mortar instead of crops. There was a little employment in service to what was left of the local gentry, but times were changing more rapidly than people were aware. Those who could afford it employed their own chauffeurs for that modern wonder, the motor car, and one-time coachmen and gardeners became chauffeur-gardeners. I remember several gardeners at the larger houses donning peaked-cap livery between pruning the roses to run the lady of the house to the latest garden party, or Sir to his board meeting, although many used the convenient train from Neston to Woodside, and paced the deck of the ferry boat morning and evening, to and from the city.

The whole area in the 1930s was slowly but surely changing, if not already changed, into the irreversible dormitory town for the city gent. He was not quite the same type or calibre as the one-time landed gentlemen of the district, but definitely the new city gent, while the rank and file of the populace had to follow suit. The city was where the new work was, and new staff were needed, from manager to office boy, from manageress to typist and shopgirl. In my childhood days the sons and daughters of fishermen, farm workers, ex-miners, cooks, and parlourmaids saw no future in their parents' occupations. To town they went on trains and crowded buses each day. A few — the brightest — studied for a profession, so lifting themselves far above their rural forebears. "The old order changeth, giving way to new."

In my young life I witnessed a strange mixture of the last remnants of the old country ways of working and thinking, mingled with the 1930s' surge into the embryo modern age. Yet no-one could then foresee the tremendous strides in technology, medical science and every possible angle of human endeavour, the outcome of the shadow of war looming on the horizon. At that moment in the mid-'30s, we still basked in the euphoric sunshine of a strangely changing system, not quite old-fashioned, yet not quite new. I clearly remember three carthorses pulling the self-binder at harvest time in the field opposite my home. Busy hands placed the sheaves into stooks in neat, straight rows. Rabbits and a covey of partridge broke cover at the last few cuts, local lads with shotguns waiting in glee. By contrast, a twin-

engined Dragon Rapide biplane droned across the evening sky, the latest method of taking mail to Ireland.

I remember walks down the Old Quay fields, as locals called them, to the site of the empty Old Quay House, silent, ghostly, steeped in its own secrets, that time alone possessed; and the old bell swinging high on its east gable, mysteriously missing on a subsequent visit. I remember being lifted up to see a huge brown bull tethered in the ramshackle barn, and feeling glad to be outside. When near the waterworks in Lees Lane I was often lifted up to see the great beam engine through the window, the big wheel half above, half below the concrete floor, slowly turning and chugging, polished, gleaming, with Harold Prince, the water engineer, in attendance to keep the works going smoothly.

Carefree schooldays seemed endless. I liked all subjects except maths, and am still of the same mind! The 24th May was Empire Day. Mr A. J. Exton, the headmaster, always saw to it that the day was marked in proper manner, with the whole school marching round the yard, and lined up rank on rank at the flagpole while he solemnly raised the Union Jack to strains of "Land of Hope and Glory". Then prayers and a hymn — perhaps "I vow to thee, my Country" —, but a different programme each year. Finally, dutiful salutes ended with "God Save the King". Those were the days before we won the War but lost the Empire.

I enjoyed art and woodwork. Mr Hacking the master taught us woodcraft: bow-tied, bespectacled, nicknamed Joey Stump because he had lost a finger on the circular saw — a fine example to the boys!

On Fridays the organ-man came round — a bearded chap from Birkenhead with his old-fashioned barrel organ, giving a tune for coppers. Milk was delivered by horse and cart. Sally Evans came round with shrimps and fish in large baskets. The onion man from France turned up each year on a bicycle laden with strings of onions. Gipsies sold clothes-pegs and told your fortune into the bargain. Leonard Roberts, the egg man, cycled round delivering essential calories before cholesterol was heard of. Andrew Cavanagh did his rounds on Monday mornings for Pearson's the grocers, collecting orders for later delivery. Greengroceries, meat, bread, coal, paraffin, almost all provisions, were delivered. Local tradespeople waited on us hand and foot for a few shillings'-worth of orders, a fact now forgotten, but what a contrast to today.

Pigeon racing was the popular sport with many local working men. Often they could be seen walking past, pushing a bike, balancing

their cooing pigeon basket on the saddle, taking them to one station or another for transport to some distant place for release on arrival. One or two went in for greyhound racing, but interest was mainly in pigeon fancying.

Children played marbles and hopscotch, while the top, hoop and skipping rope had not yet gone out of fashion. The scooter was a wooden platform between two small wheels, one foot on, one foot off, providing wondrous propulsion.

Nature and wildlife were all around us by the acre. As a young boy it was in these fields and hedgerows I sought the first primrose, golden celandine and wild iris. I knew where the lords and ladies raised their stately heads, listened for the first cuckoo and the corncrake's ceaseless grating — now the rarest sound in nature. I watched wriggling eels in many a local stream where, only about thirty years before, my own uncle had shot an otter. I gazed across the silent, still pond, with water lilies, frog spawn and ginny green teeth at its edge, azure dragonflies magnificently flitting on the wing. I have watched barn owls hunting at dusk, fox cubs playing, bounding hares in mad March mood, where now stand houses, houses, houses. Neston's countryside in the 1930s was a lively, living nature book, and one could not help but turn the pages, look, learn and love the splendour of the natural world all around us.

Just before the War seemed to be the ideal time to live: it was peaceful, the recession more or less behind us, modest prosperity slowly but surely clear to view, with more equal opportunities for all. Modern ways of thinking were now more universally accepted, with only a few old diehards still sticking to old-fashioned methods, thinking the end of the world as they knew it was at hand. In a sense they were right; by September 1939 it was the end of all placid, steady progress, as we were plunged into a new unknown. Many dreaded the footslogging return to the horrific trenches of only 21 years before, but it soon became apparent that Hitler's blitzkrieg was an entirely different form of warfare.

When one sits and thinks, so much comes to mind!

Fig. 119 The sands of Dee in 1926.

SOURCES

This chapter was written by Geoffrey Place, with the help of memories from Mrs Anyon, Cyril Cambridge, Mr and Mrs Reg Chrimes, Andrew Prince, David Scott and George Tilley.

The information about the hospital at Parkgate came from a leaflet printed for its patrons, the Gladstones of Burton Manor.

The munitions factory at Leighton Court was commemorated by a book of photographs privately printed for W. E. Whineray.

Susan Chambers researched the records of the Neston and District Council of Social Service.

INDEX

Note: Underlined figures in entries refer to illustrations or their captions. In order to avoid unnecessary duplication of entries, Churches and chapels; Farms; Hospitals; Hotels, inns and public houses; and Schools are included as main headings, under which individual examples appear as subentries.

NOTES

NOTES